About the Author...

NOW 21 BUT FAST APPROACHING 78, Aaron was born in Pennsylvania in 1923. He served in the U.S. Armed Forces (armored infantry) in Europe in 1944-45. He has been unarmed ever since. He has been, at different times of course: sheepherder, x-ray technician, professor, union organizer, malcontent, writer, liar, father, husband, paramour, single amour. He has performed in several X-rated movies because of the size of his nose. There is still disagreement about his parentage but evidence suggests he was deposited onto a fence post by a crow and the sun hatched him out. For a detailed biography, see *Who's What and Who Cares, 1995*. Then forget it. Aaron's credo, by which he lives: "Take it easy, but take it!" Those words (in Aramaic) will be inscribed on his tombstone in letters 1/4 inch high, four inches deep.

Chester, the author

Other books by Chester Aaron

Garlic is Life, Ten Speed Press, Berkeley, CA, 1994
The Great Garlic Book, Ten Speed Press, Berkeley, CA, 1997
Adult novel: *About Us*, McGraw Hill, 1967, Reprint Creative Arts Press, 2001
New Adult novel: *Black and Blue Jew*, Creative Arts Press, 2001
Ten Young-Adult novels: Several to be reprinted by Mostly Garlic, Ltd.
Short Story Collection: to be published by Mostly Garlic, Ltd.

For Lisa Merrell

The Consummate Clove
The Transcendent Tomato

For Colleen + John McCoy!!

Chester Aaron
4/3/2014

Garlic Kisses

Human Struggles
with
Garlic Connections

Chester Aaron

Cover Design and Artwork by **Molly Rose Segal, Oakland, California**

Additional Cover Artwork by **David Wolff, Milan, Ohio**

QuarkExpress Design and Typography by **Kelli Zimmerman, Lorain, Ohio**

Chapter Sketches by **Charlotte Martin, Medina, Ohio**

Mostly Garlic, Ltd.
Milan, Ohio

First printing 2001.

Although author and publisher have made every effort to ensure the accuracy contained in this book, we assume no responsibility for errors, inaccuracies, omissions, or any inconsistency. In these memoirs some names, dates, places, and other small changes have been made at the request of the people involved in the stories. The basis of each story has not been affected and thereby remains true.

ISBN 0-9701094-9-0

LCCN 00-041566

Acknowledgments

1. For information relevant to chapters thirteen and fourteen see *The Taste of America* by John L. Hess and Karen Hess, published by Viking Press, 1977

2. "Hello David," the poem in chapter two, reprinted here with permission of the poet Dusty.

Edited by:

Kelli Zimmerman, Lorain, Ohio

Ron Bakalar, Lorain, Ohio

Dennis Boatman, Hollywood, Florida

Dennis and Judy Davis, Middleburg Heights, Ohio

TABLE OF CONTENTS

Chapter One

MILLI O'KEEFE

BENGAL PURPLE

From the province of Orissa, Bengal Coast; skin reputed to be purple, four very large cloves in blue-striped skins. Taste: reported to be very hot. Salve made of this garlic is foul-smelling but is effective. Cure not scientifically documented. Shelf-life: unknown.

Definition of Shelf-life: The length of time that garlic, if well stored, retains it's unique taste. It may be edible much longer, but it's taste will become undistinctive.

In my American Literature classes at Saint Mary's College, I always included in my selection of texts two of Willa Cather's novels. I always selected the first one (it was usually *My Antonia*), but the second was selected by each student after a discussion in my office.

Milli O'Keefe was eighteen and a Freshman when we met. Five weeks into her first semester, Milli, who had rarely participated in the seminars on *My Antonia*, appeared at the door of my office at precisely ten o'clock, as scheduled. Topic for discussion: her choice of her second Cather novel.

I sat back, expecting to coast through a delivery of shallow ideas but I very soon realized that here was a mind and an attitude met infrequently at the college and almost never in freshmen. I was hearing smart interpretations not just of Cather and not just of the character of Antonia Schimerda, the major character in *My Antonia*, but also complex analyses of 19th and 20th century American morals and of the feminist movement just then getting into gear. Milli was not trying to impress her professor, she was articulating her attitudes about the world she knew and the much different world she planned to inhabit. How could an eighteen year old know so much, be so perceptive, make such mature judgments? At the end of the allotted fifteen minutes I found myself wishing the discussion would continue. I kept the next student waiting at least ten minutes beyond the scheduled appointment time.

The novel Milli selected for her individual presentation at the seminar and for her term paper was *O Pioneers !*

"Why," she asked me that morning in my office, "would there be an exclamation point after the word *Pioneers* ?"

"A good question," I said. "I've often thought about that myself. Let's see if we can find out."

We did talk about that exclamation point in subsequent private meetings but never in class because in class Milli tended to be an almost sullen, silent loner. When I indicated in a later class discussion that Cather, in taking the title *O Pioneers!* from Whitman's poem, had also taken Whitman's exclamation point, Milli said, "You make her sound like a thief. For Cather, the exclamation point is for Alexandra, not for ordinary pioneers. Alexandra is an exclamation point."

Stunned by the insight as well as by the potential of the allusion, I asked, lamely, "Is there such a thing as an ordinary pioneer?"

The heads of the students turned to see if Milli realized she had been diplomatically challenged. She was not impressed and certainly not intimidated. "Compared to Alexandra," she said, "compared to Cather, the pioneers who settled in Nebraska were ordinary. Alexandra was extra-ordinary." She separated the two words with a silent hyphen. Then, after an effective dramatic pause, she added, "So was Willa Cather."

The heads of the students then turned to me.

Unwilling to create the illusion that I was carrying on a duel with Milli O'Keefe, I said, "Let's discuss that." We did. All of us. All except Milli, who seemed to have her gaze on a distant horizon.

Over the next three-and-a-half years Milli and I went beyond the casual professor-student relationship. Two minor justifications for my behavior: I was divorced and I had no agenda.

After a marriage of fourteen years and a six-year tour of the usual trial-and-error-circus, I chose to live the solitary life in the home I had recently built on four acres in California's redwood country, sixty miles north of Berkeley. Solitary until a woman trapezed out of the trial-and-error circus to land in my safety net.

A confession is in order here: I am one of those Jewish men who finds himself drawn to non-Jewish — especially red-haired, freckle-faced Irish — women. My wife's maiden name was Callahan. Not by design but by chance, the four women I courted after my divorce were named, in order of appearance: Finnegan, O'Brien (from Canton, Ohio,) Callahan (no relation to my ex-wife,) and another O'Brien (this one from County Cork, no less.)

More than content, I was relieved to find this eighteen and then nineteen and then twenty-year-old a companion with whom I might share occasional evenings during that part of each week when I was the professor who lived in a Berkeley apartment, never my home up north and not ever my nights. I must admit, however, that I did fantasize such a blessing. But an unstated code of honorable conduct exists between professor and student, a code I have always honored. Did Milli have her own fantasies? Part of that unstated code required that neither she nor I ever pose such a question.

Milli's life came to me over the four years in occasional trickles, occasional floods.

She'd been born into impoverished Irish blue collar ("Pigshit Irish, Chester, not Lace Curtain; bricklayers, truck drivers.") South Boston. During grade school and high school, evenings and weekends and summers were given to chores and jobs to pay her way. ("To my four older brothers and two older sisters I was unsalaried hired help; meaning I did the laundry, the beds, the dishes, the cooking. My Aunt Millicent in ritzy Beacon Hill had money. Her husband, Uncle Pat, of course, was a corrupt precinct captain who earned outside his office three times the money he earned inside. "Ah, but me uncle was a loving boyo. He loved his niece dearly, he did he did. Aunt Millicent loved me too. But she loved me because I was her namesake. 'You got to get away from Boston, away from the family, to California, girl. And away from that terrible family. If I could send you further west, I'd do it; but the land ends there in California. You'll go to a foine Catholic college, Millicent, run by the Christian Brothers, not the Jesuits. You'll get a foine education. I got no daughters. You are my daughter, Millicent, even if you spell it M-i-l-l-i and your name's O'Keefe.' So here I am, Chester, and I am getting a *foine* education, thanks to Aunt Millicent and thanks to you. My Aunt Millicent told me, 'Never be poor, Millicent. Sell your soul and your pretty little Irish ass if it comes to that but never never be poor. I've tried poor and I've tried rich, and rich is much much better. That's why I'm sending you to the Christian Brothers. The Christian Brothers know how to survive'. I swear, Chester, I will never be poor. Never never never. I'm only twenty next month but I know Aunt Millicent is right : rich is better. I'll slit my wrists if I'm not very very rich before I'm thirty five. But"… (and this in a magnificent Dooblin accent) … "and after I slit my wrists and maybe my throat, how will I confess to Father McConnaghy?"

"I don't do confession, Milli. I'm a Jew. We Jews admit nothing. Not even to ourselves."

"Maybe I'll convert, me boyo. How do you say *boyo* in Hebrew?"

"I don't do Hebrew. In Yiddish : *Lantzman* , I'd guess."

"Not as pretty in the ear as *boyo*."

Can you appreciate by now why I fell in love with Milli O'Keefe?

In the four years of our friendship, Milli and I often went to movies or plays or concerts together. Neither of us ever invited the other into our homes. I took Milli to lunches and dinners in Moraga (the home of Saint Mary's College) and Berkeley and (five, maybe six times) to toney restaurants in San Francisco. By her junior year we were embracing and kissing each other (no longer just on the cheek) at meetings and farewells, sitting at tables long after dessert, walking arm in arm (sometimes hand-in-hand) along the sidewalks.

We confided in each other as lovers do, sharing hopes, regrets, anxieties. But we were never lovers. Regarding our temptations, we behaved like diplomats at the signing of a mutual-aid pact. Long-term benefits outweighed immediate pleasures.

After she graduated in 1986, Milli worked in the offices of a group of attorneys in San Francisco. Did she harbor secret ambitions to be a lawyer? ("Never, Chester. I don't want to defend laws I don't believe in.") We talked occasionally on the phone the next two years, exchanged holiday greetings, met less and less frequently. We went our separate ways and lost contact with each other.

About six years after Milli graduated, I received a long letter from her from Boston. The letter arrived three days before Christmas. After the holidays she'd be returning to her apartment in Paris, where she was trying to write a novel. "About, of all things, a woman determined to make it in a man's world. Can I send it to you when I finish it, Chester? If I finish it? Whatever *it* turns out to be."

I sent Milli a Christmas card at her Paris address, urging her to send the manuscript. She did not reply. I nursed my disappointment for several months and then secured other, more immediate disappointments ready and willing to take their place in line.

Three or four years after that exchange of letters to Paris, about ten years after she graduated (which made Milli thirty-two years old,) I was in San Francisco to attend a meeting at the Clift Hotel. As I started toward the entrance, I saw a woman rushing out of the hotel, frantically signaling for a taxi. She was surely a model or an actress. Poised, self-assured, glamorous, she was a woman of class, a woman of authority. The woman glanced up. On seeing me, she shouted, "Chester! Chester, is that you?"

I recognized the voice before I recognized the face. When she ran from the waiting taxi and leaped at me and kissed me and I held her, I wanted to rush her off to my home in Occidental and talk and talk and talk. With Milli no longer a student and with ten years having passed, I had no reason to punish myself with codes of conduct.

But Milli was in a hurry. She had an appointment, she said, and she was already late. "Will you be at Saint Mary's tomorrow?"

"Yes."

"I'll call you early afternoon."

We embraced. She hurried off and then ran back to grab and hug me again. It was not just her clothes, nor her manner that assured me she was not poor. Her scent had to be very rare, very exotic, very expensive. I am not a connoisseur of wine, but (the only poor member of my family on both sides back fifty years) I am a connoisseur of wealth. Milli was wealthy, very wealthy. Unconcerned about my insights, perhaps unaware of them, Milli planted a long wet kiss on the tip of my nose. "Oh," she laughed, "I miss that big beautiful schnozzola." As the taxi left the curb she waved through the open window and shouted, "Tomorrow. One o'clock. Your office. You better be there, sucker."

Milli called at one o'clock sharp. Was I still living on my farm in Occidental? I was. Wasn't the semester almost over? It was. In fact, I informed her that starting the following week I'd be in Occidental all summer.

"Chester, would you be willing to have a no-touchee guest for an overnight in the middle of the week?"

"Name of guest?"

"Millicent. Last name with-held on advice of counsel."

"Will you bring your manuscript?"

"It's not finished. Incidentally, the title is *Alexandra's Daughter*."

"Bring it."

"I don't have it with me."

"You bring it or I flunk you."

"I'll bring it."

"What day next week is best for you, Millicent O?"

"How is Wednesday, oh, master?"

"Do you know how to get to Occidental?"

"Hey, I am a college graduate. I have my own web page. I also have one of those high-tech thingeys in my car. I push a button and I get a virtual map that leads me to your virtual door."

"Milli, I'm glad you're back in my life." Why, I'm not sure now; but the reference to her having her own web site had no impact on me. Since then, starting a few years ago, I went on the internet, trying to locate her website but I was never successful.

"I'll be at your home in Occidental at noon next Wednesday. You should know that I am now a gourmet chef, graduate of Tellevant, Paris, France, Europe. I'll bring food. I'll cook you up a mess, maybe of greens."

"And you should know that I am now a famous garlic grower, two garlic books out there and a big poster. To hell with academic papers and books."

Silence.

"Milli?"

"Wait a minute. You grow garlic, Chester?"

"I told you. Been growing garlic for about ten years. I have eighty-seven varieties from twenty-two countries, all different. Last October, I put thirty thousand cloves in the ground. I'll be harvesting in a few weeks. I have two books published about garlic and a poster and they're selling all over the world."

"Eighty-seven varieties. Thirty thou … Chester, do you believe in synchronicity?"

"Is that an Aramaic word?"

"Chester, I have a story to tell you. Are your garlic books and your poster at your house? In Bookstores?"

"Of course, both house and bookstores."

Silence.

"Milli? You there? This connection …"

"Do you write about garlic and health in those books?"

"I do."

"My God. Wednesday. Noon. Chester … my God, talk about synchronicity."

I was in the field most of Wednesday morning, trying to iden-tify the garlics that would be the first to be harvested in the coming days. At exactly noon a blue Mercedes convertible came oozing down Lapham Lane. It could not be Milli O'Keefe. The Milli I knew ten years ago had driven an old battered Honda.

That long naked arm waving above the blue Mercedes body and the laughter sailing down across the field could only belong to Milli O'Keefe. My heart racing I pretended nonchalance as I walked up across the field to the parking area behind my curing shed. A laughing red haired hurricane was out of the Mercedes and sweeping down the sidewalk. And there was that buoyant, rich, audacious Milli voice: "Hey, Farmer John, think the rain'll hurt the rhubarb?"

As we hugged and kissed, I could no longer feign noncha-lance; but I did manage discretion. My cat Sadie had accompanied me along the concrete walkway to the meeting. Milli grabbed her, lifted her high, sang out all sorts of endearing words. Sadie, who usually clawed strangers who dared to touch her, clung to Milli as if the tall redhead were her long-lost mother.

Milli was wearing shorts that consisted of not much more than a belt, and a halter that was, it appeared, composed only of straps. She kept adjusting body parts, I kept gasping and admiring, she kept on laughing and adjusting. "Damn," she said, "coming up Highway 101 those truckers way up there above me kept leaning over and looking down and honking their horns, and I kept waving. I swear there were almost ten wrecks. Oh, Chester, I'm so glad to be here with you. Let's eat. I brought a picnic basket full of goodies, includ-ing champagne and wine." She deposited the now enchanted Sadie on the ground, returned to her car for the basket, and then the three of us walked through the redwoods to the house.

I carried the wicker basket, which was fresh out of some expensive mail order catalogue, probably Williams of Sonoma. The bottle of white wine and the bottle of champagne had been riding in the trunk in buckets of ice and freezing bags for two hours. The ten or twelve plastic containers and plates and silver, and red checkered napkins, were covered with a red checkered tablecloth.

In the house, while Milli (Sadie at her heels) toured my rooms and used the bathroom, I opened the champagne. Outside on the south deck, I spread the cloth on a table from which we could, as we ate, look toward the far redwoods and watch the late afternoon fog roll in from the ocean just about, I guessed, when we'd be having our coffee.

Milli, talking, singing, laughing, moved in and out of the house, setting places, distributing bowls and platters and silver, asked about me, about my life as teacher, writer, farmer. "Forget *lover*. I don't want to hear it."

She'd taken off her shoes and while we ate and drank she stretched to take the afternoon sun. Her body appeared to be at least ninety percent legs. Sadie, stretched out on the nearby railing, was certainly dreaming of being once more, perhaps even forever, in Milli's arms.

The conversation was chaotic until we reached the dessert, a lemon tart Milli had made that morning. "Sweets for the sweet," she said, "tarts from the tart." The coffee was Arabian Mocha Sanani, which she'd bought at Peet's in San Francisco just for me.

Then, out of her chair, Milli dragged a redwood recliner from another part of the deck and, pretending to purr like a kitten, she settled down into the cushions. "OK, now we talk. First: are you in love? Do you have a new woman?"

"No woman, new or old. Am I in love? Yes. With you."

"Not allowed, old timer. Honestly, let's be straight-arrow here. Can we sleep together tonight without fucking?"

"I doubt it. We can sleep together, yes. But without ... I want to call it making-love. No, we can't. I will get down on my knees and beg."

"Chester, be good. You promised. I'll leave right now. No I won't."

"I promised ten years ago."

"Promises are for eternity. Alexandra Bergson believed that. OK, let's talk garlic. That's garlic in those boxes down there in the field. Right? Oh God, you won't believe ... Eighty-seven varieties of garlic. I want to work in the field tomorrow. I want to dig and smell and taste and eat. Garlic, garlic, garlic. Tell me what you've done, what you're doing, then I want to see your garlic books and that poster. But first things first. Health talk. Tell me everything you know about garlic and health, the proven stuff, not the folklore."

I talked for about twenty minutes, reciting most of the information I've included in my books, information received from a variety of sources, almost all of them respectable universities in the U.S., Germany, India, China, Japan. When I mentioned that during World War Two, before they had antibiotics, Russian soldiers treated wounds with raw garlic, Milli sat up, eyes wide. When she tried to talk, she stammered. "Is that … is that honest … honest to G… God true, Chester?"

"That's not just anecdotal; it's documented history."

She sat up very slowly, left the lounge, hugged herself and shivered. The fog had started in over the redwoods, and the breeze had turned cool, almost cold. "Let's go inside," Milli said. "I need to be warm when I tell you what I have to tell you."

"Did you bring your manuscript?"

"You asked me to. Don't I do whatever you ask me to do? Wait, don't you dare answer that. Yes. And it's finished. At least this draft is finished. It's not *O Pioneers!* but it's … ." And Milli broke into tears. "Oh, G… God, Ch… Chester."

I held her in my arms for some time and then all but carried her into the house. I placed her on the sofa and covered her with a blanket. I brought her a box of tissues and sat beside her until she stopped sobbing.

"I'm sorry, Chester. May … may I have a cup of coffee?"

"You can have my life, Milli."

She cried again, not so hysterically this time, until her strength was gone. I stayed at her side. She shifted her body so she could lay her head in my lap, and she promptly dropped into sleep. She did not stir when I shifted her head onto a large pillow.

I was working at my computer in my study when a light tap on the door was followed by a, "Hi."

Milli stood in the doorway, sleepy-eyed, smiling, a pale faced, anxious child apologizing for some offense. "Mind if I take a shower?

Any wine left?"

"Sure. You'll find towels and soap in the usual cupboards. You strong enough to stay up for a while? It's cool enough to build a fire."

"A fire would be lovely. In fact, a fire's required. I'll be right down." She started to leave and then returned. "Forgive me, Chester. I didn't intend to be so dramatic. Promised myself I'd not do that. I hate people who break promises. Don't go away." Then she stepped up behind me and, from behind, she put her arms around me. "I hope you won't hate me."

I thought she was referring to her insistence that we not be lovers and I said, "Milli, you can never make me hate you."

"Don't be too sure," she said. A few minutes later I could hear the shower drumming on the walls of the upstairs bathroom. I built a fire in the iron stove, washed the dishes, cleared the remains of the meal, readied two wine glasses, put on my favorite CD, and after a brief debate with myself decided to let Milli have my bed for the night. I would sleep on the sofa. Sadie normally appreciates my presence on the sofa so she can settle in at my shoulder, but tonight I knew the fickle feline would forsake me for her new love.

When Milli danced her way down the steps, she was once again her effervescent self. She was wearing a pale blue t-shirt (and, my God, look at that mass of red hair!) and faded jeans. Her bare feet were long and strong, with magnificent ankles. Nails on toes and fingers glowed with a pink that was almost but not quite red.

"Damn," I said, "even your feet are beautiful."

"I want a copy of that CD," she said.

"That's not your generation's music. That's mine."

"The reason I want it," she said. She read the title on the plastic jacket. "Knew it was Ray Charles. Never heard of Betty Carter. She makes me think of a luscious chocolate cake."

"You ought to be a writer. When do I see your novel?"

She dropped onto the sofa and accepted the glass of wine and accepted Sadie's bulk. "Let me talk," she said. She stroked Sadie's head and back and concentrated, as if preparing herself for a launch into an alien sky. "No interruptions. No questions. After I'm through, you can tell me if you want me to stay or go, if you want me to come back some time or stay away forever."

"Milli…"

"I'm serious. I'm going to be in San Francisco for three more weeks. I'd love to come up once a week, overnight, and work with you in the field. I want to see and feel and smell and taste those different garlics. But if you don't want me to after … after I talk, just say so. No. Stop. Don't say anything now. I know you want to say I'm always welcome but don't talk. Not yet."

I sat back, willing to let her decide the evening's program.

She studied the flames in the iron stove as she continued stroking the now sleeping Sadie, and then after a deep breath she started. During her recital which went on without a word from me for about fifteen minutes, I filled her wine glass twice. Sadie never stirred.

"While I was working for those San Francisco attorneys … remember? right after I graduated? … I met a man from London. Very rich. A banker. European-American investments. He set me up in an apartment in New York. I was free to do what I wished except I was to be available whenever he came to town. He came to town once a week, sometimes once every two weeks. He paid me a very high salary. I mean very. Yes. A salary. I was an employee. I was one of about five such employees he had stashed away in various countries. Each of us listed as a consultant. Tax write-offs. After a year or so I was twenty six years old. Too old for Alber'. He gave me a big bonus and I was out. I decided that day I'd create my own fate. Like Alexandra. But I didn't have a farm. I did have other benefits. Beauty and brains. I'm a great dancer and I speak three languages almost fluently. Didn't know that? No reason you should. I put an ad in the International Herald Tribune. Escort service. One thing led to another, one rich man led to another even richer man. Word-of-mouth so to speak. In five years I had half a million bucks in the bank. Thanks to my clients I also had a primo portfolio. Went back to Paris, lived there for two years, worked on my novel. My parents didn't own the clothes on their backs, they were deep in debt. I bought them the apartment house I was born in plus three other apartments in the building. They're receiving rent money now instead of paying it. So I'm not all evil. Whenever they asked about my job I said it was International Relations, which was the truth. Last year, after I finished the first draft of the novel, I started my own escort service. Thirty-two years old now, I can't command as high a fee for myself as I could when I was twenty-four. That's right. Fee, not salary . I'll continue one more year, maybe two. By then I'll be too old to earn much more than a check-out clerk at a super-market. I'll quit and live the rest of my life however, wherever, I wish. Probably in Paris. Maybe Florence or Siena. Are you disgusted, Chester?"

Shocked, yes; disgusted, no.

No, not shocked. Not even especially surprised. I guess I should have known. Hadn't there been clues I'd not so much missed as refused to see?

"You're very quiet, Chester. Are you trying to think of a way to be kind without being honest? Do you understand why I could never sleep with you? I mean not sleep but make love to you? Not *make love*, I mean *fuck*? You deserve better than Milli O'Keefe. I'll find someone some day whom I'll marry and we'll have two and a half kids and live in a gated village and own a dog, a cat, and two canaries in a cage; and then we'll divorce. I love you, Chester. I won't ever love any other man."

"Will you marry me, Milli?"

Milli's face (no other way to describe it) sent tears into the air like bomb fragments. She leaped from the sofa with such force that Sadie ran beneath the sofa to hide. Still weeping, Milli kneeled in front of the sofa, drew Sadie out and scooped her up in her arms. She continued sobbing into the willing Sadie's long gray fur. When I turned Milli around and took her into my arms, she did not resist but she kept hold of Sadie, as if there were strength to be drawn from the tiny buffering body between us.

"There's more," she said.

She sat on the sofa again, Sadie still in her arms. I rebuilt the fire and poured more wine.

"The garlic," I said. "And the novel."

Milli drank the wine as if it were water, in one long swallow. I opened another bottle, one of my own, and returned to the sofa to pour again.

"You grow garlic."

"I grow garlic."

"I've been using garlic to cure myself. A garlic salve."

"A garlic salve?"

"Is there an echo in here?"

"Cure yourself of what?"

"O.K. Here goes. I was in India, Bengal, a province called Orissa, with … with one of my clients. I got sick. Very sick. Sores all over my body. I know, I know, but wait, don't rush to judgment. A British health worker told me it was the water. My client, a Belgian industrialist, just ran. He left me there, stranded. The British health worker brought an old Indian woman to see me. She looked at my body and took out one of several jars she had in a sack. She opened the jar. It was a yellow-brown salve that stank like, worse than, the foulest shit you can imagine. She rubbed it on my body, all over my body. She came every morning, every evening. Five days. Her hands were so soft, so tender. In six days the sores were gone. And not a single scar. The Brit managed to get the woman to understand I needed to know what it was, and I'd pay for more. The woman invited me to her shack to watch her make the salve. Garlic. I recognized it, of course. She peeled the cloves and mashed them in a bowl with curry and some other herbs. She poured in honey. That was it: garlic, curry, mysterious herbs, honey. Dark honey, almost black. The Brit said she said she only used that specific garlic. There were several other garlics in the market stalls but the other garlics were no good. That's what she said."

I waited, trying to say something supportive, something that would not sound arrogant. If I were asked to put into a book all the stories I've heard about secret mixes containing garlic and how they cured this or that disease, I'd need four or five hundred pages. "Have you used the salve since you left India?"

"Promise you won't laugh."

"I promise."

"One of my occupational hazards is, as you've been thinking, disease. As you've been thinking: aids."

"It crossed my mind."

"Two years ago, about three months before I went to Bengal, I tested HIV positive. I've been using the garlic salve for two years. Every day. All over my body. I put it on in the morning, keep it on for four or five hours, then I shower, with lavender soap, lavender shampoo. My blood tests three months ago showed me clear and clean. No HIV. Not a trace."

"I suspect you know, Millie, that recent research indicates that there is a minority of people who've been diagnosed as HIV positive who are clean three or four years later. Their immune system has apparently absorbed and neutralized the virus. There are all kinds of arguments about how and why. And there are many scientists who have many doubts."

"I've heard. Every month I send the woman in Orissa money. She sends me the salve. I thank God, or maybe Vishnu, for that Brit and that Indian woman and that garlic salve. Would any garlic work? Could I make it myself? I don't know. I don't want to take a chance."

"Do you remember what the garlic looked like?"

"I remember it as if it were my child's face in front of me, if I had a child."

"Color of skin?"

"Purple. Dark dark purple?"

"Remember how many cloves…?"

"Every bulb had four cloves, each clove was big and every clove had purple striped skin."

"Did you taste it?"

"Of course. Sometimes when she sends me the salve, she sends me bulbs, too. It's also the only garlic I eat. I usually eat it the same morning I use the salve. The Indian woman gave me green leaves to eat. The Brit said it was parsley. I use mouthwash a lot. And I own stock in a licorice factory in Spain."

"They serve parsley in Spain with raw garlic to cut the bite and the odor."

"It was very hot. The Indian woman said the honey took away the heat."

"Right. Sweetness will counter the heat of herbs or spices like garlic or chili peppers. Do you have any bulbs or cloves at home?"

"Chester, my home for the last three years has been a flat in about five different countries. No, I don't have any with me, but I can get some. It will take a week or two. Do you want to plant it?"

"Very much. And taste it."

"You don't think I'm one of these New Age loonies, do you, Chester? Are you humoring me?"

"I believe you."

"But? I hear a *but* in your voice."

"No *but* in my voice or my heart. OK, maybe I have a big butt, double t, but the but doesn't matter."

"But? But? But?"

"But you might be cured as much by your mind-set as by the garlic. But, but, but it doesn't matter how you've done it; you've done it. You're clean."

Milli, slightly drunk now and tired, yawned. "I better go to bed. Can we work out in the field tomorrow?"

"You bet. I want to watch you bend over. To pick weeds. Let me get your bed set."

"You don't want to sleep with me now, do you?"

"I want to so much I could scream. I'd marry you three minutes from now if you said yes. But you will decide if and when it ever happens. And I am serious ..."

"I know you are. When you ask me to marry you, I know you're serious. I might marry you twenty years from now, Chester, when my kids are out of the house and you need a firm female hand to help you find your dick to pee."

"I love you, Milli. I've loved you ever since you walked into my office that morning at ten o'clock to talk to me about *O Pioneers!* and..."

"And that exclamation point. Emphasis, professor. Pioneers are explorers, adventurers, independent, self-reliant, professor. "Exclaim their courage, exclaim their importance, exclaim their superiority to ordinary people. That's why Whitman and then Cather used that exclamation point, professor. God, Chester, how could you love such a strident, self-righteous, naïve voice as that eighteen year old... ."

"Miss O'Keefe, Alexandra's father was the pioneer."

"Professor, Alexandra Bergson was the pioneer. She was a strong independent American woman who took on the world, Professor."

"Why is the feminist movement scorning Willa Cather, Miss O'Keefe?"

"Because, professor, Willa Cather is a woman who has equal love for men and women."

A long pause during which Milli's eyes filled with tears. "We have recreated the class almost word for word, Chester. Oh, God, I yearn yearn yearn to be Alexandra."

"You have just received an A plus."

"Can we talk about my manuscript tomorrow? Before I leave?"

"Only then? Not tonight?"

"You haven't read it, and I'm exhausted."

"Tomorrow. Will you let me read the manuscript tonight?"

Milli tenderly settled the still sleeping Sadie onto a pillow, went upstairs, and returned, coming down the stairs this time slowly, quietly. After she handed me a small box that had once contained a ream of paper she leaned over to kiss my mouth. "I love you more than I've ever loved anyone in the world, except Alexandra Bergson." She stumbled as she climbed the stairs and then she returned. "Your garlic books. I want to see them. I might not get into them tonight; but when I wake up, I always have time to read while I let that salve cook my body."

"You brought some salve with you?"

"I told you. I use it every morning."

"Can I see it?"

"Tomorrow morning. You'll know when I open the jar." Then, carrying a copy of each of my garlic books and grunting with exhaustion, Milli climbed the stairs. Sadie, the creepy little traitor, followed her.

I read until dawn, turning over the last page of *Alexandra's Daughter* two minutes before Sadie came down from her lover's bed to be fed. Not quite six o'clock.

As quietly as possible, I opened a can of flaked fish for La Chat. After she ate, she and I tippy-toed out-side. I brought Milli's box of pages with me. Needing to sit over coffee, to think about *Alexandra's Daughter*, I drove down the hill to the Union Hotel Café. I could bring back some of Barbara Gonnella's muffins and scones for Milli's breakfast. She would probably sleep for another hour or two.

With the manuscript in the box before me, I sat at a table in the early morning sun and tried to convince myself that the story I'd read all night was not a memoir, was not an autobiography. Milli O'Keefe was not Catherine Sullivan. Catherine Sullivan had used her beauty and her brains to satisfy a score of carefully selected, very wealthy, businessmen and politicians, and had satisfied herself by securing a fortune currently ensconced in two banks in the United States, one bank in Geneva and one bank in Tokyo, with stocks and bonds greater in value than the annual budget for Rwanda. Catherine Sullivan: a still young woman who, as she built her fortune, remained in firm control of her soul. Catherine Sullivan: now, having terminated her final liaison, will live only to read and write. That is all she desires. Catherine Sullivan will lead a life of solitary pleasure, perhaps in New Mexico, perhaps in Vermont, perhaps in both.

On the last page of *Alexandra's Daughter*, the last two words: *Hello, life.*

When I drove down Lapham Lane, I realized as I approached my home, that Milli's Mercedes was gone.

On the dining table: a page.

> *Dear Chester. I can't talk about it. I'll call you. I*
> *love you, Chester. Why didn't I marry you?*
> *Maybe some day I will. You'll hear from me. I*
> *held Sadie for ten minutes before I left. I took the*
> *liberty of taking your two beautiful garlic books*
> *with me. Thanks. I'll send you an address*
> *because I want a poster. I saw the one you have*
> *on the wall. It is beautiful. So are you. The jar on*
> *the table is for you. I'll send you the garlic when*
> *it arrives from Bengal. Always and forever: your*
> *devoted Milli.*

I called the Clift Hotel in San Francisco later that morning, thinking that by then she would be back in the city. No guest named Millicent O'Keefe was or had been registered at the hotel.

Milli O'Keefe, I cannot endure your dropping into and out of my life. I want you here now, to live with me. Now!

Two years.

I have not heard from Milli. I have not received the purple skinned garlic.

I have kept the jar of salve. It is upstairs in my medicine cabinet.

Milli, please come back to me.

Chapter Two

ELLEN SAUNDERS, R.N. Ret.

SPANISH ROJA

A Northwest heirloom brought to the Portland area before 1900. Often called "Greek" or "Greek Blue" by Northwest gardeners. Performs poorly in mild winter climates. When well grown it's flavor describes true garlic. Peels very easily. Shelf life: three to four months.

It is March, 2000; and instead of looking forward to next April, I think back to last April. That's April, 1999.

April is the cruelest month. An eternal truth but I always forget it.

Every year, all through the storm-drenched months of February and March, I anticipate the arrival of April, one of the four months I have to persuade myself to love. Like all promises exchanged by lovers, April's promises are designed to be broken.

The first three nights of last April were so warm that I opened both bedroom windows and replaced the heavy down-filled comforter I'd been using all winter with a single cotton blanket. The following days I worked five or six hours in the field every morning. In the afternoon and evening, I sat at my computer. I have been trying to complete a novel. As of today, it has advanced perhaps thirty pages.

Friday evening, April 7, 1999 was still warm; and contrary to so-called typical April weather, it was still dry. Weather predictions for the next day: clear and warm, and probably clear and warm through the rest of the month and into summer.

I worked outside all day that Friday. Late afternoon, I put the tools away and went into the house to treat myself to a long hot shower. Back downstairs in the kitchen sipping my gin-and-tonic, I started preparing my supper. When the phone rang, I hoped it would be Elizabeth, my ladylove from San Francisco. I rushed to catch it before it cut to the answering machine. It was a woman but not Elizabeth. The voice, cautious but firm, asked, "Chester Aaron?"

"Speaking."

"I saw the TV program two weeks ago. Victory Garden."

This would be approximately the fiftieth call I've had in the two weeks since the local presentation of Victory Garden, the smart, informative, imaginatively produced garden series out of WGBH-TV in Boston. The program's crew of six, preceded and set up by Hilary Finkel, had visited my farm last year and had spent the day producing what would become a ten minute sequence documenting my work with garlic in northern California. Another ten-minute sequence was devoted to a corporate garlic farmer in Gilroy, down in central California. Different variety of garlic, different variety of farmer.

Within hours of that first show and over the following days and weeks and months, calls and letters came from all over the country, as well as from Alaska, Hawaii and Puerto Rico. There were four letters from Germany, two from France and two from Spain. They all wanted garlic. After the re-run two weeks ago, letters and calls were coming again.

Usually the phone messages went onto my message machine because in March and April I was in the field much of each day, working to prepare for the work of the harvest, which leads into the work of curing and shipping, which precedes the work of preparing the soil, which is necessary for the work of the fall planting. It's like being a father or a writer. I wouldn't do it if I didn't love it.

"You saw the show and you want to buy some garlic."

"Yes, I saw the show and I want garlic. I don't have a TV myself. I was at a neighbor's house. We're both gardeners. I'd like to have some garlic to plant and eat. I'll buy it if I have to, but I'd like to work for it. I mean work a lot for just a little garlic."

How should I respond?

Before I could decide, the woman on the phone said, "I live in Sebastopol. I work at home. I have a small garden every year. The only exercise I get is hiking the coast and doing volunteer work with the Marine Mammal Rescue Center in Sausalito. I want to work in the soil. I'm good with my hands and I'm strong. I'd be very happy to work for free. You'd be doing me a great favor if you said yes. Maybe you can try me for a week; and then if you don't want me around, you can say so and I'd leave. No hard feelings. It could be a real benefit to you."

"How the hell can I refuse that kind of offer? The part that convinces me is your working for the Rescue Center. I volunteered there for about five years when I was a professor."

"I know. I read your mini-bio on the jacket of your *Garlic is Life*. I liked the book very much; and when I saw the TV show, I thought I have to try this. One *caveat*, however, about this offer."

Caveat? Who uses the word *caveat* these days but a lawyer or a writer? "Are you a lawyer or a writer?"

The response was a faint melody that might have been a chuckle. "No," she said, "I'm a painter."

A painter. Sebastopol . An abrupt memory of something ... a face? a place? a song? a story? ... ah, *a painting.* San Francisco. That exhibit. "What's your name? It doesn't happen to be Ellen, does it? Can't remember the last name."

Her turn to pause. "How did you know?"

"I saw a painting at an exhibit in San Francisco ... what? ... eight or nine years ..."

"Ten. For the VWMP."

"What's the VWMP?"

"Vietnam Women's Memorial Project."

"That's it. A fund-raiser for the memorial for the nurses. My God, I remember. You're that Ellen?"

"I'm that Ellen."

"Is the memorial going up?"

"It went up in 1993, not far from The Wall. I went back when it went up, and I've gone every year since."

"You were a nurse in Vietnam."

"I was a nurse in Vietnam. What about my working for you?"

"Your painting tore me up."

Slightly defensive here: "My painting is not smiley-face, but I can be gentle in public."

"Let's do it."

"Thanks, Mr. Aaron."

"Call me Chester if I can call you Ellen."

"One thing ... certainly, call me Ellen. One thing, Chester. This is that caveat. It's important you know. I'm not trying to set you up. For a romance, I mean. I'm not interested in a romance. I'm content living alone, but I do want to work outside. I mean work hard. Reading your book and then seeing your fields and what you're doing, well, I just had to call. I'll arrive on time and leave on time. Is that OK?"

"I accept your terms."

"I was in a bookstore in Santa Rosa yesterday. It didn't have your *Great Garlic Book* or your poster. I've seen the poster. Do you have that book and the poster at your home?"

"I do."

"May I buy them from you?"

"No, I'll not sell them to you. I'll give them to you. A down payment on … "

"I want to buy them Mr. … Chester. I have the money."

"We'll talk about it. I wish I could say we might work out a trade but the work I saw ten years ago reduced me to jello. It would be too difficult for me to live with. Sorry."

"No problem. Sometimes it's too difficult for me to live with. But I want to be sure you heard me. I said I'm not interested in romance. That's not why I want to do this."

"Ellen, I have a lady. I am very much in love. She lives in San Francisco."

"I'm glad. Thanks, Chester."

I could not have known at the time of that conversation that two months later in June I would no longer have a-lady-with-whom-I-am-very-much-in-love.

"Let's talk salary, Ellen. I don't feel comfortable not paying you."

"Chester, being out there in the field, working with you, will recharge my batteries. Tell you what. Do you smoke a pipe?"

"Used to. Now it's cigars. One a week. Sometimes two."

"Are they good cigars?"

"The best."

"OK. My non-negotiable terms: coffee breaks, no rock music, a free meal now and then, an occasional whiff of one of your cigars. When do I start?"

"You ought to be a union negotiator. How about starting two days from today? Monday. Nine o'clock O.K.?"

"Too early. I paint in the mornings. The morning light's the best for me."

"One o'clock?"

"One's fine. Quit at five? Two, three, days a week?"

"Quit at five. Let's start with two days a week."

The next day, Saturday, no sweater or jacket was necessary for the first time in months, I had a piece of bruschetta; and after one cup of coffee, I carried my second cup onto the deck and down the path through the grove of redwoods. Spring, I was certain, had sprung. But the moment I left the redwoods and stepped into the field a north wind hurled ice crystals at my face. When I jerked back, raising my arm to protect my eyes, coffee splashed over the edge of the cup onto the front of my shirt and my jeans, both laundered just the day before.

After changing my shirt and pulling on jacket and boots, I drank the remaining coffee. Back outside on the deck, convincing myself that the weather had no choice but to be more agreeable, I tried again. Gray skies, no wind. But the air seemed to have thickened while I'd been inside changing my clothes. Breathing was difficult. I'm not generally allergic to anything, but this certainly seemed to be an allergy symptom. Had pollen seeped into the air to make me cough? Acacia all over Sonoma County was in heavy bloom, and Tan Oak was in the nearby brush. Both had created serious illnesses recently among local allergy victims. I loosened the buttons of my jacket to release the constriction in my throat and set out to scout the garlic. With Ellen Saunders coming in two days, I had to decide on how to best take advantage of her offer of free labor.

Out of the redwood grove and into the field, moving carefully through the dense wet grass, I lifted my knees high with each step to try to stay dry; but before I reached Box 1 in Row 1, my legs were soaked from the top of my boots to mid-thigh. I considered returning to the house a second time for rain-gear, at least for the rubber pants. Why did I hesitate? Why, even with the loosened buttons, was my throat so tight I had trouble swallowing? Was that a threat in those dark clouds on the east horizon?

Then, as if a switch had been thrown, the sun appeared but disappeared almost immediately. The tumbling mass of dark clouds absorbed the sunlight. As if caught in a sudden crosswind they stopped tumbling and they merged, forming a single cloud. Then the mass separated into several rolling portions again, each portion struggling to possess the gray-tinged reds and the blues that bloomed in the sky above them.

Racing across the horizon, the clouds, fueled by the exploding colors, grouped together like animals building each other's courage to charge against the enemy. The muted blues, golds and reds flowed and shifted to create an almost black purple. Then the sunlight boiled up inside the purple to create an eruption of intense burgundy.

Were I still a boy and still the precocious artist ("You will be a famous artist some day, Chester.") trying to capture that light, I would squirt a bit of umber into the clot of thick cobalt blue waiting on my board. I'd knife in globs of ivory with a thin strip of sky-blue, perhaps even a dash of black. Eventually I would give up.

No possibility of this famous-artist-to-be or any artist capturing even a hint of that sky born on the eastern horizon that morning. Could it perhaps be captured with pastels? Too dusty, too soft-edged,—no not the pastels but the clouds the pastels would produce. Depth was needed, a solidity that only oils could produce. Perhaps Turner could have done it. Homer, maybe. Constable? Definitely Constable. English seas are forever swarming beneath chaotic skies like those clouds of last Saturday. Tiepolo? No. Tiepolo's clouds would be too tender, too ephemeral, a home for aging angels. No angels would dare survive in that only-in-California early-morning-in-April sky.

The rains came again, harder than before, and colder.

Defeated, I retreated one more time into the house where, as tired and as hungry as if I'd been working all day, I made another cup of coffee. Searching inside the refrigerator, I found the remnant of the blackberry pie Suzanne Adams had given me the week before when I had supper with her and Roger.

For that pie, Suzanne had used a quart from the gallons of blackberries she and Roger had picked in my field last summer. She canned a total of twenty quart and ten pint jars, some with full berries, some with jam. Of my share, I still had two jars of berries and one jar of jam on the shelf.

I studied the remnant of pie, thinking that there was enough there for two lunches, that day's and the next. Needing an immediate and substantial sugar-hit, I ate it all.

Rain continued through the afternoon and into the evening. The reports on television predicted Sunday would be clear. It rained hard all day Sunday.

Sunday at noon I called Ellen Saunders to suggest we delay the start of her work for one week. "But can you come to supper tonight? You can eat and run. We can talk garlic. Maybe painting too."

Ellen hesitated, wondering, I'm sure, if this were a ploy to lure her into the romance she very definitely did not want. "Remember," I said. "I'm in love with another woman. This can be an introduction to the work you'll be doing."

"If I bring rain gear and boots can we tour the field?"

"Sure."

"Can I make a request, Chester?"

"You're a vegetarian."

"No, no. I eat meat. I just … well, can we not talk about painting?"

To appreciate Ellen Saunders (and also, perhaps, appreciate me more than you already don't) you first need to know about that San Francisco exhibit.

The exhibit was not the usual glamour-fashion circus. In fact, I recall now that the reviews I saw at the time commented less on the art being exhibited than on *the cause* the exhibit celebrated. The Vietnam War was still a topic to be graciously avoided, like using a dirty word in front of your grandmother.

The audience was composed mostly of women. Very few baby-boomers, few Gen-X's. No glitz, no string ensembles, no wealthy debutantes, no chic volunteer guides.

I'm usually a cynical puritan at galleries or museums or poetry readings. An artist or writer ought to pick his nose or scratch her crotch in private. If I cry at a movie I pretend to be laughing even if I'm alone. But here at this San Francisco gallery, I surrendered; and I suffered as I'd once suffered in Jerusalem, at Yad Vashem, the Holocaust Memorial.

Given *The San Francisco Chronicle's* announcement of the exhibit (fourteen artists represented, all of them former nurses in Vietnam), I had no reason to expect the exhibit to be light-hearted or fanciful. I was not surprised that every piece gave itself to death and agony but I was surprised to discover death and agony on the battlefield clothed in mercy.

Over the years, when I lived in Los Angeles and in Berkeley, I'd seen a fair amount of gallery and museum art created by soldiers who had served in World War II and Vietnam. War is an ancient and ongoing heritage, as are its symbols. Death in battle is always brutal, whether by lance, bullet or atomic dust. A fire-gutted city in the Peloponnesian Wars looks not too different, I'd bet, than did Lidice after the German bombing or Dresden after the Allied bombing. Freed of armor or khaki or jungle-camouflage, absent of national markings, one corpse looks like another.

On the entry wall, in charcoal with a subtle overlay of pastels (defined on the title-card as *a sketch:*) a battlefield, a soldier in camouflage hugging the legless torso of another soldier in remnants of camouflage. The anatomy of the battlefield, of the face and hands and leg-stumps, was too precise, too detailed, for the work to be considered a sketch. In iconic posture, the soldier who would survive was not just screaming out against death; he was screaming out for life, as was the artist. The card on the wall to the right of the sketch indicated the artist to be *Maj. Pamela Dorothy Lane, R.N., Toledo, Ohio.* Additional relevant identification: *85th Evac, Qui Nhon, Pleiku, 3rd Field Hospital.*

Had I anticipated what would happen to me in that gallery, I would not have gone. I suffer neither embarrassment nor humiliation easily. In that gallery among the mementos of the Vietnam War, I could not see those tortured soldiers and nurses as residents of another place, another time. Those soldiers in the arms of nurses were comrades in the arms of other comrades. In the paintings, sketches, sculptures; faces, arms, uniforms, covered with blood, the nurses (the artists) were pleading for expiation.

The painting on the next wall — an oil in bold, brilliant lightning colors — just destroyed the strength in my legs. I put out a hand to the wall for support. In the background was a helicopter unloading stretchers with a team of attendant doctors and nurses. In the foreground was a single nurse, bent over a soldier on a cot just set on the ground by two blurred corpsmen running back to the helicopter for the next casualty. In precise anatomical detail, the soldier's arms wrapped around the nurse's neck; the soldier's face distorted in pain, perhaps terror; the nurse's hands on the soldier's cheeks, her face torn by the knowledge of her patient's, her comrade's, inevitable death.

They were both, soldier and nurse, so young.

I rushed to find a rest room and locked myself in a stall.

I was sobbing for that nurse, for that soldier, for all the nurses and all the soldiers who had ever served in battle. I was sobbing for those old men behind whose backs I had snickered as a boy when they had confessed their torments in the First World War. I was sobbing for those soldiers whom, less than thirty years later, I held in my own arms on another battlefield in another war (now already forty-five years in the past). They were not just soldiers, then or now, but men — young men! Dear, God, how young! They were comrades with whom I had formed a union more intense and more loving and more durable than I had formed with any one before or since except, per-haps, my mother and my father.

Sitting there in that locked stall of that gallery — and think-ing, now, as I write — Dear God, grant me the power to bring them all … my mother, my father, Frederick and Kruyevich (whose head had been torn from his neck by a piece of shrapnel and tossed into my lap). Dear God, grant me the power to bring them all back to life. I remember thinking then, in that locked stall, the words *Dear God*, I formed the words even though I was a devout atheist convinced that God did not exist. Now, today, grown old; and thinking too often about the unforgivable mistakes of my past, I trip occasionally over the question I dare not ask: *But what if She does?*

Recovered, I returned to the painting to see, on the wall, at the side of the painting, the artist's identity card. *Capt. Ellen Saunders, R.N. Ret., Sebastopol, California. 312th Evac., Chu Lai; 67 Evac., Qui Nhon; 3rd Field Hospital, Saigon.*

Sebastopol … twenty minutes from my home.

Back home that night I searched the Sonoma County phone book. No *Saunders, Ellen* listed. I called the gallery the next day. The owner informed me that Ellen Saunders had requested that her address not be offered to anyone who might inquire about her.

For several days I sat at my typewriter trying to put into words my confusion about my reincarnated memories of my attitudes and activities during that war in Vietnam.

I had been married at the time and was teaching at Saint Mary's College. Male students, as long as they were students, could stay out of the army; all of those male students were white. Twenty year old Black and Hispanic men had taken their places in Vietnam.

A professor-friend at Berkeley had gained a lot of intellectual currency in graduate school by protesting the war as an example of corrupt American capitalism. Spared Vietnam, he had time to win his degree and become a professor. He is now a rich and much honored literary icon, hustling the same American capitalism he condemned in the '60s. Why do I want to vomit when I see his books admired by critics whose white asses were also saved by Black and Hispanic men they never met in the '60s and the '70s? Conscientious objectors? Men who defied their draft boards and risked or went to prison? I salute them.

My wife and I marched in numerous anti-war demonstrations. I was strongly opposed to that war (I still am); but when the young war protesters began demanding consideration for the humanity of the Vietnamese by demeaning the humanity of the American cops and then of the American men and women fighting and dying in Vietnam, my need to protest faltered. Something — I could not define it and didn't want to try — was wrong. When the people at the rallies and in the streets and the local and national underground press referred to cops as "pigs" and American soldiers as "baby-killers," I found excuses to avoid participating in the marches. Even more humiliating today: I don't remember ever confessing my sentiments at the time.

I did know that I could not and would not demean any man or woman who served in combat. We — those soldiers and nurses — those men and those women and I — shared a heritage that did not deserve contempt.

All day previous to that Saturday, that day of the clouds, the day before Ellen came to supper, there had been alternating spells of cold wind-driven rain, clean blue skies and brilliant sun. I knew that thrilling purple-burgundy light would never return again.

Sunday night at supper, telling Ellen Saunders about those clouds and those colors that had appeared and disappeared the previous morning, and finding words inadequate, I settled for, "I guess you had to experience that mass of color." She waited patiently, silently. "I have a sense," I said, "of how mystics must feel trying to describe to non-believers the vision they saw on a village wall."

"How do you know I'm a non-believer? You sound like a

painter who wants to be a writer. Or maybe a writer who wants to be a painter."

"Strange you should say that. When I was eighteen years old and graduating from high school, my drawings and paintings won me a scholarship to Carnegie Tech in Pittsburgh. It's called Carnegie-Mellon now. I went into the army instead. After the war I went to UCLA on the GI Bill. Of my six brothers I especially admired one. He was a writer. During the war I sent him letters from Europe. He convinced me I was already a better writer than he'd ever be. Heady praise from the master to his twenty-two year old disciple. In college, after two of my stories won prizes in national contests, I realized I'd never be more than a fair painter if I stayed with art. I decided to concentrate on writing. As they never said, the rest is not history."

I did not know that night of Ellen's visit that I would soon discover what I already knew: words can be trusted no more than paint to capture reality. It would be words, after all, which, months in the future, would kill the love that had (has) enriched my life for so many years.

Ellen asked, as if she found the reality hard to contemplate, "You have no urge at all to ever paint again?"

"None. Words are enough."

"Skies," Ellen said with a deep sigh. "I don't ever try to paint skies. Any kind of sky. Clouds? Forget it. I can't even remember the last time I painted a tree. I spend hours every day at the coast but I've never painted a seascape. No interest." She waited, continuing to gaze out through the window at the fields and trees beyond. I did not know how to invade her mood or even if I should. She was depressed, it seemed to me, and I just didn't know what I should say. Then she shook herself as if the depression, having deserted her, had left exhaustion in its wake. She nodded at the fields and the blossoming plum and apple and pear and the redwood trees struggling to ignore the rain. "Or all that." She shook her head. "The pastoral life. Can't do it."

I could not find it in my heart to tease her about her earlier plea that we not talk about painting that night.

We'd had time before supper to spend an hour in the field, both of us in rain-gear and boots. I offered a mini-lecture and led

Ellen on a tour, demonstrating what I was trying to do and why I was — am still, today, despite the occasional pains — more content than I have ever been in my seventy-six years, eleven months, fourteen days of life.

Ellen stopped to wipe the rain from her face as she stared at me. "Are you really content, Chester?"

"Yes. I know things could be better. They always can. But I sleep very well every night. I don't think I've had a nightmare since I started growing garlic."

Ellen wiped the rain from her face again and shaking her head in astonishment, perhaps with a touch of envy, said, "Let's go in. I'm cold."

I'd built a fire before Ellen arrived, so we lazed in front of the iron stove for a half-hour before I put supper on the table. Not a bad meal. Simple. A garlic appetizer, a garlic soup, a garlic pasta. "I just took for granted you'd like garlic," I said.

"Please," she said. "I do. In or on everything except my coffee and my ice cream."

"Agreed. The one childhood treasure I, like General MacArthur, will never surrender. The root beer float. Can you imagine a root-beer float with garlic ice cream? Never."

As she had promised, Ellen did indeed work hard. The original two-day week lasted for two weeks. From then on through the next five weeks it was a three-day week. She always arrived at one, always left at five. Arriving and departing, she was filled with such energy, such high spirit, that I could not resist infection. I even sang as I worked, hoping it wouldn't dampen her spirits.

After a brief introduction to the weed-whacker, she used the machine as easily and efficiently as I did. Whacking high water-logged weeds at the soil line does not cut the stalks. They just wrap around the gear, binding it, locking it. The nylon whips stop whirling; the engine roars and then stalls. There is nothing to do but turn off the ignition, untangle and unwind the grass, free the whips, start the motor again, and start cutting again. I taught Ellen what a Mexican worker taught me. "Watch. Cut the top third of the grass on the first sweep. Return and cut the lower third on the second sweep. Return and cut close to the soil on the third sweep. Then step forward and start all over: top third, middle, bottom. Step."

This process takes three times as long as it might were I to wait until the grasses dried, but by then they would be so high the job would take twice as long. All this time they'd be throwing shade over the garlics, hiding the essential sunlight and creating seed that would be carried by the winds all over the rest of the field. Another problem: the high grasses would permit gophers easier access to the tops of the boxes and the crop inside.

After using the weed whacker as I taught her and after she worked without complaint for about a week, Ellen came up with a suggested improvement. "Why don't you rent a tractor, Chester? Or a mower? Don't get me wrong. I love doing this. But it takes so long. And you have so many other jobs to do."

"Because I was an amateur when I built my boxes. The boxes lie in long rows. Right?"

"Right."

"Boxes are four feet apart, rows are four feet apart. Right?"

"Right, Chester."

"Enough space for a wheel barrow and a weed-whacker, not enough space for a tractor or a mower. I was stupid. But to redesign and reconstruct would require a year or two. And three or four thousand dollars for lumber, soil and wire. I'd have to hire a lot of help to do it all. Now you know why I abuse myself and my weed whacker each April and May. And why I now abuse you."

"You're not abusing me, Chester. No one will ever abuse me. That's my job."

An odd and even troubling analysis but I chose not to pursue it.

Together over time we cleared a path between the boxes and the pile of rabbit manure. We took turns with the wheelbarrows and the shovels and the machetes until the garlics in all sixty boxes had received a side dressing of the nitrogen-rich manure. Whenever necessary we chopped and hoed and shoveled around the base of each box to lower the soil line to eliminate potential springboards the gophers could use to climb up over the tops of the boxes and into the precious crop. We cleaned the shed and hung and tightened the wires both inside the shed and outside under the roof of the carport. There, in another month, in the cool shade, each wire would be supporting hundreds of bunches (every bunch neatly labeled) of garlic stalks hung immediately after being freed of the soil.

Ellen was as supportive and as interested in the entire process of growing garlic as a good foreman should be. When I brought in extra help (usually students from local colleges) Ellen was motherly and fatherly and farmerly, but always thinking about me and my needs, which she'd learned quickly and easily. She was as firm and considerate and as frustrated with the student-workers as I was.

Alone, she and I often shared our dismay that the young students I hired, as well-intentioned as they might have been, were simply not reliable. Almost without exception they had to be watched. In their youthful arrogance they were certain that their two classes in soils and ecology gave them the right to ignore my advice about how and what to do in the field

From the first day Ellen and I enjoyed our shared coffee breaks. Along with my coffee from Peet's in Berkeley we would have either the goodies I bought at the Union Hotel Café or she brought from her own kitchen. Over the following weeks that Ellen worked with me we had supper at my house three times. I took her to the Union Hotel for bruschetta once and, once, to 101 Main in Sebastopol.

That day we started to cut the weeds the sunlight had been warm, almost hot, on the back of my neck. It was the first week of June so the possibility of rain was very slight; but after a heavy roll of thunder, the sky just simply exploded. Before I could run through the field (the weed-whacker over my shoulder) and reach my house, the rain poured out of a sky-size bucket. I called Ellen and suggested she not come back to work until the weather improved.

Would summer ever come? And when it came, would it be as bizarre as the spring had been? And would it be as disappointing as that day?

Late in the afternoon Elizabeth called from San Francisco. "Chester, I've been trying to think of the best way to tell you this. I have to be up front. It's over. I love you, I will always love you, but I want a family. You have insisted you are too old to start a family. Please try to forgive me. I have to do this, and I have to do it this way. Cold Turkey. If I am in front of you, I can't say it. I will miss you forever."

I will miss- Elizabeth forever, that woman who had promised to be with me forever, no matter the crisis, no matter the distance. Feeling alone, isolated and vulnerable, I called Ellen Saunders. "It's still raining. I still want you to hold off coming to work on Monday. I don't want to cook for myself tonight. Or for you. How about being my guest for dinner at 101 Main in Sebastopol?"

"Oh my," Ellen said. "Dinner in a real restaurant. What shall I wear?"

"Do you have any clothes? If you don't, I can bring a t-shirt and a pair of jeans. I don't think my cowboy boots will fit you though."

"Sandals OK? Not Birkenstocks. Don't own Birkeys. I do have beautiful sandals from Italy and I have a new skirt. Guess what? It's purple, dark purple, almost black purple."

When Ellen opened the front door and stood there in her white silk blouse and her purple, almost black purple, skirt and her Italian sandals she was the most beautiful fifty year old woman I had ever seen. I did not say a word but my thoughts were obviously on my face. There was not the slightest doubt that Ellen read my thoughts. She reached out and placed a tender grateful slap of mock punishment on my cheek. "Shame," she said.

"You've been painting?"

"Yes." She made no move to say more than that or to invite me in. She came out, closed the door behind her, and said, "Want to go dancing after supper? I'm kidding. I dance worse than I cook."

"I bet your cooking's better than mine."

"Flattery will get you … a hug. That's as far as I go."

Last year, in early March after the final (the 32,345th) clove had gone into the ground, I went out every day, no matter the weather, to patrol the fields. Mounded on each of the sixty boxes was a six-inch blanket of wheat straw and under the wheat straw were layers of newspaper. Inside each of the three-inch-deep holes punched down through the paper was a garlic clove. On top of the paper and deep inside every punched hole around each clove were the pellets of rabbit manure. By January, in ten or fifteen of the sixty boxes, as the rabbit manure began to disintegrate, sending its delayed spurts of nitrogen and other goodies into the soil in response to the pleas of the lengthening and very hungry garlic roots, the first tentative tip of a green spear pushed up through the mulch of wheat straw.

By late March in every one of my sixty boxes, green spears were pushing up through the wheat grass mulch which was now compacted to three or four inches from its original six inch thickness. In April I knew that some varieties of the garlics would be three feet high, some ten to twelve inches. On a certain dry day I would pull on my jacket and my rubber boots; and I'd go down through the redwoods, moving in cautious patrol around each box as if they'd sprouted during the night. I would now see the first scapes.

The third week Ellen was here (she was working three days a week by then) we stood with our knees against the redwood walls of one box. I heard Ellen gasp and murmur, "Oh, my God, look at them."

The garlic stalks in Section A of the box were hip-high, dark green, firm; the bottom leaves beginning to turn brown. I pulled the plastic tag out of the soil and read the details I'd written (with weatherproof ink,) in October, 1998, the day the garlics in that section had gone into the soil.

1A— Spanish Roja —75 — 10/1/98

"A" refers to the first of two sections of box one. "Spanish Roja" is the variety of garlic planted in Section A. "75" is the number of cloves of Spanish Roja planted, and October 1, 1998, was the date of the planting.

"Birds." Ellen whispered the word with quiet reverential awe. "They're called…"

"I know. You describe them in your book. They're called scapes. But look at them. They're glorious. Just … glorious. They're flying. They're everywhere. They're so, so beautiful."

"All the Hardnecks produce them."

"Chester, they weren't here when I left last week. Look. They're dancing in the wind. They're beautiful birds flying in the wind."

"Remember my poster? Remember the first night you came for supper, before you started work...?"

"You showed me the photographs of scapes on your poster and in your book."

"We have to cut them. They take energy out of the bulb."

"Cut them? Kill them?"

"Right. The longer they stay, the more energy they take. If we cut them at this stage, the bulb is saved and the scapes are edible. If they're cut later, they're too woody to eat."

Ellen looked at me with a mix of anger and shock. "You eat them?

"I use them like asparagus, or I make soup out of them. They can be stir-fried with other vegetables."

Ellen's face sagged; she gulped and bent forward. I thought she was about to be sick. Then she straightened. "Chester, these are more beautiful than they are in your poster. They're like angels flying over the field."

"In another week or two when other Hardnecks send up their scapes, we'll have thousands of angels flying over the field. Now, let's break some off, and I'll make us a pasta sauce for supper."

"You can't; you can't. Don't hurt them."

It took some bargaining to convince Ellen that even after I cut enough scapes for supper there would still be hundreds of angels flying in the wind. And after those were gone there would be a thousand more. "My granddaughter calls them butterflies."

"Chester, you have forty-five years to come up with a difference between angels and butterflies."

Ellen's experience with the scapes required she stay for supper. But only if I did not cut up the scapes. She could not endure their elegant beauty being marred. Would she stay if my pasta sauce were made with the clove and not the scape? Yes, but only if she could use my bathroom and take a shower. No problem. I loaned her clean socks and a shirt and even a pair of jeans that would have been a perfect fit had her waist been twelve inches thicker and her legs twelve inches longer. At the table we talked about garlic, about what we'd be doing for the rest of the harvest, about the possibility of her braiding wreaths and selling them at the farmer's market in Sebastopol. We worked together to wash the dishes and clean up the kitchen; and when she prepared to leave, she asked if she could take some of the scapes home with her.

"Of course. Take as many as you want. They'll be coming up in various boxes for the next several weeks."

"I'm so sorry they have to be cut off," she said. "They are so gorgeous. They fly like birds released from their cages."

I felt a pang of anguish, almost fear, at the expression on her face. She seemed so vulnerable, so defenseless against a brutal world. I wanted to grab her and wrap her in my arms and protect her, but I remembered her earlier *caveat*.

She went through the supply of scapes I'd brought in from the field, holding each one close to her face and then at arms length to judge its shape, its color, its flair. She finally gave up. "May I take them all?" she asked. "You're not going to use them anyway. May I?"

"You bet. In fact, I'm almost ready to say I'll never cut another scape, but I won't. Say it, I mean."

After storing the scapes in a bag I walked Ellen to her pickup. Once in the cab, she rolled down the window. "Thanks for supper, Chester. And thanks for the angels."

"I'll see you Monday, Ellen."

"One o'clock. Chester, working with you in the field, working with the garlic ... these beautiful birds ... well, it's a distraction I need these days." She took a deep breath and, her voice catching in her throat, she said, "I'm having a hard time with the painting right now." Then she raced the motor and rushed off, the tires throwing gravel.

I kept watching the truck move down the road until the red taillights disappeared. I wondered (knowing I would never ask for clarification) if, when she had said *the painting*, she meant she was having a hard time those days with painting in general or with the specific piece she was working on.

That night I read pages out of two books I had borrowed from the Sebastopol library. The title of one, by Lynda Van Devanter, with Christopher Morgan, was *Home Before Morning*, subtitle: *The Story of an Army Nurse in Vietnam.* The title of the other book by Winnie Smith was *American Daughter Gone to War.* Its subtitle: *On the Front Lines with an Army Nurse in Vietnam.*

The books had been lying on my bed. Had Ellen seen them when she went upstairs to take her shower?

I worked alone the next three days. On Sunday night I called Ellen again, wondering if I might invite her to supper. I needed company.

She answered on the fifth ring, just as I was about to hang up.

"Ellen, I'm sorry. I woke you."

"No… no … Chester? Is this Chester?"

"Yes. Ellen, what's wrong? You sound strange."

"Chester, can you … no, no … Chester… can you help me? Can you come over right away?"

She was crying.

"Twenty minutes. Did you have supper?"

"I had … no…. I didn't. I haven't eaten all day. I don't know when I ate last. I … no, I didn't … Please hurry."

"I'll bring some food. Turn on the porch light."

The light was on. No one answered my knock so I tried the door. It was unlocked. As I walked in I called, "Ellen? You in here?"

No answer.

I kept calling as I walked through the house. The kitchen, the living room, the little alcove that served as a study, the bedroom, the bathroom, all were empty. I went down the hall beyond her bedroom, past the bathroom, to a closed door. I pushed it open. Ellen was lying on the floor. She was dressed but wearing no shoes or socks. Her jeans were open, as if she'd been in the bathroom and had simply neglected to put herself together. Her eyes were closed. I felt her face. Her skin was warm. I called her name several times but she did not respond.

I called 911. An ambulance arrived in about ten minutes with two Paramedics. They took her to the Emergency Room at Palm Drive Hospital in Sebastopol, about ten minutes from her home.

I waited in the lobby, trying to find the ancient magazines

interesting. When the doctor finally came out, he asked several questions before he decided it was appropriate to tell me that the patient had taken an overdose of sleeping pills. The patient was very sick. The patient would recover, but she would be kept in the hospital for two or three days for observation.

The doctor flipped open the chart and took a piece of paper from the clip. "The patient regained enough consciousness to give me this. She asked me to ask you to call this number. The patient said it's her daughter."

"The patient's name is Ellen Saunders," I said.

I called from the pay phone in the lobby. The area code (212) I knew to be New York City.

A woman answered the phone. She'd been asleep.

After identifying myself, I told her as much as I knew. The daughter whispered something I could not catch but then she said, "I'll catch a plane in the morning."

"I'll meet you in San Francisco…."

"Thanks, but I'll take a bus. I know the routine. I've done it several times over the years when I visited Momma. Who are you? What's your name?"

"Chester Aaron."

"You're the garlic guy. Momma told me about you."

"Yes. What's your name?"

"Marlene Johansen. I'm married. I was married."

"Marlene, your mother is…"

"I know. I know. My mother is a wonderful woman."

"I'll stay here at the hospital tonight as long as I can. I'll come over in the morning. Please call me when you get in."

"I will. But, Chester?"

"Yes?"

"She's not having an affair with you, is she?"

"No."

"OK. I thought maybe, after the way she described you, you might be good for her. But it was just a fantasy. I have lots of fantasies about Momma. I'll call my sister in Chicago. She'll come out too. I think this time we're going to take her back with us. With one of us. She can't be lucky every time. I mean lucky to have someone like you around when she goes down like this. I can't stand it any more. I just can't … just can't stand it."

It ended very quickly.

The two sisters came to Sebastopol the next day. Ellen, obviously concerned about the damage she assumed she had done to herself and perhaps to me, did not want me to see her. I accepted her rules.

Three days later when Ellen was released from the hospital, the sisters helped her pack. I called her house in Sebastopol and told Marlene I'd be glad, over the next few weeks, to pack up everything left behind and send it along.

The morning they left, Marlene called me. "Momma's left something on the breakfast counter for you, Chester. Thanks. For everything."

The *something* Ellen left on the counter was a small pastel sketch of three of the Spanish Roja scapes, elegant birds flying up into an azure sky.

I have not tried to communicate with Ellen. Marlene called me three months after she took her mother to New York. "Don't be surprised if Momma calls you soon."

It is now September, 2000. Ellen has not yet called.

An Afterward

Working to be as correct as possible in the details, I talked to a friend who'd endured two tours in Vietnam. He told me about a relevant Vietnam-nurses web-site. I went there and, by accident, found the poem "Hello, David." I managed to get in touch with Dusty, the poet, to ask for permission to include that poem in this chapter because it captured in a moment the emotion I needed twenty-four pages to try to capture. Dusty gave me permission.

Dusty's "Hello, David" helped me complete the last pages of this chapter.

The poem (copyrighted by Dusty in 1987) was included in *Shrapnel in the Heart* (Random House, 1987.) Dusty's "*Battle Dressing*: Poems about the Journey of a Nurse in Vietnam" won the 1999 Houston Writers League Poetry Chapbook Contest.

Hello, David

Hello, David — my name is Dusty
I'm your night nurse.
I will stay with you.
I will check your vitals
  every 15 minutes.
I will document
  inevitability.
I will hang more blood
  and give you something
  for your pain.
I will stay with you
  And I will touch your face.

Yes, of course,
  I will write your mother
  and tell her you were brave.
I will write your mother
  and tell her how much you loved her.
I will write your mother
  and tell her to give your bratty kid sister
  a big kiss and hug.
What I will not tell her
  is that you were wasted.

I will stay with you
  and I will hold your hand.
I will stay with you
  and watch your life
  flow through my fingers
  into my soul.
I will stay with you
  until you stay with me.

Goodbye, David — my name is Dusty.
I am the last person

you will see.
I am the last person
  you will touch.
I am the last person
  who will love you.

So long, David — my name is Dusty.
David — who will give me something
  for my pain?

Chapter Three

TEENY BIAGGIO

TRANSYLVANIAN
Softneck Silverskin/Artichoke

Seed from Professor Robin Miller, Brandeis University. She had gone through Transylvania on her way home from Russia. She'd bought garlic in a village market. I offered to trade her five different varieties of my garlics for one head of her Transylvanian. She sent me two heads. Each head contained double layers of twenty very small cloves that were difficult to peel. Taste: mild. In three years of effort, I have now planted and lost more than five hundred cloves, never harvesting more than a few stalks. More recent bulbs have contained ten to twenty larger cloves. Taste now: deceptive, ranging from mild to hot, bland to moderately rich. Because of mystique of mythology/folklore, resistance to control, this is the most provocative, most dramatic, and most requested of my current collection of garlics. Difficult to peel. Shelf life after harvest: three to four months.

At the age of twelve Crystal Biaggio was no taller, wider, or heavier than she had been at the age of eight. Her parents, brothers and sisters, and every student and teacher in Occidental's Harmony School called her Teeny, Teeny Biaggio.

I have been giving the Biaggios various garlics for several years. They ate them, planted them, loved them. They also bought my various books for birthday gifts for relatives and always had me autograph them. A poster, signed and framed, hangs on the wall of their kitchen. On my seventy-fourth birthday party at their house, they poured Dago Red wine (made by Grandpa Ernesto) on my head and declared me an honorary Italian.

I have known Teeny from birth. She has always been a serious, almost somber child. She completely stole my heart a year ago, when she was eleven years old.

She called one afternoon in late September to ask if she might interview me for a project initiated by her fourth grade English teacher. "It's the first project for the new semester," she said. "We're supposed to interview a living, famous person who lives in Occidental. Your books are in the Occidental library and the Sebastopol library, and my Mom and Dad have bought very, very many copies. You're famous. So could I interview you?"

"I'd be flattered, Crystal. In fact, I'd be honored."

"You can call me Teeny if you want to. Everyone else does. And you're sort of family."

That evening after supper, Anna Maria Biaggio brought Teeny to my house.

At Anna Maria's request, I took them on a quick tour of my garlic shed, which contained, hanging from the walls and ceiling, mesh bags filled with garlic bulbs. In a week or two, the bulbs would be broken into cloves and the cloves (14,000 of them) planted in my sixty boxes.

Teeny's passage through the shed was delayed by her fascination with the identification tags tied to each mesh bag. She recited aloud the fragments of information written on each tag she fingered. "Purple Caul... Cauldron; Bitero's North Italian, yeah, Bitero sounds Italian; Japanese Hok ... Ho ... Hokkaido; look, here's one called Georgian Crystal. Was it named after me?" She laughed at her wit and then kissed the leaves.

When she spoke the name of each country specified on the tags she delivered the syllables with the studied cadences of an actress in training. " ... China ... Bolivia ... Mexico ... Ooze ..."

"That's Uzbekistan."

"Oozebeckastand? Where's Oozebeckastand, Chester?"

Her mother suggested that perhaps she should call me *Mister Aaron* since I was to be the famous person she'd be interviewing and writing about.

"No, no," I insisted. "Chester's fine. After all, Crystal permits me to call her Teeny. Uzbekistan is in Europe, Teeny, near Russia. It's an independent republic now, like Georgia or the Ukraine or Belarus."

"There's a girl in my class called Bella. Her last name is Goldman."

"No relation to Belarus," I said.

Anna Maria said it was getting late, and Chester had work to do so maybe they should get the interview on its way. Teeny, reluctant to leave the shed, dallied over one last bag. She read the plastic details aloud. "Polish Car... Carpathian Red, 150, Box 31, October 27, 1997. What's all that mean, Chester? Is it a secret code?" Her eyes widened at the possibility of romance or mystery.

"Well, it is a code, Teeny, but it's no secret. Here goes. The garlic in this bag is a red skinned garlic from a village in the Carpathian mountains in Poland. The 150 means I planted 150 cloves. That number two in the corner of the tag means I planted the cloves in box 2. October 27 means I planted the cloves on October 27, last year, 1997. Next month, when I harvest, I'll keep the Polish Carpathian garlic separate from all the others. In my harvest log I'll note the date I harvest — let's say it's July 18, 1998. Knowing when it was planted, I'll do my arithmetic and I'll then know how many months, weeks, and days the Polish Carpathian Red garlic took to mature. That information will help me decide when to plant Polish Carpathian Red next fall, or if I want to plant it at all. Next year, when I harvest the Carpathian Red that I will plant next month, I'll compare the number of bulbs I take out of box 2 with the number of cloves I put into the box. That will help me decide if it's worth the time and labor to plant Polish Carpathian Red garlic again next year in this soil in this Occidental weather."

"Wow. This is very, very complicated, Chester. I thought you just put the garlic in the ground and it grew."

Anna Maria reminded Teeny that Chester was a busy man. "Paul tells me you write every evening," she said. "Everyone in Occidental, of course, knows you don't like visitors in the evenings."

"You know, Anna Maria, as I get older, I find I don't like visitors in the morning. Or the afternoon either."

Teeny laughed. "You are very, very funny."

"Are we intruding now?" the flustered Anna Maria asked.

"Teeny's right. I'm joking. There's time. I do try to write every evening."

"Then let's get the show on the road, honey," Anna Maria said, prodding Teeny as we moved down the path toward the house.

Apropos of nothing, Teeny, turning and walking backward, said, "I read three of your books."

"Three? I'm flattered, Teeny. Do you have a favorite?"

"I loved *An American Ghost* very, very much. The story was very very sad, though. I wish they hadn't killed the cougar. Albie was very very brave."

"I wish they hadn't killed the cougar, too, Teeny."

"Then why did you have them do it? You wrote the book. You could have saved the cougar."

"Teeny, you've struck at the heart of the problem writers have to live with. I wanted the death of the cougar to make Albie's struggles, successes and failures more important to Albie as well as to the reader. Like a farmer, an author has choices. Some will be right, some will be wrong. Maybe I should have saved that cougar, just like I've saved a few varieties of garlic I should have given up on or given up on a few I should have saved."

Teeny continued to consider that idea as the three of us sat on the deck, drinking the cold Henry Weinhardt root beer I'd brought from the refrigerator. It was the edge of autumn, but there were still occasional evenings like this one, warm enough for cold drinks and still warm enough to sit out on the deck. "I'm ready, Teeny."

The interview went well. Teeny, with grim concentration, took notes as I answered the questions she read from her teacher's instruction sheet. After a half hour or so, as the September twilight slid from blue to purple to dark gray almost black, Teeny had to squint when she read the print or wrote in her notebook. "Three more questions," she said, tilting the page to catch as much as possible of the last spray of light.

"Let's finish this in the house, Teeny. You'll ruin your eyes out here."

As if the word *here* were its cue, a bat darted out from beneath the eaves of my roof, followed by a second and a third and a fourth. Each of those four and then five or six more flapped and swooped across the deck a few feet above our heads, chopping at the air like tiny helicopters. Their high pitched chirping, just barely perceptible, seemed to scrape the eardrum, like a fingernail on a blackboard.

At the appearance of the first bat, Teeny had leaped from her chair, screaming. With the rush of the others, fluttering and chirping, Teeny, arms closed over her hair and her notebook and papers scattering, ran toward the front of the house, where, sobbing, she struggled in vain to turn the doorknob. I caught her in my arms and held her as Anna Maria opened the door. Teeny stumbled inside, her arms continuing to protect her hair.

A few minutes later on the sofa, settled into her mother's arms, Teeny accepted the hot chocolate I prepared. She was struggling to control the sobs still living inside her throat. "I'm afraid of bats," she said. "They're very, very evil. They get in your hair and suck your blood."

I tried not to sound like a teacher or a preacher. "Teeny, that's an old wive's tale, and you're not an old wife. Of course, neither am I. What would you think if I told you I love bats?"

She glanced at her mother for verification of what she thought she'd heard.

Her mother shrugged. "Chester said it, not me. As Grandpa used to say, *Stai scherzando!*"

"What's *stais zando* mean?"

"*Stai scherzando!* It means *you've got to be kidding!*."

"I'd think," Teeny said, "Chester, *stais zando!* I'd also think you are very, very sick." In spite of her doubts, a smile played at the corner of her lips. "Are you teasing me, Chester?"

"No. If I remember correctly, you suffer every summer from mosquito bites. Right?"

"I am very, very allergic to mosquito bites. Last summer I went to the Emergency Room at Palm Drive hospital. I use about a hundred pounds of anti-mosquito stuff on my skin every summer."

"Teeny, do you know that one bat will eat as many as three hundred mosquitoes a night? In a week, that's 2,100 mosquitoes. In a month that's about eight thousand mosquitoes. There are about ten bats sleeping under my eaves. Those ten bats — multiply 8,000 by ten — eat 80,000 mosquitoes a month. Mosquito season is about three months long. That's 240,000 mosquitoes."

Teeny mouthed the word *Wow!* and said aloud, "And there's still enough left to eat me up."

"Will you do me a favor, Teeny?"

Teeny had the child's natural suspicions of the grownup, but she also had a trusting nature mixed with the canny capacity for self-preservation filtered through twenty generations of peasant ancestors. She waited for clarification, just in case.

"In two weeks," I said, "on October first, when I start planting my garlic, will you come down to help me?"

"Oh, sure. Gee, I thought you were going to ask me to kiss a bat or something."

"It's, well, it's complicated. Don't laugh now — I'm serious — but this year the first full moon comes on September 30th. Lots of local farmers plant with the moon cycles, especially the old Italians. I never have. This year I'm going to. Those old Italians might have something. The night of the full moon I'm going to plant one variety of my garlics. Just one. At midnight. Will you come help me?"

"Teeny," an almost apologetic Anna Maria said, "is in bed by nine o'clock."

"Just this one night, the night of the full moon. Actually, you should be here about fifteen minutes before midnight."

"Chester, this is the weirdest thing I've ..."

"Anna Maria, please. I'll put your name in my next novel. I'll put Paul's name in the next novel. I'll make Teeny a hero in my next novel."

"Oh Momma, please? I want to be a hero very, very much. Let me do it. Please? I'll do my homework right after school. I'll nap for three hours. Then I can wake up and ... midnight, the full moon ... it sounds like Halloween."

"Well," I said, "there could be a connection."

Her mother, with great reluctance, conceded. "That means Paul or I have to get up and drive you down. Thanks heaps, Chester."

Teeny clung to her mother's hand from the moment they left the deck until we reached the curing shed. "I'm sorry I screamed, Chester, but I am very, very scared of bats."

I stopped Teeny and Anna Maria at the door of the curing shed and turned on the ceiling light. "A detour," I said. I untied a bag of garlic bulbs from the overhead wires that contained hundreds of other such bags. "Can you read the tag on this bag, Teeny?"

"Sure," she said. "*Transylvania. 51. 11. Nov. 13, 1996-July 29,1997. Box 13.* Hmm, let's see. That means the garlic's from Transylvania. You planted fifty-one cloves, November 13, 1996. July 29, 1997 you got eleven cloves."

"Eleven bulbs, or heads. A head is a collection of cloves."

"You planted fifty-one cloves and you harvested eleven bulbs."

"Right."

"And you'd planted the cloves in box 13."

"Right. Do you know anything about Transylvania?"

"Isn't that the place where werewolves live? And Dracula, that guy that sucks blood? Very very spooky things happen there."

"You got it. The three heads of garlic in this bag come from Transylvania."

"Yucko, take it away."

"Wait a minute. Werewolves are terrified of garlic. So is Dracula. Wave a head of garlic in front of werewolves or spooks or Dracula and they scream louder than you did. And you know what?"

"What?"

"Bats love garlic and garlic loves bats. Cupid, the god of love, wears a necklace of bats around his ... or is Cupid a she? ... around his or her neck."

"You're kidding."

"Well, it depends on what translation you read. But it's true."
She contemplated this information, unwilling to even try to process its implications. "Does that mean I'm supposed to love bats?"

"For starters it means that tonight your mom's going to make her famous pasta sauce with this Transylvanian garlic. Anna Maria?"

"It's OK with me. I'm always willing to try something new."

I opened the bag and removed four of the precious cloves. Precious because after three years of effort to cultivate and expand the Transylvanian garlic all I had to show for my work were these three bulbs, a total of about sixty cloves. If I failed again this year, I would eliminate the Transylvanian garlic from my collection.

"After tonight," I said, "you will be safe around werewolves and spooks and Dracula until October first. And bats will love you. Think of all those dead mosquitoes. No more ointment on your skin."

"What about after October first?"

"Remember what we're doing at midnight September 30th?"

"We're planting. The full moon."

"We're planting this Transylvanian garlic and only this Transylvanian garlic." I slid into my well rehearsed Bella Lugosi voice: "Who knows vat good events occur ven such a 'ting occurs? Nevar again you worry *pippsilucti*. In Transylvanian *pippsilucti* means mo-skee-toes." Normal voice again: "Fifteen minutes before midnight September 30th."

Teeny said, "I'm very, very pleased I interviewed you."

On the night of September 30th, Paul delivered Teeny at 11:45. I met them near the curing shed and waved off Paul's suggestion he stay. I would drive Teeny home in a half-hour, perhaps less. Paul drove off.

I did not need my flashlight. In the light of the full moon, I led the giggling and jumping Teeny down into the field where I had everything prepared.

The air was cold, but the wind had not come up. There had been two relatively heavy rains the past week so the soil in box 13 was perfect for planting, not dry, not muddy, but moist with perfect tilth.

"You better put these on," I told Teeny, handing her the hard fiber knee-protectors. I tightened the velcro straps so the protectors would stay in place when she bent her knees. "Now we can kneel in the mud and not get our jeans muddy."

The moonlight seemed to brighten even more as we stopped at box 13 where I'd already laid out the items I'd be using: two saran-wrapped sterilized sewing needles; two flat-bladed shovels; two rakes; two wheelbarrows, one filled with soil, one with turkey mulch (cedar chips mixed with dried turkey manure); a bag of bat guano; the plastic bucket containing the three Transylvanian garlic bulbs, cloves not yet broken free; the metal dibble (a ten inch long piece of steel an inch in diameter) for punching holes in the soil; a stack of wet newspapers; a clear clean plastic marker; and a pen with water-proof ink.

"Do you know what bat guano is, Teeny?"

"No."

"It's bat dung."

"What's baddung?"

"Bat-dung. Two words. It's bat manure. Bat shit."

"What do we do with ... with bat-dung?"

"We put it in the soil because it's very high in nitrogen and because, in this box, we'll be planting my Transylvanian garlic. Garlic loves bats and bats love garlic. Bat guano is the essence of bats."

"Yucko."

I poured the guano over the soil in the northern end of the box, and the two of us turned it in and over with our shovels.

"Hold out your finger, Teeny."

The trusting Teeny held out her finger. Before she could react, I pricked the fingertip with one of the needles. She said, "Ouch. What did you do that for? That hurt."

"Love requires both pleasure and pain," I said, squeezing her finger until a few drops of her blood fell onto the soil. Then I pricked my finger and dripped some of my blood as well. "For thousands of years under a full moon, the peasants in Transylvania put their blood into the soil just like this, to guarantee a good harvest."

"Weird," Teeny said, sucking her finger. "Now what?"

I reached into a small paper bag. "You know what this is?"

"Of course. A crucifix."

"Right. A silver crucifix. It belongs to my lady friend. If a vampire or a werewolf comes at you and nothing else works, you wave a silver crucifix in front of it. It will scream, turn and disappear."

I dug a hole in the soil, buried the crucifix and covered it up. We raked the top layer of soil into a smooth flat surface. "Now," I said, "the only dull but practical part of tonight's voodoo performance." I spread the newspaper, five pages thick, across the top of the soil. "While I punch holes every six inches through this wet newspaper, you break all the cloves free of their bulbs."

"Very, very weird, Chester."

"You wait. The Transylvanian garlic is whispering, 'Thank you, Teeny, thank you, Chester.' Can you hear it?"

"I can't hear anything except your breathing. You have a cold?"

"Teeny, don't make fun of your elders. Just break the cloves free and let me know how many we have."

I punched holes in the newspaper at six-inch intervals and waited while Teeny opened each of the three heads. "Sixty," she said. I punched another row of holes to make a total of sixty, four rows of fifteen each, the rows six inches apart, the holes about two inches deep.

"Now, take a clove and put it in a hole, flat end down, pointed tip up, like this. Keep going. One clove in each hole."

After every hole was filled, we covered them with an inch or two of soil from the wheelbarrow, then covered that with three to four inches of turkey mulch. "Now," I said, "take this hose. I'll turn on the water. Spray the whole area while I write on this plastic tag. Remember what I write?"

"Yes. Box number ... what number?"

"Box 13."

"Box 13. Transylvanian. 60. Today's date, September 30, 1997."

"Perfect. I'm also writing the word *Teeny*. You just might bring better luck than the bat guano or the blood or the silver crucifix."

When we were finished, I took Teeny into the house. While

she went to the bathroom to wash her hands, I fixed us both a cup of hot chocolate, which we drank while I drove her home through the redwoods. Neither of us spilled so much as a drop of the hot chocolate in our laps.

The full moon was so bright I turned off my headlights. We drove through the redwoods that surrounded Teeny Biaggio's house and I said, "Isn't it beautiful? I love redwood trees, I love full moons, I love Sonoma County, I love bats, and I love Teeny Biaggio."

"I'll remember this night a very, very long time," Teeny said.

Teeny called me a few days later to tell me her teacher gave her an A+ on her report. "Chester, guess what she wrote on my paper. She wrote, 'The best paper in the entire class. Congratulations.' Chester, it's the only A+ I've ever had."

"There will be more," I said.

Off and on over the fall and winter, whenever I visited the Biaggios, Teeny asked me how the garlic was doing, especially the Transylvanian. I did not confess my fears. The heavy rains put the entire crop, all my varieties, in danger. In March the stalks of the Transylvanian were thin, not promising.

In April and May I invited the Biaggios for supper twice. Each time they went into the field with me to help me weed. The supper in May came near the end of the month, two weeks before the semester ended. We were sitting on the deck having our coffee and dessert, an apple pie Anna Maria had baked. Teeny put down her half-eaten slice of pie and her glass of milk and walked along the deck to stand at the edge. Instead of gazing down across the field, she glanced up into the eaves.

"I hear them," she said.

"Hear what?" Anna Maria asked, but Paul placed a hand on her arm to silence her.

Teeny drew closer to the wall and stood on tiptoes, peering up under the eaves.

A bat flew out, passed over her head. Teeny ducked, started to run, then stopped. She walked on tiptoes back to where she'd been standing. She pursed her lips and made a sound, several times, not too unlike the chirp of a bat.

A second bat flew out, passed over her head. This time she did not move to escape but stood there, grinning, defiant. She chirped again, three times, and each time a bat, as if in response to her call, came flying out from beneath the eaves and sailed over Teeny's head.

After twelve bats — Anna Maria counted them in an ongoing whisper — left the eaves to begin their hunt for food, Teeny returned to the table and, with the aplomb of a connoisseur, said, "This apple pie is very, very good, Momma. The very, very best you ever made."

That summer Teeny had only twelve mosquito bites. She simply wiped them with alcohol and went on to finish her month at Camp Sunshine.

I received a card from her in the third week. "I am having a very very good time," she wrote. "I swim and hike and roast wieners at night in the campfire. How did the Transilvanyen garlic turn out?"

"The very best ever," I wrote her the next day. "Sixty cloves planted, fifty-seven heads harvested. Every head is big and firm and healthy and beautiful. Very, very much like you, Teeny Biaggio."

Chapter Four

SU XIAOLI

XIAN
Hardneck Purple-stripe

Seed from Filaree Farm and an unknown lady in San Francisco's Chinatown. A rare garlic from the province of Xian, in China. Tall thick stalks with wide heavy leaves. Very large bulb with thumb-size cloves covered with skin that can be colored rose to dark red to almost black. Taste: mild at first, then very hot, then mild, melting into a rich earthy taste. Peels easily. Shelf-life after harvest: 3-4 months.

THE 1995 GARLIC HARVEST — I HAD FIFTY-NINE VARIETIES THEN — was probably the best harvest in my fifteen years of trying to survive as a farmer. A small farmer, I might add. I am four inches short of six feet and only have four acres.

Think about Gilroy, California, where the members of the garlic consortium cultivate farms of hundreds and thousands of acres. Gilroy produces about 95% of all the garlic used in the United States. I am less than a pinprick in their bubble, but even they admit that in every way my garlics are superior.

That productive summer of 1995, after having planted 12,350 cloves the previous fall, I suffered the usual loss of about 3%, harvesting 11,507 full bulbs. *Full bulbs* means bulbs that are large, firm, and completely headed (all cloves physically and visually defined) and that are distinctly colored specimens of their unique varieties or sub-varieties.

Even in 1995, that year of my best harvest, some varieties performed better than others, meaning that they met and often exceeded the distinguishing factors of their genetic ancestors of previous years of residence in my field. They were not only larger but also those with red skins, for example, presented skins that were darker red. On the skins of those classified as "Purple Stripe garlics," the purple was darker, the stripes more obvious, and the entire appearance more dramatic. Finally, the variation in the tastes of the different garlics was more intense, meaning that the hot garlics were hotter, the mild garlics milder, and the rich garlics even richer than those same varieties had been in previous years.

Such variation of accomplishment is not unique to garlic. It happens in your family and mine.

Alert farmers or home gardeners or ordinary *aficionados* know that a certain fruit — the Gravenstein apple, for example, or the Indian Blood peach or the Winter Nelis pear — can be smaller or larger than the Gravenstein or the Indian Blood or the Winter Nelis of previous years, with the skin lighter or darker and the meat or pulp sweeter or not as sweet. The reasons: weather, soil, pruning, good or bad luck, or a combination of some or all of these factors.

Out of that 1995 harvest specimens from four varieties I selected for show won gold ribbons at three different County Fairs and two gold ribbons at the State Fair — Choparsky (from the Siberian Botanical Gardens,) Kitab (from Uzbekistan,) Persian Star (from Samarkand,) and Inchelium Red from the state of Washington. In those same fairs four other varieties (Mchadidzhvari, from the Republic of Georgia; Creole Red, from Louisiana/ California; Duganskij, from the Czech Republic; Maiskij, from an Ashkabad bazaar in Turkmenistan) won blue ribbons.

CNN and NET, contributing to America's continuously unfolding and ever expanding obsession with new and supposedly healthy foods, presented a five minute *docudrama* of what one of the reporters described as " ...this unlikely garlic farmer: a seventy five year old veteran of WWII, a former x-ray technician, a former professor of literature, a current writer of fiction for adults and young people, and an ongoing curmudgeon who declares himself more at ease with dogs and cats than he is with people, especially men."

Well, most people, most men, including that reporter.

After those programs, subsequent magazine and newspaper articles, and the publication of two books about garlic (and a poster displaying forty of my most photogenic varieties), I have had to hire a friend to respond to the phone calls and letters from within and outside the United States requesting my garlics for gardens or kitchens.

But back to that 1995 harvest.

As supreme as the harvest was, a few varieties in their second or third generation in my soil and my climate had appeared and were taken from the soil, suffering decline. They were either smaller than the previous year's first or even second generation or they appeared weak with evidence of rot at their bases. Several of the necks were soft or broken. Certain bulbs (often called "heads") had begun to open, their cloves well on the way to decomposition. The hair-roots of several garlics were often very short, completely missing, or were simply fetid gelid masses. Inspection under a magnifying glass and later microscopic inspection by a plant-pathologist friend demonstrated no fungus, no insect or nematode damage. On some bulbs the short, neatly clipped hair-roots presented evidence of the ever-present, and ever-famished gophers.

After collecting those failed specimens, I knew I had to make a decision. Did these garlics deserve another year of effort in my limited space? Might they perform better in a different box filled with a different soil mix? Should I replace those unreliable varieties with other varieties that had already proven themselves, varieties that demanding patrons (customers) had already savored?

I delayed the decision for a month. I needed more evidence, not of the gopher damage (I knew what had to be done about that) but evidence of the failure of the capacity of those specific garlics to survive.

Three of the four potential victims of my concern were first generation, meaning that was the first time I'd planted those varieties. I hung them in a segregated area inside my curing shed to see how or if they might recover during the drying process when they would be losing 30%-40% of their water. If they or their sickly mates survived without further evident damage, they might deserve another year to prove themselves.

Two garlics already in their second and third generations deserved neither sympathy nor probation. They had to be eliminated. So I ate them.

Over the next five or six weeks I served many cloves of these garlics in pastas, salads, soups, and sandwiches. Farewell Argentine Bolero, farewell Siberian Snow, farewell New Guinea Storm, farewell Nigerian Purple.

There comes to mind an old chant about home-made wine from my childhood in the coal-mine town of Sundown, Pennsylvania: "First to the mouth, then to the gums, look out guts, here it comes."

At mid-summer I set aside, in special net-baskets in my curing shed, the healthiest, fattest bulbs of the fifty four varieties I would definitely be replanting in the coming fall. On the morning of September 10, twenty days before I always start my planting (October 1), I received and recorded a call that would lead to my fifty-fifth variety.

My voice: Yeah?

Woman's Voice (with a heavy accent:) You rike garic.

My voice: Is this Donald? You can't fool me. Your accent is lousy.

Woman: I come China. Xian. Shanghai. I smuggrl garic this

country. I hear about you. You rike garic. You buy garic? I here San Francisco.

Me: I'm sorry. I thought this was a friend. Garlic from China?

Woman: China. Xian. I grow. My father grow. Best garic world.

Me: I happen to be coming to San Francisco tomorrow. Where can we meet?

Woman: Jus minutc. Cousin terl you prace.

Woman's voice: Hello, my name's Lucy Su. I'm cousin Su Xiaoli. My restaurant Chinatown. Green Lotus. You know my restaurant Green Lotus?

Me: I'm sorry. I don't. I hardly ever go to San Francisco anymore.

Lucy Su: Best Chinee restaurant Chinatown. 205 Sacramento. Tomorrow morning. No crowd.

Me: Is ten o'clock OK?

Lucy Su: Ten o'clock OK. Name?

Me: Chester Aaron.

Lucy Su: Tomorrow ten o'clock Chester Aaron. 205 Sacramento Street, San Francisco.

At that time I had two Chinese garlics, one called Beijing and one called Xian, both of which I had bought from Filaree Farm in Washington State. Both were second generation, and both had produced even larger bulbs this year than they had at last year's harvest. Both were covered with beautiful skins, the Xian's red skin much darker than the Beijing's. The Xian tasted much richer, with the heat (or "bite") not lingering quite as long in the mouth.

A third Chinese garlic (even if it also came from Xian, as long as it would be different) would be interesting indeed.

In China, the selections and presentations and quality of food from province to province varied more often and to a greater degree than in any other country in the world. It would follow that China should offer a greater number of different garlic varieties.

At the time, because of my own ancestry, my selection of garlics represented Europe more than any other continent. Of my fifty-four garlics, twelve were from Russia and eight of those twelve were from the Republic of Georgia where my father was born. Perhaps I would have three Chinese garlics next year.

The trip to San Francisco took an hour and a half; the search for a parking space seemed to take three days. I arrived at the Green Lotus ten minutes late.

Inside, men and women were rushing about preparing for the lunch crowd. A grim little woman sitting at a table near the cash register was tapping the tabletop with long-nailed fingertips. "You garic man?" she called.

"Yes," I said, joining her at the table. "I'm Chester Aaron."

She might have nodded, though the movement of her chin was too brief and too faint to be sure. With a deft and apparently practiced little maneuver, she whipped her hand into and out of the pocket of her Mao-style green silk jacket and deposited a garlic bulb on the table. Then, her hand moving in and out of a different pocket, she produced a second bulb, which she deposited next to the first. "Xian," she said. It sounded like *tsch-ee-en*.

I picked up one of the bulbs, about the size of a baseball, and judged its weight to be about five ounces. "I have two garlics from China," I said, "including one from Xian. This doesn't look like the Xian I have now."

"This best garlic, Xian, best China, best worlrd."

"It is beautiful," I said.

The Xian garlic I was growing was about this size, but this one appeared to have two or three more cloves. The skin was much darker than the skin on my current Xian. "Very nice," I said. "How much for the two heads?"

"Sixy dorars."

"Sixty dollars? For two heads?"

"Sixy dorars."

"No, thanks," I said, rising from the table. In rising I bumped into a woman I knew had to be the cousin, the proprietor of the Green Lotus. I hadn't noticed her standing behind me. "You taste!" she ordered.

The woman from Xian picked up one of the bulbs, ran her fingernail along the two edges of skin enclosing a very large clove, and lifted the clove free. "Taste!"

"Yes ma'am," I said. I think I would have been *chop suey* had I refused.

I bit the tip from the clove and picked it from my lips as if it were a fleck of tobacco. Then, after running my fingernail along the edge of the clove and peeling the skin back from half the body, I bit a sizable chip from the end. I held the chip on my tongue and waited. No heat, no taste, nothing. I took a larger bite and slid it along my tongue to the back of my mouth.

No bite, no heat, no taste.

These two bulbs of unimpressive garlic were not worth sixty dollars. They were not, in fact, worth thirty dollars. Ten, perhaps.

Suddenly, my head and face felt as if both women had stuffed a burning match into my nostrils and down into my throat and up into my ears. I choked. My eyes watered. I wanted to find sugar. (Sugar will ease the pain of heat on the tongue.) But no sugar appeared on any of the nearby tables, and neither of these two dragon ladies was about to indulge me. They waited, impassive.

Then, as suddenly as it had struck, the heat disappeared. In my mouth was the taste of rich, loamy earth, the same sort of taste offered by a fine fresh Morel or Chanterelle mushroom. That taste not only lingered, it swelled. "Yes," I said, pulling three twenty-dollar bills from my pocket.

I handed the money to the lady from Xian. "Delicious," I said. "Thank you."

She stuffed the bills into her jacket pocket. "Xian."

"Where in Xian? A city? A village? Where?"

She looked at her cousin, the proprietor of the Green Lotus.

"No tell," Lucy Su said. "She smuggle garlic. You want tea?"

"No, thanks," I said.

I now had my fifty-fifth garlic in time for the October planting.

I planted the twelve cloves and guarded them lovingly through the next nine months. After I harvested in June, I hung the twelve stalks in the curing shed.

Three weeks later, about seven o'clock in the morning, I braved the freeway traffic and drove to San Francisco to have breakfast with my friends Leo and Carolyn. I went first, however, to Chinatown, which was already bustling. Parking at this hour was easy. I walked into the Green Lotus restaurant. Standing behind the cash register scanning several ledgers was my lady from Xian. She nodded. "Garic man."

"Yes," I said. "I want to thank you for that Xian garlic. It is beautiful. Here is a little token of my gratitude."

I'd gift-wrapped a collection of five of my garlics: a head of Celaya Purple, a head of Ukrainian White Artichoke, a head of Creole Red, a head of Spanish Roja and a head of Armenian. They ranged in size from medium to very large and in color from silverskin white to red to tan with purple stripes.

Su Xiaoli, with a surprising tenderness in her voice, said, "You sit." She disappeared behind a curtain. She stuck out her head once, saw me sitting and nodded. "You wait." Then, as if she suddenly remembered how to pronounce the word, she said, "Prease."

About five minutes later she appeared again with her cousin Lucy Su, the owner of the Green Dragon. Each carried one dish. Both dishes were set before me, along with a large flat plate and a napkin and a pair of chopsticks. "You want fork?" Su Xiaoli asked. "No, you chopstick. This best dish Xian. This one best, this one best."

It would be difficult to decide which of the two best dishes was the best. Or the most best. Or the greatest best. The best of the best?

The first dish contained several different offerings of different textured meats, probably fish from different levels of the sea as well as rivers. There were also shellfish: mussels, so small and sweet they melted in the mouth like chocolate truffles; and oysters, large and small and dense as cork as well as soft as marshmallows, all of it simmering in a broth tasting and smelling like a distillation of ocean water. Fine noodles, red as blood and redolent of candied ginger, bound the seafoods together. On taking in the first mouthful, I heard mermaids singing each to each.

The second dish contained tender slices of four, perhaps five, varieties of the same vegetable. Broccoli? Cabbage? A mutant radish? The leaves and roots were stir-fried in an oil tasting of anise. The aromas kept coiling back on themselves, helping produce layers of new tastes.

I could weep at the knowledge that I could neither ask for the details of that meal nor expect to receive such secrets.

Lucy Su and Su Xiaoli and their family (six adults, seven children) have come to Occidental the past two summers to help me harvest. I have sent them home with bonuses of several varieties of garlics, most of them from Europe, one from Japan, and one from Guatemala. I now have five Chinese garlics, three from Xian, one from Hunan, and one from Shandong Province.

Su Xiaoli, her chopsticks waving faster than humming bird wings, intones after every dish, whether they or I made it, "Xian best!"

This summer, along with the food, there was much laughter. Either their English has improved, or I am learning Chinese as I absorb their food. There was an exchange of stories about childhood in Xian and childhood in Pennsylvania. Their children listened. In time, these children will relay these stories, with appropriate supplements, to their own children. History marches on.

I catch myself thinking every now and then how my mother and father would respond to these magnificent people sitting at my extended table on my deck beneath the redwood trees. How they would react to my mother and father? Oh, what I would give to experience that exchange of awe and admiration and laughter and love, of which there would certainly be more varieties than fifty-four or fifty-five or even eighty.

Chapter Five

SADIE

SIBERIAN
Hardneck Purple-Stripe

One strain (via Filaree Farm) from Russian fishermen trading green leafy vegetables with poor peasants who grew only root crops; another strain from Kalmyk-Russian farm family near Tacoma, Washington. Very large bulbs often credited to the existence of weak flower stalks at U.S. latitudes (though my flower stalks are not what I would call "weak".) Skins of the eight to twelve very large dark brown (sometimes almost glossy black) cloves: mottled with purple or covered with purple stripes. Flavor: rich with initial heat fading fast. Shelf life: six to nine months after harvest. One of the most durable of all my garlics. A survivor.

TWO KISSES HERE: ONE KISS FOR SADIE, MY LONG-HAIRED, green-eyed, insufferably self-indulgent beauty of a mongrel cat (*Felis Domesticus*) and one kiss for my beauty of a garlic (*Allium sativum*, variety Purple Stripe, sub-strain Siberian.)

They share a history. Like cats, my Siberian garlic is a survivor.

I forget. The word *my* should never be used when speaking of either cats or garlic. *My* — as in *my* car, *my* computer, *my* wife — implies possession.

Chester's First Law of Nature states that cats will not, can not, be possessed.

Siberian garlic? Chester's Second Law of Nature states that weather, latitude, soil can alter certain elements of genetics, but the power of DNA is virtually immutable. I can send cloves from my Siberian garlic to growers in five other states. The Siberian bulbs that come up in their soils can be smaller or larger than the bulbs here in northern California. Their cloves may have skins that are mottled or striped with a lighter or darker purple and theirs can be hotter or milder. Rarely, if ever (enter, Stage Left: DNA) will the number of cloves in the Siberian planted here in California or in any other state be less than four or more than ten. Never will the scape (the central stalk), especially here in California, be "weak."

Chester's Third Law of Nature states that because each person has different body chemistry, mouths can respond differently to the same stimulus. Something that tastes hot to me can taste mild to someone else, that tastes rich in my mouth can taste like gym socks in others. As Einstein said: *Vive la différence!*

The short and long of it: neither cats nor garlic can be completely possessed or controlled by you or me. You and I have no choice but to yield to fate. Not Sadie.

Sadie, eighteen years old today, continues to prowl through life as if every dawn and every dusk is her very first. Over the years she has tangled in field and forest with raccoons, badgers, foxes and coyotes. One evening as Sadie strolled across the field, she saw me waiting on the deck and began to run. She did not see the red-tail hawk drop out of the clouds and plummet down through the sky. I did not have time to scream.

Apparently alerted by the feel and sound of compressing wind or windy doom, Sadie at the last moment flopped onto her back and clawed at the chest and belly of the hawk. The astonished bird lifted herself out of range of Sadie's claws and, deserting several of its floating feathers, climbed in dizzy spirals back up into the clouds.

Sadie rose, shook herself, and continued her run toward home.

I jumped from the deck, caught the rumpled ball of fur into my arms, and held her. I was prepared to call my vet. No need. There were a few minor scratches on her belly, a bit of blood oozing from her chin, but she was purring. In the house, I applied to each scratch the garlic ointment I have created for just such emergencies, Sadie's or my own. When I put her down, she walked to her bowl and waited while I prepared her food, which she scarfed up with special delight. Then she strode jauntily across the room and up onto the sofa and from there onto to her private pillow, which lies on the wide windowsill. She cleaned her whiskers, she cleaned her ears, she cleaned her belly, and only then did she curl up to sleep the sleep of exhausted warriors. Another day, another dolor.

Now, today, even as we speak, this eternal cat sits on the railing of my deck, studying the field for gopher activity. Twice in the last hour when a tall weed shivered (even though there is not the slightest breeze), Sadie left the deck to investigate. Her patrols were mainly of box 44, in which eight months ago I planted two hundred cloves of Siberian garlic; and box 45, in which I planted 150 Siberian cloves and fifty Red Toch.

According to cat mathematicians, Sadie's eighteen years is the equivalent of 240 human years, thirty years for each of the eight of her nine lives. She has one more life available in this first series. Then comes another series of nine times nine and, after that, another series.

I will be seventy-seven years old next May. I've appointed Sadie, if I ever die, to officiate at my funeral. After my two friends and forty-seven enemies consign my ashes to whichever box contains my Red Toch garlic that year (Toch standing for my father's village of Tochliavri, in the Republic of Georgia,) Sadie will go down into the field to patrol the other fifty-eight boxes; and just as if I were still around to be impressed, she will dig up and consume most of another gopher and place the bony remains on the deck at the precise distance in front of the door that will require the drop of a naked foot of whoever is then living in this house when he or she opens the door to enjoy the deck I built thirty years ago.

Sadie happens to be the fifth cat to share my life.

Meet Eddypuss, my first cat.

I was married then. It was Eddypuss who, with his perpetual good humor, converted me from a benign tolerator of cats to a cat-lover. My wife showered him with affection, but he brutally ignored her and shamelessly courted me. Once, losing my patience, I brushed him aside with my foot, and the anguish on his face pierced my heart. I picked him up, and for the next two years sought forgiveness by enslaving myself to his every need. I swear, once I caught Eddypuss looking back over his shoulder at my wife and grinning. Six months after Eddypuss mysteriously disappeared, I was pruning a hedge in the rear of our Berkeley house and found a collection of fur-covered bones that had been without a doubt Eddypuss.

The second cat to inhabit our house was procured from the Humane Society. Large for a female, this kitten had a jauntiness about her that defied anyone to have any feeling for her but love. My wife named her Mammakatz in honor of Mamma Cass Elliot. You will have to be in your fifties now to remember "The Mammas and the Pappas" and Mamma Cass. Remember my dictum about varied responses to the same stimulus? For me the most beautiful tune and the most hauntingly beautiful voice born in the '60s were Mamma Cass joining her comrades in *California Dreamin'*. I have forgotten all the shrill revolutionary slogans of those days and years, but I still hear and love that song, especially the voice of Mamma Cass. Mamma, wherever you are, I'm still in California and I'm still dreamin'.

After I was divorced and living in northern California, the tables turned. I was adopted by my third cat. He appeared on my porch during a storm and would not leave. I named him Wellenuff so I could warn my Border Collie Chuck to "… leave Wellenuff alone." Wellenuff was a Manx and woke me up every morning at exactly six o'clock by seeking out my right hand, spreading my fingers with her nose, and sitting in the open palm. Never the left hand. Wellenuff was a right winger, the only conservative cat I ever knew.

The cat just previous to Sadie was the inimitable Ariadne Obnoxious, named to honor the opera *Ariadne auf Naxos* by Strauss/von Hoffmanstahl. Balanced atop a fence, silhouetted against a full-moon, the amorous Ariadne's voice could force a shamed Jesse Norman or Kathleen Battle into a retreat from the Metropolitan Opera stage every time they (Norman or Battle) might strain for a high C. When the moon was round and full of silver, Ariadne Obnoxious, without the slightest effort, could ascend in glorious crystalline tremolo to far above high C, clear up to high R and even on occasion high S. Take that, Norman; take that, Battle.

Most people tolerate cats, not love or like but *tolerate*. Very few people believe, as did the ancient Egyptians around 2,500 BC, that cats are the furred and animated spirits of goddesses, each endowed with a unique persona. As with gods and goddesses, so with cats and cat-lovers. Unique, meaning *eccentric*. People think I'm eccentric because I would rather have my cat on my bed than a human of the female persuasion, a possible character flaw that could explain my current bachelor status. Four years ago I did consider marriage again to a woman who was allergic to cats. When the time came to choose between cat and wife, I chose cat.

It is the insufferable independence of cats, that ineradicable contempt for human arrogance that endears cats to people like myself, people who love being reminded that man does not live by being bred alone.

When a century or so in the future I decide to go, Sadie will search out one of her two favorite haunts from which to launch herself into feline eternity. Haunt number one: the grove of giant redwoods north of my house where on hot summer days Sadie loves to soak her bod in the dark aromatic humus. Haunt number two: whichever of the sixty boxes in my field contains, that year she decides to depart, my Siberian garlic.

Several of the garlic varieties I grow (generally the ones native to the higher latitudes) can suffer from the heat of a Sonoma

County summer. Other varieties (from the more tropical countries) struggle to survive the moderately severe Sonoma County winters when temperatures can fall to twenty degrees above zero, Fahrenheit. If it isn't the weather, it's the soil. In most local fields viable soil, referred to as Burbank Gold, is not much deeper than ten inches before it gives way to clay. Supplementing and covering the Burbank Gold with my own mix of soils and my own secret amalgam of compost can be very beneficial, but it can also introduce legions of villainous insects or maggots or nematodes or viruses or funguses. Every October, as I start planting I tap wood, burn incense, throw salt over my left shoulder, pray, and hop Hopi Dance of Fertility.

Occasionally one or another variety of garlic will, for no identifiable reason, simply succumb. Current examples are the Sahara White from Egypt, the Nicaraguan Rose, and the Mayan Red from Yucatan. Over the last several years I had treated all three of these rare varieties (rare at least in the U.S.,) with patience and generosity, consigning them after harvest to special containers with controlled temperature, controlled humidity. Each season I harvested fewer and fewer bulbs, every October I had fewer surviving cloves to plant. Last October I gave up, I did not plant even one of the three varieties. I ate them all.

As I ate, I convinced myself that I was wise to desert these former friends. After all, I have neither the time nor the patience for self-indulgence. *Tempus fugits*, as Sadie will tell you. At seventy-six, my *tempus* is *fugiting* fast.

About ten years ago, in the late eighties or early nineties, in mid-September (I was planning to return home in a week or two to start planting,) I was traveling in Washington State, visiting friends teaching at the Evergreen campus of the University. I'd been growing garlic for about five years and had, at the time, fourteen or fifteen varieties and twenty-five boxes.

At the Pike Street market in Seattle, I approached a beefy garlic-farmer who displayed in large bins mounds of white skin garlic. The variety, I guessed, was the Softneck called California Late from Gilroy, California, the garlic sold in every supermarket in the U.S. This man had been growing this same white-skinned garlic for years.

The bulbs were large and firm. I asked him about red-skinned garlic. His reply, in an unmistakable (to me) Russian accent: "You go my uncle. He got farm this side Tacoma ten mile. Me, him, my wife, his wife, we Kalmyks. Best Siberian *chesnok*, Kalmyk. Best *chesnok* every world. We eat only Kalmyk Siberian *chesnok*. This" ... I think he said something foul in Russian ... "this (expletive) *chesnok* we sell here this place to dumb pipples. Kalmyk Siberian *chesnok* too good dese pippples, dese pipples know nottink. Is a vaste give dese pipples Kalmyk Siberian *chesnok*."

Have you guessed by now that in Russian *chesnok* means *garlic*?

Following the man's directions, I found, four hours later, this side of Tacoma on a dirt road, a wooden house with a combination tent-hut that shielded a counter; and, on the counter, three wooden crates filled with what I thought at first were eggplants. Standing next to the crates, I realized the eggplants were garlic. I have never before or since seen such deep-purple skin on any fruit or vegetable. As I stared, two people came out of the house, a man and (I think) a woman, one of them wearing a *babushka*, a headscarf. With stiff black hair, yellow-brown skin, slightly tilted eyes, they could have arrived from Outer Mongolia that morning. Both of the squat little people were wrinkled, wizened, like dried raisins, like Disney gnomes, but so full of energy, of life, I wanted to grab them and dance a *kazatsky*. As a child I had squatted and leaped through many a *kazatsky*.

The two gnomes were in their eighties, maybe even their nineties. They spoke with an even heavier accent than had their nephew in the Pike Street Market. Was it Russian?

"*Chesnok*. Goooode *chesnok*. Siberia *chesnok*. Kalmyk Siberia *chesnok*. Best *chesnok* anyvere everyvere all vere."

I had not seen such beautiful garlic since my introduction to my Red Toch garlic five or six years before. The agent on that occasion had also been ... no, not a Russian, he had been a Georgian. If, in the Independent Republic of Georgia, an individual calls a Georgian a Russian or uses the term *Russian Georgia*, he or she will go home to his or her spouse with his or her throat slit, making it difficult to ever again taste a clove of *chesnok* of any color.

This Kalmyk Siberian garlic, thirty or forty large bulbs in each crate, was covered with purple stripes. Each bulb I held in my hand contained eight to twelve cloves, each clove as large as, or perhaps even larger than, my thumb.

As if anticipating my question, the old man, chuckling to the raisin that had to be his wife, tore one clove free. Peeling it quickly and easily with the nails of thumb and forefinger, he handed me the snow-white crescent. I bit off half and chewed. Nothing happened for five or six seconds and then the stab of heat brought tears to my eyes. As quickly as the heat had struck, it faded. I grinned through my tears. The old man and his wife chuckled. Within a few seconds I could swear I'd just been eating berries soaked in snow. I, the geezer with the palate of an iron skillet, almost swooned as the taste of this Kalmyk Siberian *chesnok* settled in my mouth and oozed back into my throat.

The Kalmyk gnomes hopped about on their fat little legs and clapped me on the back as they sang in Russian in well-rehearsed harmony. I bought ten pounds of the Kalmyk Siberian garlic. Ten pounds meant forty-three bulbs.

Talk about survivors. Consider the people known as Kalmyks. The forebears of the Kalmyks came from Inner Asia during the thirteenth or fourteenth century. Their history has been interwoven with other Turco-Mongol horse-riding people who lived in round felt tents. They herded sheep, cattle, goats, horses, and Bactrian camels. From different regions with different histories but united by language, they were committed to the Buddhism of Tibet or to the Faith of Mohammed. Over the centuries the Kalmyks were enslaved, killed, or deported by an array of tyrants of increasing evil from Ghengis Khan to Joseph Stalin. Hundreds of thousands, perhaps millions, died in Soviet slave-labor camps. In 1943, a half century before the birth of the term *ethnic cleansing*, the USSR deported every single remaining Kalmyk. A few thousand have survived, some in France, some in Germany. A few hundred live today in Pennsylvania and New Jersey. Wherever they are, they have revived their language, revived their religion, and revived their culture. As their fervor for survival increases so does their numbers. The Kalmyks will endure.

Here now, I admit to the single error I have made in my life. May the Kalmyks, wherever they live, forgive me.

Three years after I obtained my Kalmyk Siberian garlic, I supplemented it with a garlic also called Siberian from Filaree Farm in Okanogan, Washington. The skins of Filaree's Siberian were mottled rather than striped with purple, the heads had smaller but fatter and browner cloves. My Kalmyk Siberian heads were larger, the cloves so dark brown they were almost polished black.

Over the years my predilection for unnatural selection (I keep only the fattest, firmest, healthiest bulbs for the next planting season) has given me a final Siberian garlic crop that is a mix (I also plead for forgiveness from the twelve goddesses of garlic) of the best of the Kalmyk Siberian and the best of Filaree's Siberian. I can no longer be sure which of the bulbs I grow have descended from which source.

I am sure only that they are Siberian. Each of the big firm heads offers eight to twelve crescent-shaped thumb-sized (my thumb) cloves covered with purple-striped or purple-mottled skin. Not bulbs and cloves with skins both mottled and striped. It's one or the other. I suspect that the mottled bulbs are born of the original Filaree bulbs, the striped of the garlic from those hospitable Kalmyk gnomes outside of Tacoma, Washington. Taste of either or both: beyond compare, compeer. Once in the mouth there is no possibility of calling this garlic Spanish Roja (it is not in the slightest what can be called "mild") or Creole Red (its bite is less intense and its heat does not remain as long) or Asian Tempest (it is nowhere as hot.) In size and color and shape of the head and the shape and number of cloves and certainly in taste, the garlic is Siberian.

I tear one clove free, peel it, bite into the smooth cream-white meat, and wait. Once past the bite, the taste is richer and tangier than almost any of my other garlics. Almost.

For me the taste of the Red Toch from the Republic of Georgia is richer, even tastier. The Persian Star, also a Hardneck, from a bazaar in Samarkand in Uzbekistan (thriving in my soil now, thanks to that genius and allium devotee, John Swenson,) is, for me, just as tasty but much hotter.

Remember: *you* might sneer at the heat of the Persian Star, *you* might find Persian Star milder even than the Inchelium Red garlic from the Colville Indian Reservation in Washington State. A garlic which, in a 1990 taste-test at Rodale Kitchens, was rated the top of the Softneck Garlics.

One more item of interest: all of my Siberians share certain Hardneck traits. The central stalk, or scape, shoots up in the spring and makes a perfect 270-degree curl with, at the tip, a pod (called an umbel) that dips and weaves in the wind like a butterfly. Inside that umbel: not a hundred tiny aerial cloves (called bubils) as are in the umbels of almost all other Hardnecks, but only twenty or thirty bubils the size of my little fingernail. If I plant these bubils, fifty times out of a hundred, I will harvest what is called *a marble* (a bulb without clove divisions). If I plant that marble and keep planting subsequent marbles, after three or four years, I will get a fair sized bulb. Fair sized. Why bother with this laborious technique when I can plant a single large healthy clove and, one year later, not three or four, bring out of the soil a large healthy bulb?

A friend who has a Ph.D. in Plant Pathology informs me that if the bubils the Siberian garlic produces in the umbel are removed early, a purple flower with purple anthers will occasionally produce pollen. And then, possibly, viable garlic seeds. These characteristics, common to Purple Stripe garlics, convince my friend that Purple Stripes might be the oldest of all existing garlics. Perhaps he's correct. The theory not only proves the survival instincts I so admire in the Siberian garlics but I also admire in the Kalmyks.

Back, finally, and thank God, to Sadie.

Sadie was about eight years old when I started adding garlic to her food, not to her kibble but to her once-a-day (evenings only) serving of wet food, my own concoction of leftover meats, rice, greens, the whole collection chopped fine but not mashed.

At first the garlic was also leftovers; what some people might even call crumbs. Sadie obviously liked the garlic additive because each serving was always consumed over a span of several hours.

One evening, without crumbs at my disposal, I used a clove of my just harvested Siberian. Sadie attacked the bowl with a growl as if the contents deserved not just all her attention but all her ferocity generally reserved for gophers. The entire serving was consumed in about ten minutes. After that meal, Sadie would never even approach her bowl unless its food was infused with Siberian garlic.

I'm fortunate (as is Sadie) that the Siberian has a long shelf life. Under prime conditions I can keep the Siberian in my kitchen for six to nine months after harvest. That's usually a month or two before the next crop is available. At the first signs of deterioration in a Siberian bulb, I press a clove into a single serving of my prepared food concoction and freeze the accumulated multi-servings in ice-cube trays. Long after I have no viable Siberian garlic available in the field or on the shelf, I have it in the freezer. Each evening a cube or two at a time, thawed and brought to room temperature, is Sadie's appetizer, main course, and dessert.

From her kitten days, Sadie has always loved my garlic boxes, and for good reason.

In the early summer there remains in each box after it is emptied of its garlic, a fluffy mound of soil. By mid-August when all the garlic has been harvested from all the boxes, there are sixty fluffy mounds of soil, each mound offering different textures, different aromas, and different densities, sixty boxes, sixty mounds, and sixty very promising cat-boxes.

Remember Sadie's diet? Whether it's chopped chicken gizzard or shredded salmon or cream-covered corn flakes, the bowl is ignored unless it is redolent with raw Siberian garlic.

My theory regarding Sadie's addiction?

The gophers, having tunneled beneath the boxes (and, since birth, having dined on the garlic roots that have penetrated the wire floors of the boxes) have been thoroughly and permanently marinating themselves with garlic from gut to fur. Is it accident or coincidence that the gophers practically drive themselves insane trying to penetrate the two boxes that contain my Siberian garlic? Every summer when I suspect gopher penetration through the aviary wire (Has it rusted? Has it been torn by the tines of spades?) in any box, I have to empty that box and turn it over. If there are holes or tears, I replace the entire sheet of wire.

Last summer I had to examine one of the two boxes that had contained Siberian garlic. Reason: two gopher holes spotted early in the season. I had, as soon as the evidence had come to my attention, inserted two traps four times. Result: seven dead gophers. No more gopher signs all season. But could I risk the next year's planting? No. When I emptied the box (four hours of shoveling) to examine the wire, I found myself gazing down at a miniature but detailed three-dimensional topographical depiction of the New York subway system.

Along with the presence and the taste of the gophers and the presence and the taste of the Siberian garlic, there is another reason Sadie practically lives in those two boxes in the summer, *especially* the summer.

The stalks of my Siberian, especially my Kalmyk Siberian, are thick and tall. The leaves are wider and thicker than the leaves of other varieties and grow at oddly oblique angles to the stem. All these unique features contribute to the presence of denser and more prevalent shade than the shade available in other boxes. In the summer when she's not in the dark cool humus at the base of the redwood trees, Sadie seeks shelter beneath the leaves of the Siberian garlic. I have on the wall of my study a close-up photograph showing the dense almost jungle-like thicket of stalks and leaves. Just stalks and leaves. Everyone who looks at the photo wonders why I consider the leaves and stalks so special as to … and then: there! "Look at Sadie."

Almost lost inside the web of green is Sadie's gray face. There rests one cool cat.

Last winter was a serious challenge to Sadie, to my garlics, and to me.

El Niño brought us days, weeks, and months of heavy rain. Along the road leading to my house not one or two but ten or twelve big firs and oaks fell over, blocking entrance or departure sometimes for hours, sometimes for days. Neighbors worked together to clear enough of a passage for cars to come and go and then another tree would fall. The neighbors would be out there again with roaring chain saws, sawing trunks, dragging branches, and drinking an ocean of hot black cowboy coffee made on an open fire because the power lines were down.

Sometimes, when I walked down in my fields to lament the fate of my garlics, I sank to my ankles in muck. In every box, the garlic lay in pools of water. Not much hope for a harvest this year.

At night, after working on the roads and the fallen trees, I would come back to find my iron stove filled with cold ashes. I'd wrap myself in towels and blankets and wait for the new fire to spill its warmth. Power was out for two and three days at a time, so I often had no light, no water, not even cold water. Without power the pump in my well was useless. Nine buckets of rainwater was enough each day to wash my face and work the toilet. Eating beans out of a can and drinking water from a jug became routine morning, noon, and night. Sadie's frozen food thawed in the so-called freezer, spoiled, and went into the garbage can. Fortunately there was kibble, left over from the months of reliance on my garlic-mush. Sadie managed to chew a few chunks of kibble but then went out on her own.

Because of the underground water washing through their tunnels, gophers had no choice but to float up to the surface. Sadie, though she hates the rain, could simply not resist the temptation. She ate her daily gopher and brought home the four or five others she caught. During the worst two weeks, I dropped dozens of furry little bodies into the garbage cans stacked on top of each other near the garage because it was impossible to travel the road to deliver them to the County Dump.

Both of us, Sadie and me, were forever wet. Odds and ends of clothing covered the railings and the backs of chairs to dry in the heat from the iron stove. During the night Sadie slept peacefully near the stove, but during the day she was out in the field, sheltered inside the jungle of Siberian garlic.

I caught her one of those days converting instinct into action. When her inner cat-clock alerted her, she left her Siberian jungle shelter to sit on the rim of the box. That cool cat had been secretly watching those Wild Nature shows I had been appreciating on television, especially the program showing the bears standing patiently knee-deep in rushing water, and with left or right paw, casually scooping up a swimming salmon and heaving it onto dry land. Sitting on the edge of the box, inches above the bubbling ooze, Sadie, with the swipe of a paw, lifted one and then another gopher out of the muck and tossing them, one and then another, up into the box. The gophers were probably glad to have their miseries brought to such a quick and merciful end.

The cat had limits. There were more gophers than hours available. Those she missed or scorned or surfaced when she was sleeping in front of the fire were gathered up in early evenings by owls and in early mornings by hawks and buzzards.

Thanks to the floods, to the bats and hawks and owls, thanks to Sadie, a huge portion of the gopher population in my field was destroyed, much as the Soviet Union had destroyed the Kalmyks. This year, like the Kalmyks, the gophers were back in force.

The rains slowed and thinned in early May. The ground began to dry. By late June I could predict that every one of my eighty-seven varieties of garlic was so damaged I'd be lucky to harvest half of the crop I harvested the year before.

My guess was correct. Of each of eighty-six varieties, a half to a third of each planting was lost, except for the Siberian. Remember, I'd planted a total of 350 Siberian cloves. I harvested 197 out of box 44 (I planted 200), I harvested 148 out of box 45 (I planted 150), and of the fifty Red Toch I planted in box 45, I harvested twenty-four.

Last October, at the First International Garlic Festival in Tulsa, Oklahoma, a grower from Texas told me he'd lost about 80% of his garlic in one day to grasshoppers. They flew in, took the stalks down to the ground, and then went after the bulbs. For some unknown reason they never touched the Siberian.

I mentioned that fact along with my own experience in the flood to Dr. Gowsala P. Sivam, Director of Research at Bastyr University in Kenmore, Washington. Dr. Sivam had presented a paper at the festival, describing her research on the interaction of garlic and breast cancer. She asked me to send her a few Siberian bulbs. I have sent them. Will they offer special genetic information about their ability to survive disasters? Will they present, in plant form, the Kalmyk genes that have armed their struggle to survive?

It is now mid-May. Sadie sits here with me on the deck. She moves away from me because she cannot stand the smell of my weekly ration of one cigar.

Down in the field every box is filled with lush garlic. As I puff on my Macanudo Maduro, my seventy-six year old eyes see a blade of grass shivering on the ground, not three feet from the edge of the deck. Sadie's 240 year old eyes saw the shivering weed before I did. A graceful dive lands her near the weed. She crawls, hovers, waits.

It is a glorious evening. The sun is red above the western redwoods. The breeze coming in from the ocean carries a scent of brine. Down in the distant field, two does and three fawns enjoy the wild grasses. All five heads lift to gaze up across the field. The does are probably indicating the twenty-four trees scattered across the intervening field. Wait, the does are whispering, soon those trees will be dropping delicious overripe apples and pears onto the ground just for us.

The deer were here last summer; they will be here this summer, too, and probably every summer from now on as long as I am here. And long after. Sadie will be observing them from the shade of the redwood grove, observing them and remembering me. Won't you, Sadie?

Chapter Six

BEN BREUNER

CALIFORNIA EARLY
Softneck Artichoke

Originated and commercially grown in California. Large, occasionally flat-round bulbs. Ten to twenty-one cloves usually in four layers. Color of clove: tan or off-white, often with pink blush. Very vigorous and productive in warmer parts of California. Fewer stem bulbils than California Late and much milder, much sweeter. When my own garlics are not available, I choose to rely on California Early. Shelf life: five to seven months after harvest.

Until I was nineteen and went into the army, I lived in western Pennsylvania, south of Pittsburgh, in a village called North Butler, an appendage to a town called Butler. Soft-coal country.

Six days a week, including Saturday, I walked to town, picked up 50 copies of *The Butler Eagle*, stuffed them into the canvas bag and carried them on my back through the city and up the hills to North Butler. About five miles.

Every Saturday morning, after my last swallow of coffee and jellied bread, I stored two dimes in my pocket and walked the five miles to town. To the Majestic Theater, which showed cowboy movies all day every Saturday.

My first dime went to the Majestic Theater, my second dime was reserved for a hot dog and a bottle of soda pop, both consumed after the movie on my way to the Butler Public Library, where I collected my weekly allotment of four books, all four devoted to cowboys.
On the evening of my fourteenth year I started writing my own cowboy stories.

I rode and talked and dreamed the life of a cowboy. Every morning, when I brushed my teeth, I spent ten minutes before the mirror massaging my round cheeks and thin neck in an effort to win square jaws, those symbols of American virtue owned by every movie cowboy from Buck Jones to Tom Mix to Tim McCoy to George O'Brien.

I walked with bowed legs, thumbs hooked in my belt, and always wore an old straw hat painted white. I greeted everyone every morning, even my brothers and my sister, with a, "Howdy, pardner."

Cowboys were everywhere: at the movies, in my library books, in every story in every issue of Street and Smith's *Wild West Weekly* and, every night at the kitchen table in the pages of my own stories. The title of my collected stories (in big black letters across the first page:) *A Cowboy's Life*; in smaller letters in black script, the subtitle: <u>An autobiography</u>.

During the seventy-five years of my life I have known noble and courageous men and (politically correct here but also truthful) noble and courageous women. I've known only one real cowboy.

Contrary to the myth accepted by the unaware, this cowboy, Ben Breuner, had no difficulty with his conversion to sheep. Of course, he didn't have much choice. He'd fallen in love with and married Millicent Stinson who had inherited her father's sheep ranch.

"Chester," he told me one day at the supper table, snapping his fingers, "I converted like that!"

Every sheep rancher in the west who knows Ben Breuner does not forgive him for his single offense: he keeps Girl, primary member of his current family of Border Collies, in the house day and night.

I hate to think what his friends might do if they were to discover that Ben has a bed for Girl in front of the fireplace, a thick soft sack of aromatic eucalyptus leaves.

Girl is now fourteen years old. That's old for a dog, especially for a Border Collie. The dog does, of course, have major problems. She copes, but just barely, with occasionally severe arthritis. Another serious infirmity: she not only has a delicate stomach these days but she frequently offers Ben and Millicent gifts of flatulence. These gifts try Millicent's sensibilities but not Ben's; he considers Girl's offerings symptoms of continuing good health, spiritual as well as physical. Gifts for them as well as for Girl.

Girl' most serious affliction: she is totally blind, a victim of P.R.A. (progressive retinal atrophy.) Born too long ago to benefit from the advances in contemporary genetic research (which have led to almost complete elimination of the inherited criminal gene) Girl just keeps on keeping on, as Ben says.

Those who are strangers to the world of sheep and sheep dogs would find it difficult to believe that this little black and white bundle of indolence sleeping on the eucalyptus cushion is the first California Border Collie ever to win the Silver Cup at a Grand National Sheepdog Trial. That was in 1988, twelve years ago in Texas when Girl was two years old.

1988. About the time I'd begun surrendering myself to my obsession with garlic.

I'd been growing the ordinary Gilroy garlic for years (California Late and California Early) but by the late '80s I was building my supply of exotic garlics from other parts of the United States and from other countries. I had eliminated the California Late variety for two reasons: it was available in all the commercial markets and it burned my mouth so badly I could not appreciate the garlic taste.

By 1988 I had a total of twelve different varieties of garlic, most of them from the United States. One had come from France; two had come from Georgia, one of the independent republics of Russia.

Before Girl's vision was completely gone (about two years ago) and she could no longer compete in national trials or even work the fields at home, I had often accompanied the Breuners to the state and county fairs where Ben's calls and whistles and hand signals were still able to fire up in Girl those ancient instincts born of the wild dogs of Scotland and Wales, instincts that have flowed down through countless generations directly into her and into her one son and two grand-daughters, Ben's current family of working Collies.

Until Girl entered Ben's life his philosophy about his dogs had always been simple and practical. If the dogs worked hard and efficiently after the first ten months of rigorous training they would continue to have the best food, the best care, the warmest and driest pens, the cleanest runs. Before Girl, the younger Ben used to shoot any dog, which, for whatever reason, promised vet bills that would outdistance that dog's value. Older now, and more aware of his own mortality, and dealing with the sons and daughters of his beloved Girl, Ben can not dispose so easily of dogs that fail. He has been selling the more promising to other ranchers and offering the least promising to friends and relatives.

"Just like any piece of farm equipment, Chester. It wears out, you fix it or replace it. A rancher's further ahead dumpin' a dog than spendin' time and money on it. Ranch dogs gotta earn their keep. You can afford to be sentimental about your stinkin' garlic, Chester, but I can't afford to be sentimental about my dogs or my tractor or my pickup. They put the food on the table."

Millicent, Ben's wife, never fails to chuckle at Ben's repeated attempts to convince an audience that he is still the tough, bitter, hard-nosed realist he used to be when he was a young sheriff and then a not-so-young marshal, guardian of all things right and just.

During the early years of our friendship I used to admire the two framed photographs of the young Ben Breuner on the wall of the kitchen: one of the photos showing a sheriff (lean, young) astride a chestnut mare, Stetson low over his eyes, Sharpes rifle in the saddle scabbard, a posse strung out behind him; and the other showing a slightly older Ben Breuner, a U.S. Marshal, standing erect in front of a row of flags, receiving the citation of Lawman of the Year. Ben had tracked a killer into the Sierras and dropped him with a single shot when, refusing to surrender, the killer had come out of his cabin, arms extended, firing his revolvers. The caption on the frame of that photograph reads: "Ben Breuner, Man of Stone."

"A man of stone," Millicent says. "That's Ben Breuner. Go ask Girl, you don't believe me. I swear, he's the last of the old softies, Chester."

Ben's response: "That's sentimental cow puckey, Chester. And cow puckey smells worse than your garlic."

"Mind your language," Millicent warned him, waving her spatula in the general direction of his gray hair.

Ben lowers his head so, he hopes, neither Millicent nor I can see his grin.

Since Girl's retirement from the world of dog trials, Ben, for his benefit as much as for Girl's, has devoted a half hour every morning of every week to the perpetuation of Girl's pride in herself. Before he begins his work in the field, he puts the little Collie through a brief exercise not too unlike her training when she was a pup. It would be difficult to say which of the two, man or dog, enjoys the early morning activity more.

When Ben finishes breakfast and pulls on his boots, Girl waits, ready and willing, at the back door. Despite her blindness she is poised in the classic Border Collie stance: belly almost touching the floor; tail curled under; neck stretched out; head forward, nostrils alert; blind eyes concentrated on the wood-paneled door leading to the outside pens and the distant fields beyond. In that posture: the concentration of Border Collie intensities described as *the eye.*

The eye.

A phrase to be heard wherever (California, Texas, Scotland, Wales, New Zealand) shepherds or ranchers (men and women) gather to discuss the dogs they own or would like to own or had once owned or have heard about in tales handed down through generations like heirloom jewels. Tales that do not honor size or speed or strength or even endurance but honor some vague mystical legacy called *the eye*. "Oh, you ought to see my new pup. He has *the eye*. He's out of Joan, she's out of Champion Toby..."

The phenomenon, like the beauty of a daffodil, is impossible to describe in words. You have to witness the phenomenon in operation at trials or in the field to appreciate it: the little Collie standing there, crouched, head extended, every gram of its strength and cunning and authority concentrated in that stare. A stare so intense, so tyrannous, that even the most rebellious ram has no choice but, eventually, to submit.

Ben insists that Girl, even now, totally blind, still has *the eye*. I used to have doubts. I don't any more.

Four months ago at dawn, I went over to help Ben bring in the sheep for worming and dipping. Before we let the other three dogs out of their pens, Ben led Girl out of the house to put her through her brief morning routine.

After settling Girl at his right heel, Ben gave her a few moments to adjust, to get her bearings, then he snapped his fingers and muttered, "Come by."

Girl strained to lift her rump. When she finally succeeded she tried to whirl about, to run behind Ben, but she lost her balance. She began a slow labored walk that did become a trot that did ease into a run. Once her feet were active and she was speeding over the field, she aimed herself at the barbed wire fence that separated the Breuner ranch from the Bandini ranch. When it seemed she must surely strike the barbed wire, some assembly of sounds and scents alerted her and she turned.

Nose up to take the breeze, Girl went into a long straight run designed to take her to the grove of eucalyptus trees and the six sheep resting there in the early morning frost. She paused for a few seconds every thirty or forty feet to catch her breath and, as she sat, steam poured out of her mouth, rose in clouds from her body. Then she was up again. And running.

She would follow this course and maintain this speed until

ordered to change by Ben's whistle-signals which, given Girl's unimpaired hearing, both she and Ben relied on for her fulfilling her duties. Ben had once suggested to me that to compensate for her loss of sight, her sense of hearing and especially her sense of smell were better now than when she was a young national medal-winner.

Ben's plastic whistle, held on his tongue, sent out a pattern of high-pitched calls. Girl responded by moving away from the straight-ahead approach that would have brought her directly onto the sheep. Stopping three times to catch her breath and to rest her legs, she finally closed her curved approach so she would come up behind the sheep, all six of them suddenly alert to that black and white ball of energy floating above the high grasses.

A sharp single note from Ben's whistle brought Girl to a halt about twenty feet behind the now restless sheep. She promptly dropped to the ground, body flat, head stretched forward. She stayed in that position without even a flick of an ear until, on the next signal, she very slowly rose and moved, very slowly, very cautiously, forward.

In fumbling with the focus knob on my binoculars, I missed some of Girl's progress. I wasn't sure if she'd stumbled or fallen but when I found her again she was lying flat. Resting again. Another signal from Ben brought her onto her feet and forward for *the lift*, the actual assertion of authority that would compel the sheep to move forward, toward us.

Girl, head down and stretched forward, moved the tightly bunched sheep out of the Eucalyptus grove and into the field and south, toward us. Belly low, muzzle out, she walked, raced to right or left, crawled, sat. As a thin, leggy ewe attempted to bolt, Girl, not waiting for Ben's directions, responded immediately, racing in front of the rebellious ewe and in front of her, compelling her, by shift of nose, lift of tail, jerk of right foot, left foot, into submission. So that she turned almost gratefully back into the submissive group.

To help guide Girl now, Ben whistled her to the left of the herd, then to the right, forward and back, around to the right, around to the left. She responded each time almost before the signal was completed, knowing better than her master what had to be done. She was as precise and authoritative this morning as she had been that day in Texas when the crowd rose and, for five minutes, sang, "Girl! Girl! Girl!"

The sheep, heads up, trotting slowly but gracefully, came on toward Ben and me. Girl, black head so low in the grasses it was lost to my view, ran, walked, rushed, slowed, darted. Carefully, daintily, her almost serpentine body easing to one side, to the other side. One moment she was up and racing, the next she was flat on her belly. One ewe — no, it was not a ewe, it was a ram, a Suffolk fifteen or twenty times the size of Girl with magnificent horns designed for forceful impact — turned from the huddled submissive flock and decided to face down his tormentor.

How did Girl know the ram was preparing to charge? What was in the air or on the grasses that alerted all of Girl's instincts and all her senses except her sight?

Or did she not know and did some inherited, some intuitive, force take over and move her forward?

The little Collie approached the ram, foot by foot, inch by inch, arriving within seconds at within inches of the lowered head, the large curved horns. There, lying flat on her belly, all four legs splayed out, neck stretched out, she dragged herself forward another inch. And another. Until her nose was close enough to the ram's muzzle so that the dog must surely have smelled the ram's breath, must surely have heard his snorts and grunts.

As it stretched even farther, Girl's neck seemed to have gained several extra vertebrae.

Through my glasses I saw the muscles quivering in the ram's haunches, I saw the great body preparing for the charge, that horned head preparing for the impact.

"Ben, call her in. She can't see the ram. He'll kill her."

Ben grunted. "Nope. She gotta die, she oughta die out there, workin' her sheep."

Angry, frightened, I watched the exhausted little Collie drag herself forward once more to what I knew would be her destruction.

The ram's front feet stomped the ground: the first signal of danger.

As Girl moved closer, the massive chest and body of the ram lifted. The rear legs prepared themselves for the leap and thrust.

At that moment Girl pulled her body forward, pushed out her tongue and licked the ram's nose. Twice. Three times.

Shocked, humbled, the mighty ram stepped back, turned, and then led the five ewes to within three yards of where Ben and I were standing. All six sheep, including the ram, stood in meek submission, waiting for whatever fate had in store.

The soaked and steaming Girl stretched out in the grass a few feet behind them.

Ben muttered a few words I could not catch and Girl, just a tad reluctantly, pulled up her body. She staggered, stumbled, made it around the bunched sheep to Ben's right heel and, with a deep sigh, settled into a perfect sit-stay position.

Ben clapped his hands, and the sheep dispersed.

Lifting Girl in his arms and holding her close to his chest, Ben said, "Chester, you get old and blind and arthritic and you do as well as this little girl, I'll come back from wherever I'm buried, and I'll maybe eat some of your stinkin' garlic."

I'd met Ben and Millicent thirty years before, when I'd first moved to Sonoma County.

Ben was in his early fifties then. Millicent close to that. On their ranch, which sits along the coast, ten miles from my home in Occidental, they run about a thousand sheep. Their kids used to help, but both are gone now, one living in Oregon and one in Los Angeles. So Ben and Millicent work the sheep alone. No, not alone, not at all alone, they have their other children, the four Border Collies.

According to Ben, four border Collies equals forty human helpers. Though he tries hard to restrain any demonstration of affection for anything or anyone, even Millicent, Ben could never help himself with his Collies, especially with Girl.

I've seen Ben, as he penned each dog at the end of the day, lift Girl in his arms and check her fur for ticks, her toes for foxtails, and then lay her down inside her pen with an all but inaudible whisper of gratitude.

About a month after we'd met, in the late '70s, I'd spent much of one day with the Breuners helping them string wire along a new fence line. Millicent invited me to stay for supper. By then I'd already helped the Breuners with the sheep four or five times. I learned in the process to appreciate the Border Collies. Ben had imported all of them as pups from Scotland. He trained each pup and juvenile himself and, occasionally, he bred one of the more promising bitches. At the time we met he had four dogs. In the years since he'd married Millicent and started working sheep, he probably owned twenty dogs, all of them Border Collies.

A few days after that first supper I returned to help the Breuners complete the battered fence. I brought them a copy of *An American Ghost*, a novel I published about a mountain lion as well as a copy of *Catch Calico!*, a novel about a cat.

That evening, after supper, I got into my car. The Breuners came outside to wish me a safe drive home. There had been heavy rains all day, and Millicent said it would be a perfect night to sit in front of the fire and read my book.

I said I felt a new novel coming on and it had to be about a Border Collie.

"Border Collies," Ben said, the usual monotone voice possessing a rare overlay of emotion. "They work harder than any man I ever met. Border Collies live to please their shepherd. They don't complain about cold or heat or rain, they don't call in sick, they'd rather die than quit runnin', they don't have to pay into social security, and they don't join unions."

Several years later when I started growing garlic, Ben Breuner just shook his head. "Can't stand the smell of the stuff, can't stand the taste. The neighbors, Italians, the Bandinis, you stand next to them in line somewhere, like the post office, all you smell is garlic. Don't bring any of that stuff 'round here. Get yourself a couple Border Collies or maybe Blue Heelers; that's a fine dog for cattle. Go in the breeding business, Chester. You have a talent for dogs."

"I have a talent for writing fiction," I said. "Writing doesn't pay as well as breeding dogs but I don't have to leave my desk to write. And I get my exercise over here at your ranch."

"You just come here for free exercise? Well, be sure to come over Friday. Make it for supper. I'm getting' a new pup from J. Bathgate, a friend in Scotland. Four months old, so I'll have to train her to my American cowboy accent." Ben, standing straight, pulled down the front rim of his battered Stetson as he stomped the mud from his boots.

The name on that pup's papers was Lass. Ben changed it to Girl.

It is January now, fourteen years after Lass' arrival in California from Scotland.

Ben called me a month ago, a week before Christmas. I was having my breakfast.

"Need your help, Chester. If you got the time. I know you're a busy man these days, growin' that garlic; and I know you ain't the young buck you was we first met, but you've worked my dogs. You know them, they know you, especially Girl. I got a problem. My kids ain't around, you know, and I don't want to go to the Bandinis for help. I ain't puttin' them down cause they're Eye-talians but … "

"I know, Ben. They smell like garlic. Damn you, Ben, you know that's a lot of bull puckey, and you know bull puckey … "

"I could use your help, Chester."

If I didn't know Ben Breuner so well by now, I would have guessed he was seeking solace but just could not ask for it. My first suspicion was that Millicent might be ill. "What's wrong, Ben?"

"That storm last night. A fir tree came down. Broke some fencin'. Before I got out there this mornin' about fifty ewes got through the break. Ten with newborn lambs. About twenty-five ready to lamb. They're way over in Bandini's hills. More coyotes in them hills than grass. I don't get the sheep back this mornin', I'll lose them all."

He paused. Now he'd tell me about Millicent being sick.

"Chester, Girl couldn't get up off her pad this morning. I think maybe she's at the end. I might have to put the girl down today. We'll use the other dogs to bring the sheep from Bandini's."

I waited.

"The girl hasn't eaten in two days, not even a sip of water. Hasn't had a bowel movement for three days. Belly's swollen tight. She's in a lot of pain."

"Have you called the vet, Ben?"

"No use. I can tell. I've given her laxatives. Even gave her an enema. Nothin's worked. I thought maybe we'd get the sheep in and then ... then maybe you'll hang around when I put the girl down. You two, well, you two have been friends a long time. I'd like a friend to be with the girl when I put her down. Millicent just can't ... you mind ...? "

"I'll be there in twenty minutes."

Short of a death in the family — and maybe even then — I would stop whatever might be demanding my attention to help Ben or Millicent Breuner. Were the roles reversed, were I the one needing help, neither of them would need twenty minutes to respond.

And, of course, a death was about to occur in the family, in both of our families.

Within five hours after I arrived, we — Ben, the three collies (Girl's two sons and her daughter), and I — had every one of the sheep out of Bandini's fields and back across the fence and onto home grounds. Millicent's rheumatism was too painful for her to be out in the cold to help us so she stayed inside to prepare a meal.

When, finally, we were satisfied the sheep were settled and the fence repaired Ben counted seven new lambs. There would be four more, he predicted, before midnight. "Let's go in," he said.

I went to my car for my backpack and carried it into the house. There, in front of the fireplace, curled, nose in tail, on top of her bed, lay Girl.

Usually, as I entered the house and spoke one word, Girl would pull herself up off the pillow and come to lay her head in my lap. Now the only sign of recognition was a slight twitch of her ears. I knelt at her side and felt her swollen rock-hard abdomen. "She's ready to burst," I said.

Millicent, standing at Ben's side, was sobbing, wiping her eyes with one of Ben's blue handkerchiefs. "I wish you'd call Dr. Nelson," she said. "I know she can't likely help but maybe she can at least make the girl comfortable." Millicent turned away to seek escape in the back of the house.

"Can I try something?" I asked.

Ben did not respond. He had no reason to believe I knew

something he hadn't thought of. But I had to try.

"I've done something on friends," I said. "And on myself. Let me try it on Girl."

Ben started to shake his head, but then Millicent shouted from the bedroom in the rear, "Damn it, Benjamin, let him try! Whatta you got to lose? It's Girl who's dyin', not you or me!"

Ben shrugged.

I opened my backpack and removed a bottle I'd brought from home. "Can you get me a feeding tube, Ben, and one of the big syringes?"

Ben left the room and returned with several thin rubber tubes he and I had often used to force-feed sick sheep. He handed me one of the tubes, and I sat on the floor and lifted Girl into my lap. She was too sick to resist. Ben, unable to watch Girl endure this indignity, turned away.

I had had some experience tube-feeding animals when I was a volunteer with the Marine Mammal Rescue Center in Marin County. It was a fairly common procedure for seasoned volunteers to learn to feed orphan seals or sea lions when they needed nutrition but had no mother to feed them. This procedure was the same.

I slid the tube between Girl's lips and over her tongue. Very carefully but quickly, I worked the tube over the rear of the tongue and down so that as I continued advancing the tube I would not be feeding it into her larynx. The tip had to get into her stomach. If it went into her larynx and into her lungs, she could drown.

When I guessed the tip had advanced far enough, I blew gently into the available end of the tube. Girl gagged slightly but did not cough, a fair sign I had missed the larynx and had succeeded in getting the tip into her stomach.

Ben handed me one of the big syringes that he and I had used on sheep. I filled the syringe with fluid from my bottle and fixed its glass nose into the rubber tube. I lifted the syringe for Ben to hold. "Okay," I said, and Ben pushed the plunger slowly. The syringe emptied slowly. Girl still did not cough. I filled the syringe two more times, and Ben (I could hear him talking to himself) pushed the plunger.

"That's it," I said. "Let's wait five or ten minutes. It will either work by then or it won't. If it doesn't work, I'll walk out to the field with you. I'll carry the girl."

Millicent, having come in to observe our efforts, was trying hard to control her sobbing. When she put a mug of hot coffee in my fingers, her hand was trembling so badly she almost spilled it. She offered a steaming mug to Ben but he just sat there, ignoring the coffee, staring at the floor.

I had taken one sip of my coffee when suddenly there was a sound like water spurting out of a broken hydrant. Girl, howling, tried to get up. I grabbed her and tried to control her. Ben kneeled to give what support he could. As Girl continued howling and Millicent continued crying, Ben and I were slipping about in the widening pool of thick muck.

It was over in a few minutes.

Girl lay still, no longer howling. Then she whined and stood up, not exactly smelling like lavender but she was up.

Millicent ran for a bucket and mop.

After we bathed Girl, Millicent gave me some of Ben's underwear and one of his robes. While I was in the shower, she dumped my clothes and Ben's in the washer. Ben went into the shower when I came out.

I walked to the eucalyptus pillow. Girl was sleeping, or seemed to be.

When Ben came out of the shower and went over to her pillow, Girl stood up and posed at the back door, giving the wooden panel *the eye*.

Ben, not saying a word, opened the door.

I watched them from the kitchen window. They performed as they had every morning: Ben whistling, Girl running, the sheep submitting.

Millicent had food on the table when Ben and Girl returned. Girl settled onto her eucalyptus pillow and fell asleep immediately.

"Okay," Ben said. "What was it? Whatever it was, I want four bottles, for the wife."

"Garlic and olive oil," I said. "Two to one. Two cups of chopped garlic to one-cup olive oil. California Early garlic. It's all I have left. I would have used Red Toch or Siberian but they're both gone."

Millicent chattered happily as we ate. Ben and I were silent. Then, as he waited for his pie, Ben raised his chin and he looked as if he just might punch me in the head. Instead, he said, "I still want four bottles, for the wife."

"I don't need it," Millicent said. "You're the one who's full of it."

Ben still looked as if he was using great restraint with his right fist. Then he got up and walked over to where Girl was sleeping. When she lifted her head and pointed her sharp black nose at him, he said, "Don't you pretend you can't see me. You've fooled this cowboy long enough." He kneeled down, held Girl's muzzle in his hands, peered into her eyes. "What did you call that garlic, Chester?"

"California Early. The only garlic I grow that's native to California. It's the one in all the supermarkets."

"That the garlic the Bandinis eat?"

"Probably."

Millicent put her arms around me. "Will it work on arthritis, Chester? I got it bad in my fingers."

"Why not? It couldn't hurt."

Ben, still kneeling beside Girl, was shaking his head and muttering to himself.

Chapter Seven

GIOVANNI LEONI

SPANISH ROJA
Hardneck Rocambole
Seed stock from Filaree Farms (Washington State) and Jim Baiar (Montana). A northwest heirloom brought to the Portland area before 1900. Performs poorly in mild winter climates. Best selling Ophio (Hardneck) garlic. Described as "the most piquant garlic in the world" and "… when well grown, its flavor describes true garlic." In taste tests Spanish Roja often shares first place with Creole Red. Very easy to peel. Shelf life: four to five months.

BURGUNDY
Softneck Silverskin (Creole Group)
Creole Group includes Ajo Rojo and Creole Red. Source uncertain, possibly France/Germany. Bulbs, grown well: moderate to large. Eight to fourteen small-medium cloves, all covered with striking Burgundy-colored skins. Flavor: biting heat that fades fast. Shelf life: four to six months.

Time: late August, perhaps early September, 1990.

Place: North Beach, San Francisco; a restaurant called *Buca Giovanni*. (Translation: Giovanni's Cave.) Giovanni had arrived at the name for his restaurant after discovering that the main dining room was under-ground.

I had driven from Occidental, sixty miles to the north of San Francisco, to meet with my friend and attorney, Diana. I was about to meet Giovanni and was about to be reminded why I fell in love with Italy and with Italians. At least, with most Italians. One of the few exceptions: those fashion-plate Milanese, all suntan, flash, fashion, and hair oil. Giovanni's judgment of these self-important *buffoni* (Giovanni's word, meaning *clowns*) was accompanied by his angelic grin: "Cesare, *voglio romper loro le gambe, strangolarli.* I wanta to breaka their legs. I wanta to chokea their necksa."

I was, forever after that exchange, no longer Chester. I was Cesare.

Before he established his own restaurant, Giovanni had been owner and chef at Vanessi's, a famed San Francisco landmark. Born in the Serchio valley in Tuscany, Giovanni had been honored with a gold medal for his contributions to the growing fame of Italian cuisine in the United States. After his arrival in San Francisco, he had been acclaimed by chefs and reviewers and colleagues as "… a true artisan of the culinary art. The Maestro approaches his profession with a mixture of scholarship, skill, hard work, and that pure pleasure that separates great chefs from competent cooks. He has educated San Franciscans in the subtle delights and goodness of Tuscan cooking years before they traveled to Italy and discovered its roots. At Buca Giovanni, the Maestro not only served homemade pasta, home-grown rabbit and vegetables from his own ranch, but he also roasted his own coffee."

The preceding quote comes from The Gold Medal Award.

Diana had suggested this restaurant on Greenwich Street. She had spent time in Italy and had promised me that Buca Giovanni offered the best Italian food in North Beach, perhaps in the entire U.S., thanks to the owner-chef, Giovanni Leoni. Giovanni the Lion.

Not only was southbound traffic on Highway 101 lighter than usual that day but I also found space in a parking lot less than a block from the restaurant. I arrived before Diana, carrying what I had intended to be a gift for her; a bag of six garlic bulbs. Each bulb represented one of six different varieties I'd recently taken out of the ground. At that time, 1990, I had forty varieties of garlic from eight different countries.

While I waited, I watched the white-jacketed chef behind the bar. He was a ruddy faced man of sixty or so who moved not just with ease about the stove and cutting-tables but with a pleasure that suggested he might be imagining himself in some more exotic environment, an opera, perhaps, or a ballet. In truth, he was simply enjoying what he was doing and where he was doing it. At his own tempo he was preparing food for … I was about to say *his customers*, but I know now almost ten years after I met him that the term *customer* never came to Giovanni's mind. The man was preparing food for his family.

Of the thousands, many, many thousands of fortunate diners who had sat at Giovanni's tables, Diana was one of the few who early on had recognized her good fortune, who had known that when she occupied a table at *Buca Giovanni* she was perceived by The Maestro not as a customer but as a daughter, a sister, a lover, a wife, as family.

Had any restaurant-reviewer written the previous sentence, I would be sneering at his/her sentimentality. I use the double pronoun here with equal-opportunity contempt. My opinion and, I later discovered, Giovanni's opinion, of food writers, especially restaurant-reviewers, was less than admiring. If you can't earn a living at a real job, take a one hour writing lesson in a community college, memorize a few French phrases, learn the difference in spelling between palate and palette, trumpet the superiority of Chateau Lafitte Rothschild 1812 over a Mogen David 1998, and you're on your way to a career as a restaurant reviewer. Your credentials? You eat.

It was about six o'clock when I entered the restaurant. The advance scouts of the dinner crowd had not yet arrived.

I will never know what prompted me to amble over to the bar, to carry the bag of garlic bulbs with me, and to empty the bag on the bar's clear surface. One of the bulbs, I recall, was Burgundy, source unknown for certain; the other bulb was one of my five or six favorites, Spanish Roja.

The chef came to the bar, spatula in hand. His white jacket emphasized the red bronze tone of his face and hands. This was a man who loved the sun and wind, and oven.

Giovanni studied the six bulbs, each of them obviously garlic but each of them unlike any garlic he had ever seen: six different shapes, six different sizes, covered with skins of different colors. One or two had three or four cloves; others had eight or ten.

Gazing up over his bifocals to get me in focus, Giovanni said, "Whatsa this? Thisa garlic, si?"

"Si. I mean yes. I grow garlic."

He did not reach out to touch the bulbs; he did not even seem especially interested. In fact, I thought that he was about to turn around and walk back to the stove, but then he grinned and I swooned. If I had been a woman, I would have felt I was being caressed, I was being kissed.

"*Bello*," he said. "*Straordinario*. Where thisa garlic from?"

Though obviously enchanted, he restrained the urge to catch even one of the bulbs in his rough red fingers.

"I live in Occidental, up north near Santa Rosa. I grow my garlic there. I have almost five acres."

"Occidental. Italian restaurants. Union Hotel. Same fooda the Gonnella family they put on the table hundred fifty years ago for the *immigranti*. No fancy bullshit, just gooda food."

"That's it. The Union Hotel. Barbara and Frank Gonnella. They work hard. Bar, café, restaurant, pizzeria. I'm there, in one of them, at least once every day."

"I livea up north too. My wife and me, we buy a place near Ukiah."

"That's only seventy or eighty miles north of Occidental."

"We buy it three years ago. I grow fruita and vegetables. I usea everything here. Some garlic, too, but not garlic looka like this. I planta that *cacata* you buy in the super-market, that shit from Gilroy. In Italy, I throw away garlic tastea likea the Gilroy garlic. But whatta you do, you use whatta you get."

"Next week I'll send you some of the other garlics I grow. I have forty varieties from eight different countries, including two from Italy. I only eat the Gilroy garlic when I run out of my own. Taste these six. They all taste different."

"You givea me these? No chargea?"

"They're yours. Eat them. I'll send you five or ten more heads of different varieties after the weekend. Do you have a garden?"

"Garden? Ha! I gotta Goddamn thirty acre. I gotta a housea ten rooms. I pay you."

"No, no. I have five thousand more bulbs like these at home."

Giovanni lifted the Spanish Roja bulb, pulled back the outer skin and nodded as the pink underskin appeared. He pulled off a clove, and to his surprise the white body of the clove snapped free of the light red skin. Somewhat apprehensive, he popped the clove into his mouth, chewed, and contemplated the activity in his mouth. He nodded again, this time very much in approval. He selected a Burgundy bulb, pulled back fragments of the outer skin still covered with dirt, and sniffed the small tight ball of cloves. The red body of the Burgundy bulb was just a shade darker than his skin. He removed one of the small cloves, studiously removed the skin with his finger-nails, nibbled, chewed, and swallowed. *Bellissimo*," he whispered; and as the grin slid into a smile, his eyes half closed and his hand came up to grab my wrist.

I am not one of those New Age types who adorns all human behavior, good and bad, with mystical interpretations. Rather, I think about that mural on the ceiling of the Sistine Chapel, that muscular God afloat in the clouds reaching out His arm and with the tip of His finger touching the fingertip of Man and zapping him with Life. That's life with a capital L. When Giovanni grabbed my fingers and squeezed, I felt as Adam must have felt when God said, "Hey, Adam, relax, live a little for Godsake."

That day at Buca Giovanni, I was, like Giovanni, in my six-ties; but when Giovanni smiled at me, I wanted to rock and roll in every little bar and café in North Beach.

Over the next eight years every time I was to visit Giovanni and his wife Michelle at their farm, I was possessed by that urge to celebrate Life. I simply wanted to celebrate my continuing presence in these fields and hills of Sonoma County, these redwoods, these oceanside cliffs, these sunsets and dawns, a sea as wine-dark as the sea Homer offered Odysseus.

Every time sounds like I visited Michelle and Giovanni often. Unfortunately, I visited them only three times.

That first night at Buca Giovanni, Giovanni brought Diana and me a pizza appetizer made just for us: the thin crust covered with slices of what can only be described as melted onion topped with thin slices of fresh sweet tomato brought from his own garden that morning. Over both onion and tomato, a whisper of a very light garlic-scented olive oil. *"La rossa,"* Giovanni said. *"La rossa spagnuola.* I plant it tomorrow my farma."

"No, no. Eat it. I'll send you more. But don't plant a single clove until October."

Diana was correct. The last time I had food prepared as simply, as beautifully, as tastefully, as the food I had that night at Buca Giovanni had been in Italy: in a *trattoria* in Cortina, in one of the *tripe mobile* in Florence, and, also in Florence, in a *ristorante* called Il Toscano (owner: Allesandro Valentini.)

The food at the *tripe mobile* and at Il Toscano was tripe (Giovanni called it *treepa*), a dish that he and I during one of my visits discussed in detail. He made it for me on my second visit and dubbed me an honorary Italian, not just because I was an American and I liked tripe but because I also used a *scarpetta.* "My people," he said, "in Italy they very poor. Poor people everywhere, they usea everything to stay alive. Chicken feet, cow's stomach, sheep's brains, blood. Cesare," and he kissed the tips of his fingers, "you likea my *treepa so* much you usea *una scarpetta.* You know *scarpetta?"*

I remembered my elementary Italian. The word *scarpe* means *shoe.* "Isn't *scarpetta* a diminutive for *scarpe?"*

Giovanni shrugged off the word *diminutive.* "You talka like a Goddamn *professore.* Come on, Cesare, you writea booksa, si, but here," (tapping his heart), "you are *un contadino*, a farmer. *Scarpetta.* The piecea breada you wipe up alla the juices you cleana the plate." He threw a firm arm around my shoulder.

In late September shortly after I met Giovanni, he called me at home. "Cesare, it's almost October. I wanta buy *molto aglio*. I pay whatever you say, my friend."

"Giovanni, I'll send you bulbs, different varieties. A gift."

"Cesare, you are my besta friend." The voice a benediction. We talked about the space he planned for the growing of his garlic and the best techniques for planting the various garlics in his soil and his weather, which could be both hotter and colder and wetter than Occidental's. I sent him ten different varieties, three or four bulbs of each. In the box he'd built, he planted over two hundred cloves. He followed my advice and saved the healthiest bulbs from that harvest for planting the following October. I sent him five more varieties the next year, about twenty more bulbs. He built four new boxes and ended up planting about a thousand cloves. The cloves he planted the second year were harvested in July and cured down in the depths of his cool dry basement. "Cesare, my favorites stilla my favorites, that beautiful reda Burgundy and my *rossa spagnuola*. But I now gotta one even more favorite, Cesare. You know whicha one?"

"Let me guess. The Tuscan White."

"How the hella you know that? *Esattamente!*"

"What's *esattamente* mean, Giovanni?"

"It meansa ... I don't know. Michelle, *esattamente*. In *inglese?* "

Michelle, whose heritage is Greek, had picked up enough idiomatic Italian to help Giovanni over occasional linguistic hurdles. I heard her voice in the background. "I think it's *exact* or *exactly*."

"Cesare, it means *exactly*. You guessa exac ... *esattamente*. Whena you come visit? I makea your favorite dish. You wanta I guessa your favorite disha?"

"You know my favorite dish, Giovanni."

"*Corretto*, Cesare. I guessa correc ... *corretto*. Treepa."

"Next Saturday."

Giovanni's tripe that day was better than the tripe at Il Toscano in Florence. In addition to the tripe (the *trippa*, the central and most important part of the cow's stomach) Giovanni, like Allesandro Valentini, used *lampredotto*, the upper part of the stomach. "And guessa the garlic, Cesare."

"The Tuscan white or the Burgundy."

"You gotta picka one."

"The Burgundy."

"Ah! *Un bel palato!* You gotta finea palate." And over the tips of those thick red rough-skinned fingers Giovanni Leoni ... Giovanni, the lion ... blew me a kiss.

About the fourth or fifth year of our friendship, I sent Giovanni a copy of my first novel, *About Us.* It had been published in 1967, costing $5.00 at the counter. It is out of print. If you can find a copy, it will cost you about $100. I have only five copies so I hoard them, hide them, save them for my grandchildren, though I often wonder if they'll ever read it. The novel is about a Jewish boy growing up in a Pennsylvania coal mine village before and during World War II. What do my teenage grandchildren care about American life, or any life, fifty years ago? If I were six million years old and a dinosaur, my story might get their attention.

The dedication printed in *About Us* reads: *For Margaurite and Louis.* Margaurite was my wife. Officially, Louis is my stepson. He was then about fifteen years old.

Giovanni called me five days later. "Cesare, *grazie, molto grazie, mi'amico.*"

I next sent Giovanni my first garlic book, *Garlic is Life.* There the dedication reads:

For Louis Segal

Since I met you when you were ... what ... three years old,
you've been (for the last forty-two years) in my mind
with such force that you are now in my blood. You are not
my stepson anymore, you are a much admired and
much-beloved son.

About a week later Giovanni called me. "Cesare. I reada your book. Whatta you say abouta your son, I know in my hearta. I havea stepa-children. I lovea them likea they are my blooda. They are in my hearta, too, and ina my blooda. *Grazie*, Cesare."

On my third visit to Ukiah Giovanni and I took a long walk.

We talked about many things: his love for Michelle, his departure from the restaurant so he could live on the farm, his longing for Italy balanced by his love for this farmland in Sonoma County, California. He had plans for planting a variety of fruit trees and vegetables. He'd already planted over a hundred olive trees; and as we moved among them, he clapped his hands like a child when he described the joy that would be his when we — he, Michelle and I — shared the first pressing.

We talked about life and death and, of course, the current state of the so-called culinary art. "Theesa people they calla themselvesa chefs. They go to school a few years, they reada booksa, they worka six months, they open a restaurant, and suddenly they're famous chefs. They don't know gooda fooda from *cacata*. You worka many years, you planta vegetables, you cuta meata, you study the besta chefs, and you lovea people because they respect you not because they are biga names or *aristocrazia*. Cesare, I tella you a secret. I hate richa people, I hatea the *aristocrazia*, the famous people. You know what I do, Cesare, I was a boy?" He laughed. "My people always very poor. I ama hungry all the timea. I worka for *i nobili*, the nobility. Ha! You know thisa famous woman she calls herself a *contessa*? You see her biga beautiful books about Italy alla the magazines. Very famous, very rich. Ha! She buya her *contessa* title like I buya my cigarette. She no more *contessa* than you, Cesare. Chefsa, they say, '*Oh, Contessa. You sita my table, Contessa. I kissa your foota, Contessa.* Cesare, I work for people likea *la Contessa*. I cleana their barnsa, I cleana their toilets. You know what I do I was a boy, Cesare?"

"What did you do, Giovanni?"

"I cleana their toilets. They come ina the toilets. You know whata…?"

"What, Giovanni?"

"Before they come ina I pissa on the doorknoba. The *aristocrazia* they come ina the bathroom; they go outa the bathroom; they gotta puta their hands in my pissa."

We both laughed so hard we had to sit on the giant stump of an old redwood to catch our breath.

Is it because I myself come of peasant stock and grew up in a Pennsylvania coal mine village with children of immigrant peasants that I enjoy so much that uncouth peasant humor that often targets the wealthy, the powerful, the socially and intellectually *poseurs* (look that up in your Funka and Wagnalls)?

That day on our walk, I mentioned to Giovanni that I had read somewhere that many newly arrived Italian immigrants (had it been the men only?) to New York City used to band together on the weekends to travel out of the city to the deserted rural areas. There in the forests they could lower their trousers and drape their rumps over a tree limb and relieve themselves onto the grass. Giovanni nodded, thoughtful, compassionate. "Not nicea maybe," he said, "but kidsa, poor kidsa, lifea full of things not nicea."

About five months after our walk in the woods, shortly after Giovanni had planted all his garlic, Michelle called to tell me Giovanni had lung cancer.

He died about six months ago.

It is August now. I have just completed my 1998 harvest.

As I pack my Burgundy and my Spanish Roja bulbs in their bags, how can I not see Giovanni's ruddy face? How can I not hear Giovanni's laughter?

How can I not weep for Giovanni's children, for Michelle?

How can I not weep for myself?

How, especially, can I not weep for you who never knew Giovanni Leoni? Giovanni, the lion.

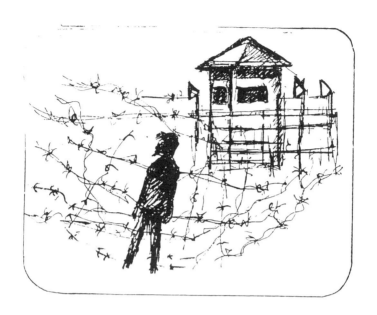

Chapter Eight

GUNTHER

SABRA
Softneck Artichoke

From a friend at the Israeli kibbutz of Ma'agan Michael. Not unusual in appearance, but with obvious sentimental value to me. After three successive bad crops, the addition of large amount of sand in the soil earned medium to large bulbs with six to eight tan-skinned cloves. Named after the Sabra, an Israeli cactus, which is thorny, durable. Native-born Israelis are called Sabras. Taste: quite hot without the subtleties of other artichoke garlics. Shelf life: four to five months.

THANKS TO *EL NIÑO*, 1998 GAVE US A HARD WINTER IN CALIFORNIA. THE rains came early, meaning in August, and, after several frosts, continued through the following June. That's June of 1999. Three months ago.

Like most humans, most garlics do not appreciate cold heads and wet feet in the last quarter of their lives.

Two of my eighty-seven garlics were not only not effected by the heavy rains, they actually thrived. One of those two was the Siberian.

Of the 150 Siberian cloves planted in October, I received, in July, two months ago, 145 beautiful purple-striped bulbs. Three bulbs were so malformed (given the well-ordered shape of the parent) I did not dare distribute them. Nor could I risk returning them to the soil because they might very well relay their radical genes into the next generation. I could eat them, though, and I did. Twisted, malformed, looking more like pine cones than garlic, they still delivered that rich dense earthy taste unique to my Siberian garlic.

At the Tulsa Garlic Festival, a Texas garlic-grower had informed me that a few months before, after a year-long drought, he'd lost 80% of his crop in one day to grasshoppers. The clouds of insects that appeared in the morning attacked the stalks and took them down to the ground. Then they went after the bulbs. But there was one variety that survived, that the grasshoppers never even went near.

"Let me guess," I said. "Was it the Siberian?"

"Yeah. How the hell did you know that?"

"I'll tell you. In the floods last year my Siberian garlic endured the floods without the slightest damage. I told that to a friend in London. She gave me this phrase. Let's see if I can remember it. *'Ya utselevshaya!'* On the shores of the Sea of Okhotsk in far Siberia that means, *'I am a survivor!'*"

I'd planted 170 Sabra cloves on October 20, 1998. On July 27, 1999, I harvested 166 stalks. Those Sabra stalks, along with eight thousand stalks of many other varieties, were hanging in my curing shed when Gretchen called from San Francisco.

Gretchen von Hoffmanschau had submitted an application for employment soon after I became Chief Tech in the x-ray Department at Alta Bates Hospital in Berkeley. That was in the early 'seventies.

I already knew enough about the qualities that make a capable technician to be aware at the time that the training of European techs was superior to the training available to American techs. And European techs, perhaps for that reason, were almost always more indulgent with patients.

Had it been possible, I would have filled the department with techs trained in Britain, Denmark, and Sweden. In fact, when Gretchen applied for work at Alta Bates, my staff of twelve full time techs and four part-timers already included two from Britain, two from Denmark, and one from Ireland. All women. Few men at that time, in both Europe and America, were interested in hospital work.

Gretchen, though European-born and trained, created problems for me. Or was it I who created problems for Gretchen?

When I invited her back to my office and we started talking, Gretchen's accent was like a dentist's drill digging deeper and deeper into an old but still troublesome cavity. I remember now how I closed my eyes during our first moments together as if not seeing her might mean I would not hear her. I discovered years later, after we became close friends, that Gretchen, when she'd entered my office, had been very much aware of the fact that I was a Jew. My face, after all, could have been the model for the illustrations of the big-nosed Jews that filled the Nazi newspapers when she was a child growing up in Berlin in the late 'thirties and early 'forties. I also discovered years later, as Gretchen and her husband and my wife and I spent more and more time together, that she'd known at the time of our first conversation that I had judged her a Nazi. Given her age and her background, and my recent past, what other judgment could I have reached?

Just fifteen years before that day Gretchen sat in my office, I had been in combat in Germany. In the last month of the war I was with the American troops that liberated the concentration camp of Dachau. Close and distant relatives of mine had been executed and cremated at Dachau and Auschwitz.

I could have found many reasons to wave Gretchen out of my office, out of my mind, out of my conscience. Her accent was only one reason. I would explain to anyone who might ask that the woman would have trouble communicating with patients. But the major reason: this tall handsome woman refused to pretend she was anything but what she was, a thirty year old woman of great beauty almost arrogantly at ease with her European sophistication and elegance.

Gretchen's papers indicated that she had trained in Berlin, she spoke four languages fluently, she had worked in several hospitals in Germany during the war years. Her references were beyond impressive: the administrator of Massachusetts General Hospital; a professor at Harvard's School of Medicine; two radiologists, one of whom was president of the National Board of Radiology.

Gretchen von Hoffmanschau. The *von*, I knew, meant that the Hoffmanschaus were Prussian, the ultimate European aristocrats and military leaders.

I hired Gretchen, and she started working on a Monday, three days after her interview. By the following Friday I knew not only that I had not made a mistake but that I had performed a service for Alta Bates Hospital and for every patient that came into the x-ray department. The following week when my wife came to the hospital for lunch she and Gretchen sat in the cafeteria long after I returned to the department. As if they'd been intimate friends since childhood, they talked about clothes, San Francisco shops, dress patterns, art, jewelry, museums.

A single illustration here of Gretchen's value not just to me but to the hospital. And to the patients. One reason why I still admire her, why we remain friends today.

I was x-raying a woman who had been brought from Intensive Care to the department on a gurney. Her chart indicated she was in her seventies, perhaps her eighties. She was very sick. While I was sliding her about on the table so she'd be centered for the film I'd be taking of her abdomen, her hands came up to cover her face. Humiliated, she started crying. Unable to control her bowels, she had messed herself, the linen she was lying on, the gown she was wearing, the x-ray table, and me. My green cotton work-blouse and my dress-trousers were soaked. I shouted, "I need help in here."

Two techs started into the room and, assailed by the odor, turned and hurried out, expressing concerns about leaving their own patients alone. Then, as if she'd been waiting for the opportunity,

Gretchen sailed into the room. Without saying a word, she helped the woman out of her gown, removed the sheets from the table and dumped all the linen in the hamper. Having messed her own always immaculate white uniform in the process, Gretchen tied a clean patient's gown around herself. While I scrubbed down the table and mopped the floor, Gretchen washed the woman's body from face to feet with warm wet towels. After we wrapped the patient in warm blankets and lifted her onto the gurney, Gretchen rolled the gurney into the hallway.

As I prepared the room for the next patient, Gretchen, using her own comb and brush, worked on the woman's gray hair, her mix of English and German reminding the woman that she was beautiful, that she would soon be home playing with her grand-children.

Gretchen von Hoffmanschau, who had been surrounded by servants all her life, was by nature far more humane than I or anyone else in the department, more humane perhaps than anyone in the hospital.

I invited Gretchen and her boyfriend, an attorney from San Francisco, to our house for supper the following Saturday night.

Gretchen worked in our department for five years. In the sixth year she married the attorney, who, shortly after, was appointed to the position of judge in Superior Court in San Francisco. Reluctant to quit work and more reluctant to commute, Gretchen applied for a job in the x-ray department at Mount Zion Hospital, a few blocks from her home in San Francisco. When the Chief Tech at Zion called me for a recommendation I said that Gretchen von Hoffmanschau Patterson was not only the most competent technician I had ever known, she was the most humane person I had ever met.

Gretchen and I saw less and less of each other over the following years, but one of us occasionally telephoned the other. After I left hospital work and accepted a job at Saint Mary's College, the intervals of silence grew longer and more frequent. When news somehow reached her that my wife and I were divorced, Gretchen sent each of us letters pleading that we continue being friends, that we continue being decent to each other, that we try to never hurt each other. I knew the language was not the banal chitchat of a simple-minded do-gooder or amateur counselor.

One evening in the early 'nineties, 1991 to be exact, several years after my divorce, I was in a book store in San Francisco, signing my just-published young-adult novel *Alex - Who Won His War*. Bent over a book and posting my signature, I heard a familiar voice with a familiar accent murmur a phrase common to x-ray departments: "Now, take in a deep breath."

Gretchen and her husband (Howard Patterson, just appointed to the California State Supreme Court) were standing at my table. Gretchen placed a large bouquet of roses in my arms and kissed me on both cheeks, twice. Howard and I embraced.

Gretchen and Howard bought five copies of *Alex*. I remember signing one of the books *To Gunther and Ilse, from Gretchen and Howard and the author*. As she turned to leave, Gretchen looked back and said, "Ach, I forget. Breathe normal, please."

A week later Gretchen wrote me a letter here in Occidental. The letter is long lost, but I remember the seventeen words above her signature as if I received the letter a few minutes ago. "Chester, only a brave and generous and decent man could write this book about Alex. Thank you." She could have added a fourth adjective: *foolish*.

I'd taken some hits from Jewish friends for *Alex* because one of the novel's characters was a "good" German. Change that to *One of its characters was a German soldier who was also a good man*. The setting of the novel: World War II, the concentration camps. The narrative: my own experiences as a young American Jew who had helped liberate Dachau.

Gretchen's friendship had helped me write that book; her simple decency had moved me to include that German soldier. I wasn't so simple-minded as to make Hans (my German character) perfect but I did try, as I created him, to understand him. Only now do I know I was also trying to demonstrate the beginnings of my own rejection of my need for revenge.

In 1992 the German publisher of two of my novels, including *Alex - Who Won His War*, invited me to a book-fair in Berlin. The event could have been important for my career as a writer, but I found myself searching for reasons to refuse. Almost fifty years after the war had ended, three years after having written the novel about Alex and Hans, I discovered, in spite of what I considered a change-of-heart, that Germany and all things German were, as my father would say, still a fishbone in my throat.

Gretchen, I knew, travelled to Germany every year to visit relatives and old friends. Perhaps if I called her, she would suggest I stay home. But she disappointed me. "You will have no problems, Chester. Germany is fully aware of its crimes. You will be honored." She offered to give me introductions to several friends and relatives.

I just couldn't do it. The ghosts I thought had been exorcised by the writing of *Alex* still had the power to haunt.

In 1996, three years after I'd stopped teaching at Saint Mary's College and began living here in Occidental full time, I read, in *The San Francisco Chronicle*, the report of the death of Judge Howard Patterson. His obituary indicated that he was leaving a wife, Gretchen, three daughters, one son and seven grandchildren. I wrote Gretchen a letter, and I remember my words as I remember her words to me about *Alex*: "Bravery, generosity and decency, Gretchen. Those are the qualities Howard Patterson possessed, as a judge, as a man, as a husband, and as a father. Your friendship has helped me grow old with greater peace. I hope my continuing admiration of you and my friendship help bring you peace in return."

Two months ago Gretchen called me here in Occidental. She'd been reading about me and my garlic books, both of which she owned and both of which, every Christmas, she bought as gifts for friends and relatives in the U.S. and in Germany. She'd seen the various magazine and newspaper articles and television programs about me and my farm and just recently she'd bought two copies of my garlic poster. "I keep one poster. It hangs on my wall in my kitchen, Chester. Beside it is a framed photograph of you signing our books that night in San Francisco. The other poster I send my friends Gunther and Ilse in Germany. You probably do not remember but you autographed a copy of *Alex* for them." The accent had mellowed but *Germany* was still *Chermany*.

"I do remember. You and Howard gave me a large bouquet of roses that night."

"Ach, yes. Chester, my two old friends come yesterday from

Germany. They own a farm in Bavaria, near München. Gunther grows garlic. He and Ilse know we are friends, you and I. They want very much they should meet you. May we visit?"

"Gretchen, give me two days to clean my house."

"You need *ein Cherman hausfrau*, Chester."

I would not have cleaned my house for anyone else.

The timing was not ideal. It was August. I was deeply involved in the harvest of my garlic, of taking it out of the soil and bundling the different varieties together and hanging the bundles in the shed for curing. I was working every day from sunrise to sunset. Interrupt that work? Only for Gretchen.

At my suggestion we were to meet at the Union Hotel for lunch. Gretchen promised they would be in front of the Union at noon. I parked my Toyota; and when I walked toward the entrance, I saw a slightly older version of the Gretchen I had interviewed standing on the sidewalk in front of a black Mercedes. She waved and ran up to me, followed by her friends who appeared to be her age. They were probably two or three years younger than I.

Gretchen and I embraced, held each other, assured each other how well we looked. After wiping her eyes, Gretchen introduced me to her friends, Gunther and Ilse.

Following the preliminaries, I led them through the café, past the walls that contained the photographic history of the Gonnella family and the Union Hotel. In the pizzeria I said, "I took the liberty of ordering for you. Hope you like garlic." That brought laughter.

I'd prepared Barbara Gonnella that morning and now, no more than a minute after we sat at the table, she served us with four plates of *bruschetta*.

The Union Hotel's *bruschetta* is just about the best I've ever eaten, except for my own. Three slices of thick French bread, topped with mounds of chopped tomato, chopped basil, chopped garlic and olive oil, all sent very slowly through the pizza oven.

My guests offered hearty appreciation, and Gunther asked if the hotel used my garlic. I explained the realities. I did not produce enough to satisfy the restaurant's needs, and Barbara could not afford to pay the price I received from subscribers. This led to an exchange of information regarding Gunther and Ilse's small farm in Germany; how many varieties of garlic they grew (twenty two) how many I grew (currently eighty seven), how they managed to survive in the European Common Market, and how I managed to compete with the garlic corporation in Gilroy and survive in the American market.

While we were lazing over our coffee, Gunther removed from his shoulder bag a copy of my two garlic books. He started to talk but paused to think. There was a brief but hurried exchange in German between the three of them until Gretchen said, "Autograph."

"Yes, yes," Gunther said, "it is auto-graph. Would you be so kind, Chester? May I be bold, may I call you Chester? It is good manners? We have read the books, ach, several times. We have ..." (again an exchange in German)..."we have given as gifts to many friend these books." The *"Oh, so good"* came out *"Ach, so gut."*

I felt the slightest of chills but they passed.

Before we went into my house. I led them on a tour through the field. Gunther asked intelligent questions, indicating that he appreciated not just the amount of physical labor I expended but the amount of planning and discipline I gave to the perpetuation of the different garlic varieties. Ilse and Gretchen conversed in German, but Gunther spoke only English, even when he talked to the two women. After an hour or so in the field, we went into the house.

It was close to eighty-five degrees outside, but inside, thanks to my solar system, which converts the hot air into cool air and then circulates it through the house, the temperature was about seventy degrees. Ilse, standing at the south wall of windows and admiring the twenty or thirty humming birds outside the glass, begged Gunther to get all the necessary information about solar houses so that when they returned to Bavaria they could enjoy these California pleasures.

There was a fair amount of laughter along with much talk about how each of us survived our days in San Francisco (Gretchen), in Bavaria (Ilse and Gunther), and in Occidental (me). I was so pleased with my guests and my own peace of mind that I actually produced the bottle of Williams and Sellyem Pinot Noir that Ed Sellyem had traded me for about a hundred dollars worth of garlic three years before. That wine was considered one of the prime Pinot

Noirs in the world. The single bottle was worth twice the value of the garlic Ed Sellyem had received, but no matter.

About four o'clock Gretchen reluctantly suggested it was time to leave. Gunther stood and said, "Before … I'd like one …" and there was a brief conversation with Gretchen in German. "Brief," Gunther said to me. "We walk in the field one time, Chester? You and I? Brief?"

"Of course."

In the field we strolled among the boxes that were now empty and the boxes in which the garlic remained, waiting to be harvested. Gunther turned at one point and looked up at the house. "You live a beautiful life, Chester. I am happy for you. My life I live, not so good." *Not so gut.*

I waited, thinking that perhaps he was about to tell me he had some incurable disease and was, perhaps, dying. After all, he had to be in his seventies.

"I read your books. The garlic books. I also read your book… your novel. *About Us* it is called?"

"That was my first novel."

"It is true, this story?"

"Yes, but like all writers I've taken some literary liberties."

"Gretchen tells it is true. Dachau. Gretchen tells you were at Dachau."

He seemed about to fall but leaned on a shovel I'd left upright in the soil the day before. The shaft of the shovel kept him erect.

"Yes."

"Chester, 1945 I am a guard at Dachau. American troops come fast. The guards run. I run. We leave the trains with the bodies. I cannot run no more, Chester." The blade of the shovel came out of the ground and the shaft tipped over and Gunther sat down hard on the corner of one of the boxes. His long gnarled fingers covered his face. "I am so shamed, friend Chester. I am so very, very shamed. All these years I hide. Ilse does not *verstehen*. Does not know. Forgive me I speak Cherman. I wish I speak a language not Cherman, but Cherman I only know. Oh, God, I am so shamed. Fifty-four years, three months, I lie to the world. Forgive me, friend Chester."

I knew that if I stayed there, looking at him, I would vomit. I walked up through the field and onto the path that leads into the shed where the garlic bundles are hung to cure. I could hear Gunther sobbing behind me. At the shed, I climbed the three steps and went inside. Gunther waited at the doorway, under control now.

"Very well," he said. "We leave. I understand you hate me? You wish to destroy me?"

I turned and faced him. "No," I said. "I do not want to destroy you, Gunther. I do not even hate you. I don't have the right to forgive you. I don't have the power, and I'm glad I don't because I don't know if I could. I don't even know if I'd want to. But look, man, it… that … was fifty years ago."

"Fifty four, Chester, and three months." He was wiping his eyes with his knuckles, like a child convinced his world is lost.

"Gunther, I don't know what to say. It's … it's the past, man. We're both of us old men, Gunther. We don't have much time left. I don't want to die full of hatred. I love my life too much."

And then, on impulse (though God must have been watching because She surely guided my hand) I reached up and untied the nearest bundle of garlics hanging from the wires. I offered it to Gunther. "Take this home and plant it and now and then, every year, when you harvest, think of me. Now and then, remember today. When you get home send me one of your garlics and I'll do the same. I'll plant your garlic and think of you."

He accepted the bundle of five stalks, turned the label over and squinted so he might read it more clearly. "Sabra," he said. "Where is this Sabra garlic come from, Chester?"

Why did I want to say it was from France or Spain or Italy? The lie would be a fishbone in my throat. "From Israel."

Gunther's grunt sounded as if someone behind him had landed a severe punch in his kidney.

The women came out of the house just then, trying to sing a German song, the words of which neither could quite remember. While they laughed and sang, Gretchen was digging inside her purse for her car keys.

Gunther, clutching the Sabra garlic, stumbled to the Mercedes and into the rear seat. Ilse paused to embrace me. *"Auf wiedersehen, mein lieber Freund,"* she said. "My husband speak of this day many months. He want very much he should meet you."

I repeated the words, *"Auf wiedersehen."*

Gretchen, her mouth against my cheek, murmured, "I call next week." Then she stepped back and assumed that pose of aristocratic elegance I remember so clearly. "Take in a deep breath, please," she said. "Now, breathe normal."

Chapter Nine

OLGA KAZHINSKY

POLISH SLUBSK
Hardneck Rocambole

From the village of Slubsk, near the Baltic Sea, Poland. Via Olga and Frank Zymansky of Berkeley, California. Large bulbs with large cloves covered with off-white skins containing copper-colored veins and a faint purple blush at the base. Flavor: Strong garlic taste with a quick rush of heat that does not fade. Shelf life after harvest: about four-to-six months.

OLGA KAZHINSKY WAS A NURSE AT ALTA BATES HOSPITAL IN Berkeley, at the time I worked in the x-ray department. That was more than thirty years ago.

I'd been staff tech for two years and then promoted to Chief Tech. Olga was head nurse on the third floor, then the repository of terminal cancer cases. Being department heads, we both attended several of the same weekly meetings. We also occasionally served on the same committees. It became customary for us to either sit together or across the table from each other.

Three or four times a week when we happened to meet in the cafeteria, we sat at the same table. If her floor was understaffed she occasionally acted as escort for patients going to the x-ray department. She'd call first to let me know she was coming and we'd stand together for a few minutes in the hallway. This casual friendship went on for four or five years. During the year my marriage was in danger, our conversations dwelled less and less on work and more and more on my depressions.

I did not think of it then, but I know now what first attracted me to her. Olga was a contemporary version of those first girls I'd loved when I was a teenager in Pennsylvania, girls who were daughters of Polish and Russian immigrants. They lived in Lyndora, near the steel mills, three miles from the center of town. I lived in North Butler, three miles on the opposite side of town, near the coal mines. We met as freshmen at Butler High School and shared our teenage lives in classrooms, gyms, auditoriums, ice cream counters.

Johnny Prebula would borrow his dad's Studebaker on Saturday nights; and he, Roman Krepenevich, and I would ride to Butler to pick up the Lyndora girls who had walked to Main Street hoping for a few hours of fun.

The names of the girls: Helen Sopel and Juley Fako and Katey Galida, Pollack girls. They were earthy, unpretentious, warm, and full of joy. When we drove to the woods on Saturday nights and parked and kissed and felt each other, we never engaged in sex and our frustrations were ringed with laughter. They were not promiscuous. They were not teasers. They simply possessed more love-of-life than their bodies could contain. It had to overflow, it had to be shared. We went up to the edge of sex but never beyond. The simple act of containing each other's body in each other's arms was as thrilling, as fulfilling, as an orgasm. Their natural exuberance was so infectious that though my friends and I would return home with aching groins packed with unreleased sexual tension, I would dream for the next six nights, until the following Saturday about Helen or Juley or Katey. They would be in my arms and I in theirs, and we would be smothering each other with kisses. We would be admitting undying love for each other.

Olga Kazhinsky swelled with that Slavic beauty I had been drawn to then and still admire: the broad face, the sharply angled jaw line, the flat firm cheeks, the liquid brown eyes with their slight almost Oriental tilt, a heritage of Genghis Khan and his Mongol hordes.

Olga had another quality that made her even more attractive to me. She moved with the grace of a dancer, which she was, or had been, for years, before becoming a nurse. She continued dancing throughout her early years at Alta Bates Hospital. During the six months I was separated from my wife, Olga and I lived together. She gave me complimentary tickets to her performance in the Oakland Ballet Company's production of *Giselle* and then to the San Francisco Ballet's production of *Swan Lake*.

Olga Kazhinsky satisfied two of my then adult requirements for an ideal mate: a Slavic face and a talent for ballet. When I told her once that if I had believed in reincarnation I'd want to return as ballet slippers to be worn by a beautiful dancer. Olga nodded and said, "Ah, yes, the new Russian dancer, Nureyev. He has large feet." And so satisfying my third and fourth requirements for a mate: wit and a sense of irony.

During that six-month period of soul-searching that ended in a foolish and very brief reunion with my wife, I survived primarily because Olga Kazhinsky loved me. She nursed me back to health, as Helen or Juley or Susan would have done had I been ill when I was fifteen or sixteen.

For those six months we shared our lives (after which I returned to my wife and Olga met and married an also Polish auto-mechanic whose wife had died and left him with two small children), I loved Olga as I had not ever loved any human being before. After my divorce and Olga's marriage, I would occasionally see her at the hospital; but it was never quite the same. Why should it have been? How could it have been?

After I left the hospital, I did not see Olga again for thirty years, that is until exactly seven months ago today, today being May 14, 1998

I was sitting at the counter of the Union Hotel Cafe. Looking up from my newspaper, I saw through the window a man and a woman closing the doors of their car at the curb. Could the *espresso* Shelly had prepared for me (Shelly joking around again!) have been laced with a triple shot of vodka? My head went heavy, then light; my heart raced, slowed, almost stopped, raced again; my eyes blurred. There, coming through the door, was the twenty-eight year old Olga Kazhinsky. She was trying, for some reason, to pretend that she, too, had aged. Perhaps she looked three or four years older than she had when I had last seen her thirty years ago.

As she and her male friend (her husband, I was sure) moved through the cafe on their way to the main restaurant, Olga saw me at the counter. Her eyes widened and her lips opened to show her large, still strong, still flashing, white teeth. Her face declared the same pleasure that same face had declared when she was a twenty-eight year old nurse-ballerina sliding naked into my bed. She stood there staring at me, then she screamed my name.

A lazy writer relying on easy language would say we fell into each other's arms.

When we finally broke our embrace, she introduced me to Frank Zymansky. I insisted, of course, on hearing Frank *Kazhinsky*; only later, after I accepted their invitation to join them for lunch in the main restaurant, did I correct my ear.

At the table in the Union Hotel restaurant, Olga and I talked with great merriment, each of us apologizing now and then to Frank for excluding him from our exchange of hospital memories and questions about friends and acquaintances we had shared during that period. Frank, more than gracious, even seemed to enjoy our recollections. Whenever a serious or ominous reference threatened appearance, it was ignored.

Frank, a big beefy man with a face bordered by heavy jowls (a face that had probably, as Olga's still was, been flat and Slavic in his youth), was not at all embarrassed by Olga's holding his hand as she and I talked or kissing his cheek or brushing his hair with that occasional almost sacrificial I-love-you-more-than-life glance of which I had once been the grateful target.

Olga informed me that she had, through mutual friends, kept in touch with my career after I'd left Alta Bates Hospital. She had every one of my young-adult novels on the shelf in their den, and their grandchildren read them during weekends or vacations.

"She won't let those books out of the house," Frank said. "Me, I read them too. And I aint no young-adult. Man, they are better than Louis L'Amour. I'm proud to finally meet you. Olga's told me stories about you are even better than those books."

Olga's eyes, as she kissed Frank's knuckles, glistened with tears.

I invited them to come with me after lunch to my home. Did they have time? They did, because they had planned to spend the day cruising the coast and even, perhaps, spending some time fishing at a few places Frank had visited as a youth. Unfortunately those old haunts were now covered with condominiums. So they had time to spare.

I apologized beforehand about the state of my housekeeping, but they couldn't have cared less. "Frank," Olga reminded me, "was a bachelor when we met."

"I aint left a pair of socks on the floor in almost forty years," Frank said.

We were, at that moment, in my car.

It would be easier, I'd explained, for them to leave their car parked in the lot outside of the Union Hotel Cafe and ride with me in my Toyota. Fortunately, I had cleared out all the old newspapers and magazines and coffee cups that morning.

After we left Graton Road and I was cautiously moving my little Tercel up Acreage Lane and around the more menacing curves, I apologized again for the condition in which they'd find my home.

"What you need," Frank said, "is a Polish wife. My sister's looking for a good man."

Olga laughed. She was sitting in the front seat beside me, but she turned to reach back and take Frank's hand. "I love you, darling; but Sophia would fill Chester's belly with so many Polish *halupkas*, so much *krupnik* and *kapusniak*, that in six months he'd weigh twice as much as he does now. Incidentally, Chester, for an old man — what are you now? Seventy? You have to be, I'm sixty-five — you're in great shape. You look like a man fifty years old."

"I'd have said fifty-five," Frank said.

"Seventy-five," I said. "What's *krupnik* and what's *kapusniak*?"

"Barley soup," Olga said. "And sauerkraut soup."

"No, thanks."

Frank said, "Seventy-five? You've got to be kidding."

"I kid you not. Seventy-five. Five days ago."

Olga dropped Frank's hand and reached over to pat my right hand, which was clutching the rim of the steering wheel. I felt as if I'd been struck by the very same lightning bolt that had struck me thirty years before. That same damn bolt of lightning had continued flashing through the universe all these years just waiting for me to expose myself so it could zap me one more time.

Olga said, "Happy birthday, Chester." She kissed my cheek.

"Yeah," Frank said. "And I hope God gives you fifty more."

We passed Liza's vineyard, and I pointed out the horses and dogs and sheep and pigs behind the fences, animals Liza had saved from extinction. Frank said, "Lord Almighty, horses and dogs and pigs. And a vineyard. Olga, can you imagine having your own pigs? I don't want to live in Berkeley any more. I want to live up here. I want to raise pigs. I'll grow cabbages and make *kapusniak*. I'll roast pigs, and I'll pickle pigs' feet."

I slowed down as we left Hillcrest and turned onto Lapham Lane. I wanted Olga and Frank to see the land as I had seen it that first day, before my house went up, before my gardens went in, before my boxes (most of them empty) spread across the fields. "Hey," Frank said. "You got redwood trees."

"I've got redwood trees," I said. "Thirty-four of them. Some of them two or three hundred years old."

Frank murmured something in Polish, and Olga crossed herself.

After a tour of my solar home and a lazy walk through the redwood trees, we lingered in the field. I introduced them to my passion for garlic. They listened to my stories of how each of my days began and ended with the work in the field, with planting, weeding, irrigating, harvesting, cleaning, selling, eating, garlic. And ended with three or four hours of writing every evening.

Returned to the deck, as I added to my garlic stories, we drank cold beer.

"What are you writing, Chester?"

"Novels. Stories. One of the novels is about my hospital days, in fact."

"Oh, Lord," Olga said. "I want to read that."

"You're in it," I said. "And I'm still writing about garlic."

"Garlic," Olga said. "Chester, I never knew. How could you have published two books about garlic and I didn't know?"

I went into the house while they rested on the deck and I returned with a laminated copy of my garlic poster, which displayed forty colored photographs of my eighty-four garlics.

They might as well have been taken into the Sistine Chapel to be offered a private view of the ceiling. They studied each garlic, compared one to the others, asked about this or that variety, where this or that garlic came from.

Olga sat in a chair facing the poster, which was leaning against the wall.

"Tell him," Frank said.

"Tell me what?"

"I have some very special garlic for you, Chester. If I'd known we'd meet today, if I knew about you and garlic, I'd have brought it. But now we have an excuse for inviting you to Berkeley. To supper."

"Where's this special garlic from?"

"When we went to Poland, we took trains and busses until we got to Slubsk, a small town near the Baltic Sea. Frank's *babka* lives in Slubsk."

"Lived," Frank said. "She died last year at ninety-one."

"What's *babka*?"

"Granny. His Grandma. She lived in Slubsk. She made a beet soup for us one night with the garlic she had gotten from *her* mother, who inherited it from her mother on back through many generations. She insisted it is the best garlic to be found in Poland. I believe her. I brought home three heads. I planted it in my garden in Berkeley. I've got seventy-four stalks growing. My God, you're the expert. Come help me. I'll share."

"I'll trade you ten heads of ten different garlics from ten different countries for three heads of your Slubsk garlic. Incidentally, how many cloves to a head?"

"I don't want different garlics, Chester," Frank said. "I only want Polish garlic. How many cloves? I don't know. What, Olga? Ten?"

"Eight or ten. Big cloves."

"Let me do something for such a magnificent gift."

"OK," Frank said. "For three heads you gotta come to supper. You gotta give us advice about growing garlic. And you gotta give us a poster. I seen it on the wall of the Union Hotel. It's like a piece of art."

Olga was outraged. "Frank, you're terrible."

"He's not terrible," I said. "It's a deal. Supper and a poster. But that's not all. I'll also give you copies of both garlic books."

Frank said something in a low growl.

"Speak English," Olga said. To me she said, "He said you don't know how to bargain. You shouldn't be so quick to give in. What kind of Jew are you?"

Had the remark come from one of the ranchers or workers that visit the Union Hotel Bar, I would probably have burned with outrage. But here, with Olga and Frank, I actually laughed; and I was pleased that I felt no impulse to explain, to them or to myself. I had nothing to fear from these two friends.

Two weeks later I went to Berkeley. Before I could go into their home Frank, who met me at the door, with Olga running to catch up, led me along the outside of the house to the garden in the rear. "Here," Frank said. "What do you think? Is it ready to come out? Each year we just sort of guess."

"I almost canceled my trip to Berkeley," I said, "because my own garlic's going brown. I'll start harvesting in three or four days. Your garlic is ready now."

"Now? We've never taken it out of the ground until July."

"Do you see how many of the leaves are brown? About half of them?"

"Yes," they said in chorus.

"That means it's ready for harvest."

Olga laughed. "Imagine. A harvest. In my back yard. A harvest in Berkeley not in Kansas or North Dakota. Slubsk. My darling, Slubsk garlic."

I picked up the shovel leaning against the wall and showed them how to insert the blade at an angle, so the sharp edge would go beneath the bulb. "Lift," I said, speaking just above a whisper. "Carefully. Now, reach under the bulb, like so, and raise up. Oh, oh."

"What's wrong?" Frank asked. He was on his knees beside me, face close to the ground.

"The ground's wet."

"I read your garlic book last night. The first one. Too late. We've been watering every morning," Olga said, her voice infected by our secretive tones.

"The soil should be dry a week or two before harvest or the bulb — see, the bulb's begun to open, the cloves are exposed. It's still edible, but it won't store very long now that the outer skins are gone."

We dug up the entire collection, about a hundred bulbs. More than half were open. "The heads, some people call them bulbs, that are still protected by all their layers of skins, will probably last three or four months. These, exposed, should be eaten now. After they dry out in cool shade."

"My carport," Frank said.

The exposed garlic cloves were eaten in the next few weeks, as I suggested, by both the Zymanskys and me.

Four times over the next month Olga and Frank came up to help me harvest. We shared meals and stories. Frank brought his home brew; I offered my best eight dollar wines.

The first week in October they came up to help me begin my planting. The first garlic in the ground? The Polish Slubsk.

This summer Olga and Frank Zymansky brought their son Anthony and their daughter Anya. We all wept when we dug up the Slubsk. Companion to the smell of garlic was a smell of history, of genetic passions.

We all continued to sniffle and make fun of our sentimentality when they got into their car that evening to drive home. I felt that I had reconnected somehow with my own Polish ancestors, as if, no matter the Polish legacy of Jew-killing, we all shared a common history, a common land. I invited Olga and Frank and their children to stay that night, to stay for a week, or for a month. Olga said she was very tired.

Getting into the car (into the back seat with Anthony,) Olga actually appeared a bit weak. She joked about it, saying she was getting too old to work like a young woman. Frank drove home. Anya, as the car moved down the lane, reached back from the front seat with one hand to touch her mother's face.

The cancer killed Olga in late August.

I have visited Frank Zymansky several times the past few months. It has been very difficult for both of us, for all of us. Anya has dropped out of college to live with her father and brother. Yesterday Anthony and Anya and Frank and I visited the cemetery.

"Two months," Frank said, standing at the small concrete cross that would soon be a large gravestone.

I looked at the fresh mound and the cross and I saw Olga in *Giselle*; I saw Olga in *Swan Lake*. I saw Olga's face merging with the Slavic faces of the girls of my childhood.

Each year now my Slubsk garlic goes into a portion of box 12, that box which receives the most sunlight throughout the year. Every plastic tag in every other box contains the appropriate information relevant to the specific garlic or garlics in their box. In the box that contains the Slubsk garlic the tag is not plastic, it is a clear clean little slab of wood. Frank gave it to me.

Printed on the wood in blue paint (Olga's favorite color), are five words: *Olga Kazhinsky's Spirit Lies Here.*

Sitting on my deck this evening, I think of the Pollack girls in Butler, Pennsylvania. Those girls of my childhood: Helen Sopel and Juley Fako and Katey Galida.

I hear a song from my childhood. Helen, or perhaps Juley, used to sing it. I always sang along.

Oh, the moon is shining bright upon the Wabash
From the fields there comes the scent of new mown hay
Through the sycamores the candlelight is gleaming
On the banks of the Wabash far away.

Chapter Ten

SADDLE BAGS HEPPENSTALL

ELEPHANT GARLIC
A Leek, Not a True Garlic

Occasionally listed in catalogues (erroneously) as Allium sativum "Gigantum" or "Monster Garlic." Sometimes called "Oriental Garlic," perhaps because, in France, it is called, "Ail d'Orient." Bulb contains four to six very large garlic-like cloves with barely perceptible garlic flavor. Shelf life after harvest: four-to-five months.

Twenty years ago Mary Glover had been one of my students at Saint Mary's College. We've stayed in touch over the years. She's survived two marriages without losing her co-ed energy or optimism. As a student she'd enjoyed literature and had even tried writing a novel; but she finally decided that whatever talent was required to be a successful writer, she did not have it.

Mary is a realist.

Born into a proper middle class home, she has chosen to continue rebelling even in her forties, relying on men who were what her parents referred to as trailer-trash. Thanks to a successful former husband (a stock broker), she now lives in a seashore home near Jenner, fifty miles north and west of Cazadero, in what used to be called logging country.

The ecology movement has so crippled the logging industry that most loggers have either left the area or searched out other ways in other areas to make a living. In Washington and Oregon and this part of northern California loggers have found an alternate source of income: the harvesting of wild mushrooms. People who were making eighty to ninety dollars a day as loggers are earning $300-400 a day harvesting chanterelles and morels and boletes. A distributor in Santa Rosa buys all the wild mushrooms that come his way and relays them to toney restaurants in Berkeley and Chicago and New York City.

Mary Glover, a teacher at Coastal Alliance Elementary School in the outskirts of Cazadero, lives with a former logger named Zeke. A mechanic, he works on all sorts of cars, but his preference is motorcycles. Bikes. He caters to a large contingent of bikers in the Cazadero area, some of them Hells Angels, some former Hells Angels and some Angel wannabes.

Mary called me one day in July about two years ago, right after I'd finished harvesting. She and Zeke had just been to Santa Rosa on a shopping trip and she'd seen *The Great Garlic Book* in the window of a bookstore. She went in to buy it and saw, on the same table, *Garlic is Life*, which had been published the year before. On seeing the poster, she bought it as well as both books.

After reading *The Great Garlic* Book, she called to invite me to her house for a book-signing party (proceeds to go to a benefit for Coastal Alliance Elementary School) and a garlic tasting. "Bring some of your garlics, Chester. Please. It would be great to talk, to see each other. And a garlic-tasting up here could be fun. Loads of people will come to a tasting who won't go to a PTA meeting. It's a good way to feed money into the school. And you could stay overnight with Zeke and me."

I went and almost didn't live to regret it.

Mary's house is one of those new shingle houses built ten years ago along the north coast but which, after exposure to the sun and the ocean storms, looks like it could have been there for a century at least.

The house is a mile from the main highway, at the end of a sandy road. This day — a Saturday in July — there were probably forty or fifty cars parked along the road. People filled the deck and swarmed over the beach that led from the deck to the surf. I'd informed Mary I'd be driving a red Toyota Tercel and would be arriving about two o'clock so she was watching for me.

Though she must have been nearly forty by now she did not look much different from the way she'd looked in her college days. The once dark long brown hair was short, gray brown bristles, the trim long legs of her youth were the same length and almost as trim. The grin that used to taunt me in class was maybe a tad less confident.

An adult now, with a bank account of sorrows, she could not so flippantly invest in arrogance or superiority. We'd met a few times over the years, twice by accident, once by intention, and our friendship had solidified so now, after a long embrace, we shared the usual inanities and then, for several minutes, we tried to convince each other there could indeed be life after divorce.

"Come on," Mary said. "People are waiting. I ordered fifty of your garlic books, both of them, and fifty of those absolutely scrumptious posters."

By now Mary had the full collection of my novels, young-adult and adult, which she had either bought or I had sent her. She was an unabashed, uncritical, fan, who every now and then had sent me copies of my books to autograph and return to her for relay to nieces or nephews.

After the requisite tour of her house there were introductions to people whose names I didn't pay attention to or promptly forgot and an offering of wines and beers and sandwiches. Finally, two sandwiches after my arrival, Mary guided me to a table heavily laden with books and posters.

For the next hour or two I signed anything put on the desk in front of me, including a copy of William Saroyan's plays and a novel by Leo Litwak, one of my friends and idols. Mary finally declared the event a huge success. Every book and every poster had been sold. "I could shoot myself," Mary said. "We could have sold twenty more of everything. You must be exhausted. You want to rest? Nap, maybe? Walk along the beach? I'm taking you to dinner at the best restaurant in Mendocino so don't eat too much now. You can sack out whenever you want after dinner. What do you think of Zeke?"

I said I'd have to hold an opinion until I met him.

"You met him, you vision-impaired old igloo. He's the big concrete truck over there talking to that river barge in leather."

"The barge with all the tattoos and hair?"

"That's Saddlebags Heppenstall. He's the meanest biker in Caleyforney. He really has a heart of gold. Come on."

They watched me approach as if I were a cockroach about to be squashed beneath one of their leather-gloved fists. Mary introduced me to Zeke again but this time I saw him. And felt him. When he crushed my right hand I refused to wince. Saddlebags was next. He wore a grease-stained leather vest over an otherwise bare upper torso that was darker than the vest and greasier. His handshake tried to complete what Zeke's had begun. I remained standing, without showing a single tear, but I knew that for the next few weeks I'd be picking bones out of my palm.

Saddle Bag's arms were so much larger than the rest of his torso I thought at first they might have been built on some lathe in a metal shop and screwed into his shoulders to replace pink skinned arms he'd been born with. The right arm appeared darker and hairier than the left but I could not miss the big black Gothic swastika tattooed on his forearm, midway between wrist and elbow. It was larger than the one on his right chestplate. The tiny replica — this one red, trimmed with a black border — under his right eye was almost lost in thick folds of dark skin.

Mary tried to engage the two men in a cheery exchange but Saddle Bags remained silent as I stared at the swastika on his forearm. "That bother you?" he said, pointing at the tattoo with a thumb the size of my neck.

In spite of the pain throbbing in my hand, I tried to be nonchalant. "The last time I saw one of those," I said, "was on the arm of a Nazi machine gunner I'd just shot in the head."

I heard Mary whisper, "Oh dear God, Chester."

Saddle Bags considered my remark for a moment, trying to decide, I think, whether to laugh or hit me. Mary's concern might have kept him under control. "You killed a Nazi?" The *you* came out with a snort, as if he were trying to blow his nose.

"Chester was in World War Two," Mary said. "He wrote a book about it. He was at Dachau. You know, the concentration camp."

Zeke, who'd been tilting a bottle of beer, removed it from his mouth and choked out a mouthful of foam. "No shit?" Zeke was grinning. "How old are you, man?"

"I'm seventy four," I said, which at the time I was.

"Jesus Christ," Zeke said. "My old man's sixty something and he can't hardly stand up. You work out or something?"

"He's a Jew," Saddle Bags said. "Jews live forever. Right, Aaron? That's why he don't like this pretty little pitcher on my arm."

"That's as good a reason as I could come up with," I said, managing to smile while I shivered on the gallows.

Zeke, in respect for Mary, lowered his voice when he asked, "You really kill a Nazi, man?"

I tried to act like a war hero unwilling to relive his trials for the people back home.

"Jesus Christ," Saddle Bags said. "It's true."

"What's true?" Mary asked.

"I didn't put it together. I read his book. Hey, Aaron, that the truth in there? About you being a Jew?"

"Everything in that book's the truth," I said, "except for three lies, one of which is the marriage. I really didn't get married to the Irish Catholic Mary Catherine. I married an Irish Catholic named

Margey."

Saddle Bags looked as if he'd just gotten off his Harley after smashing it into a brick wall. "Yeah. Right. You write about being a Jew. You write about your folks. That stuff true?"

"It's all true."

"I bought the book because Mary said it had recipes. I got 239 cookbooks, countin' yours. Those recipes. You make them up?"

"I made some of them up. Others I got from friends or relatives."

"Man, you ever do another book I got a recipe for you. I make the best Goddamn chili a man can stuff in his gut. I use maybe five pounds of garlic for a two gallon pot of chili."

"Come on," Mary said. "Five pounds?"

"That big garlic, too. The biggest you can get. Called Elephant Garlic."

"That's not garlic," I said. "Elephant garlic is a leek. It's so mild I don't grow it."

Saddle Bags showed remarkable restraint for a man who, at that moment, wanted to simply take off another man's head after first tearing out his tongue. "What the fuck are you talking about? It's called Elephant Garlic. Not *elephant apples* or *elephant grapes*. It's *garlic*."

"Nope. Regular garlic is *Allium sativum*. Elephant garlic is *Allium ampeloprasum*, which is a common leek. Leeks are milder than garlic."

The conversation could only go uphill after that, with Saddle Bags pulling me into the kitchen, where, over three consecutive gin-and-tonics he picked my brain about a variety of details regarding both garlic and recipes. By the third drink I think I was advising him on the best technique for roasting a pickup truck.

When we left the house for the Mendocino restaurant Saddle Bags insisted I ride on the back of his Harley. Everyone else went in cars and trucks. Mary showed me crossed fingers behind her back.

I think I survived the ride to the restaurant and the meal and, after the meal, the ride back, also on the Harley. I can't say for sure. I do remember trying to hug Saddle Bag's body to keep from falling off his bike and I also remember not being able to get my arms around him and I remember bits and pieces of his remarks: " ... I'm going slow here ... hold on, man ... that bump hurt your balls? ... sorry 'bout that, man ... Mary, we got a Jew passed out here ... I got him … "

The next morning, at breakfast, Mary informed me that Saddle Bags had carried me into the house. "Over his shoulder. Like you were a bag of sand. He is so impressed with you he's going to go to the bookstore in Mendocino tomorrow and buy your other books and your poster."

Four days after I returned from the party at Mary's house I had a phone call. Five o'clock. In the morning.

"Aaron?"

"Speaking. Who's this?"

"Saddle Bags. Remember me? Hey, Mary and Zeke and me are coming down there Saturday. There's a restaurant I heard about. Mary says she knows how to get to your place. We'll be there about six o'clock."

I hadn't been asked if I'd be home, if I'd be interested in going to the restaurant with them or if I even wanted to see him again. But he was a friend of Zeke and Mary's and, considering the fact that he hated everything my face suggested, he'd treated me okay. He'd even put me to bed without slitting my throat or recircumsizing me. So why not?

Saturday. Six o'clock. There they were, in front of my curing shed, revving their engines so much my deaf neighbor probably lost the rest of his eardrums. Saddle Bags grabbed me and heaved me up and into his chest. I thought he was wrapped with barbed wire but it was only his beard hanging free.

As everyone followed me around the field I explained why I didn't plant directly in the soil and how and why I had drip irrigation lines. When I took them into the curing shed, where garlic bulbs hung from the walls and ceiling and interior racks like thousands of shrunken heads not yet shorn of their beards, Saddle Bags stepped ahead of us. He inhaled and then tilted back on his heels in mock astonishment. "That is the smell of heaven," he sighed. "Aaron, you grow a shitload of garlic. And they're all different?"

"They're all different. See for yourself. Different sizes, different shapes, different colors, different number of cloves. You were at the tasting at Mary's. They all taste different. You said so."

He studied me with the first suggestion of honest appreciation. "Never seen nothin' like this, man. I mean never the fuck ever. You know, you wrote a book and it's true. Hey, what's the hottest garlic you got here?"

I searched the walls and racks and produced a bulb of my Asian Tempest. I tore a clove free, peeled it with my fingernails, stuck it in my mouth and chewed. I gave the next peeled clove to Saddle Bags. He crunched down on it, started to laugh, then suddenly closed his eyes against the spurt of tears and tried to cough, tried to gasp, tried to talk, but failed each time. He was beating his chest with his fist when I took a bowl of sugar from a windowsill, opened it, put about a spoonful to his lips. "Eat it, fast."

He had no choice.

In a few seconds he was breathing normally.

After wiping his eyes, he managed to stare at me. "Yowzah," he said. "That lil' sucker do got a bite."

I make what I consider the best garlic potatoes ever mashed but those at the restaurant were as good as mine, maybe better. Saddle Bags almost wept as he downed his third helping, supported by the second or maybe the third huge pork chop.

"The cook used Gilroy garlic," I said. "If he'd used my Red Toch garlic from Georgia the potatoes would have been so good they'd be worth more than gold."

"Georgia? They grow tobacco in Georgia, man. And weed. I been there."

"Russian Georgia. It's not called Russian anymore. Now it's the Independent Republic of Georgia. They hate Russians. My Red Toch garlic comes from a village in Georgia called Tochliavri. That's what the word *Toch* comes from. My father was born in Tochliavri."

"So you say this is Gilroy garlic in these potatoes?"

"Yep."

When the waitress came to the table Saddle Bags said, "Missie, will you ask the cook where he gets his garlic?"

"I know where," the waitress said. "He gets it from Gilroy. I take it home and grow it in my garden."

"This garlic's called California Late," I said.

She looked at me as if I'd just guessed the exact sum she had in her checking account. "How'd you know that?"

"Missie, take off your hat. This man sitting here is King of Garlic. There is nothing about garlic he don't know." He leaned closer to me after the waitress left. "Is Elephant Garlic from Gilroy?"

"They grow it there. Along with the California Late. But it's..."

"I know. It's not garlic. I'm gonna confess somethin', man. My mashed potatoes never taste like this even if I use ten pounds of Elephant garlic."

"Saddle Bags, look. You love garlic. Right?"

"I love garlic, man."

"I'm going to give you heads from ten different varieties of garlic and you're going to plant the cloves where you plant your pot and you'll have garlic that will ..."

"Wait a shittin' minute. You a narc?"

"Nope. I'm a farmer and a writer and a lover. Do you want to grow prize-winning garlic? You want to make the best food in the state of California?"

When he left me off at my house, Saddle Bags said, "I'm gonna hold you to it, Chester."

"Hold me to what?"

"You promised to give me ten varieties of garlic."

"Come on in to the shed. I'll give them to you now. Save the fattest healthiest cloves for planting, eat the rest. Thanks for the dinner and thanks for the ride. But my ass hurts."

"Rub some Asian Tempest garlic on it, man."

The next morning, when the phone rang at five o'clock, I picked it up and said, "Saddle Bags?"

"Speaking," he said. "Hey, give me the names of some books I can read about Jews."

I tried to sit up in bed but flopped back onto the pillows.

"Books about Jews. Give me some names. I want to read about Jews."

"You have a pencil handy?"

"A ball point pen do? I don't have to have a pencil to write down the names of books about Jews, do I? Is that a rule?"

"A pen will do. Write Henry Roth."

"That's the name of the book?"

"That's the name of the author. The title of his book is *Call it Sleep.*"

"Got it. Another one."

"*Portnoy's Complaint* by Phillip Roth."

"One more. Maybe more later but for now just one more."

"*About Us*. The author is Chester Aaron."

"How do you spell ... hey, that's you. You wrote that book?"

"I wrote that book."

"I'll be a sonofabitch. Aaron, if I turned Jew do you think I'd get smart and be able to write books? I could write a best seller. I got stories you wouldn't believe, man."

"I'd believe them. But you're already smart, Saddle Bags. If you turned Jew you'd be so much smarter you could teach in a college."

Silence. Then, in a quiet, almost timid voice: "Don't shit me, pardner."

"I shit you not," I said. "You'd be better for students to be around than most of my colleagues at the college. You are an honest man."

"You little fucker," he said. If I hadn't been sleepy and so couldn't hear correctly, I'd almost swear his voice contained a hint of affection.

Six months later Saddle Bags came down and picked me up and I rode north with him to the woods east of Jenner. He insisted I check out his garlic.

He guided me through some oak trees to a field that had about 500 little palm trees that were, I knew, *cannabis*. Pot. Weed. Mary Jane. Marijuana.

In furrows at the edge of his field: garlic that appeared healthier than mine back at Occidental. He'd obeyed my instructions. Each variety had its own separate plot, its plastic identification marker in the ground. "You make a map, showing what's planted in each plot?" "You said do that, man. I did it. I'll show you my map inside."

We went over the details of weeding, of keeping records, of harvesting, of cleaning, of curing when the time was right.

"You're going to have better garlic than I will," I said. I meant it.

He put a finger to his lips and led me through the oaks into another grove that contained the biggest patch of black morels I've ever seen.

That night Saddle Bags made a pasta for me and three of his buddies. The sauce had sliced morels, chopped garlic (the Red Toch cloves he'd saved) and parsley and olive oil and pine nuts. "Over linguini," Saddle Bags said. "My favorite. It's from Italy. Made with Durham wheat, man."

Saddle Bags slept outside, on the porch, in his old sleeping bag that night. He gave me the platform in his bedroom, and his new nylon sleeping bag guaranteed to remain warm to below-freezing temperatures.

"You're the first one in that bag, Chester. You got its cherry."

The next morning Saddle Bags took me home on his Harley. Four or five times, as we roared around the curves of Highway 1, with the cliffs rising to my left and the cliffs falling to the ocean on my right, I thought we'd both be killed.

When Saddle Bags braked the Harley in front of my curing shed and helped me dismount he said, "I'll call you next week. I'm gonna need some more names of Jew books. Thanks for that Red Toke garlic from your pappy's village. Man, I gotta tell you. Next to garlic, weed is bullshit." He grinned, showing one good gap between three bad teeth. "You want some weed?"

"I don't use it anymore," I said. "I smoke garlic leaves."

He considered that for a moment and then laughed. "Elephant garlic? I'm gonna kill the guy sold me that shit, man. Swear to God. I dumped every bulb and every clove of my Elephant Garlic into the pig's trough. And I swear to God the pigs won't eat it. That tells you somethin', man."

Saddle Bags lifted his hand for a high five. When we slapped I had a clean look at his swastika. I think he winked at me, I think he tried to keep from grinning. He roared the Harley, roared it again, and then he leaped the bike into the air and raced down the dirt road.

Just before the bike turned left, to disappear, Saddle Bags, without looking back but knowing I was watching, raised a right fist high above his head and punched the air three times. Then he was gone.

Chapter Eleven

BRUSCHETTA

PERSIAN STAR
Hardneck Purple Stripe

Purchased by John Swenson in a bazaar in Samarkand, Uzbekistan, in the late 1980s. Outer bulb wrapper is sometimes smooth white; inner wrappers are purple-streaked. Cloves are large, with marbled streaks on yellow-brown background. Great for cooking and roasting. Flavor: very pleasant with mild late zing. Shelf life: five to six months.

I CELEBRATED MY 77th BIRTHDAY A MONTH AGO; AND REMEM-
BERING my 76th, I'm still angry. Why is it that the older I get the
angrier I get?

It's easy to be old. I don't even have to try. It happens fast,
before you can say, "Stop."

Only yesterday I was seventeen and I ran the 100-yard dash in
eleven seconds. This morning I needed fifty-five seconds to climb the
stairs to the bathroom and another ten seconds to find the flush appa-
ratus on the toilet.

But anger? Anger is not natural to *homo sapiens* or even to
straight sapiens. Made in God's image, humans are born to be kind,
generous and forgiving. Wolves, lions, Lyme ticks, slugs, and literary
critics, made in Satan's image, are born to kill.

My friend Aristide Priappus, whom you'll be meeting, attended The Grand National Banana-Slug Festival in northern California in
1991. The dish that won first prize that year was chocolate-coated
slugs with garlic sauce. Aristide has suggested the same ingredients
for the coating of contemporary food and wine faddists. "Think about
it, Chester. Do you realize that the hearing-impaired could very easily
mistake the word *faddists* for *fascists*?" It was Aristide who came up
with the alternate title for those sections of the mighty newspapers
(*The New York Times, The Boston Globe, The San Francisco
Chronicle*, etcetera) devoted to food and wine. "Did you read the
Freud and Whine section in today's Times, Chester?"

Be prepared. This chapter (and its sibling, the following chapter) contains adult themes and adult prose, meaning that hidden
beneath the garlic is a serious mix of anger, resentment, jealousy and
revenge.

The target of Aristide Priappus' anger, which (unlike me) he
defiantly refuses to moderate, is, well, let Aristide speak for himself.
"Chester, in the culture of *Nouvelle Cuisine*, a handful of mortals
have not only been granted the status of immortality, they have been
granted bank accounts that rival the CEOs at General Motors and
IBM. You are such a Christian man for a Jew, Chester. Your major
faults? One, you forgive your enemies; two, you refuse to carry a
grudge. Me? I am beginning to sympathize with Commissar Josef
Stalin's policy of exterminating those middle-class wannabes he

called *kulaks*. I want to revive Uncle Joe if only to take care of the nouvelle *cuisiney-weenies*."

Celine, Aristide's wife, though indulgent, does not conceal her impatience. "Ari, you're not so tough, you're all huff and puff and bluff."

That not very generous declaration of Aristide's had been presented in the middle of a conversation the three of us were engaged in while sitting at a table some weeks ago in our favorite restaurant in California: *101 Main*, at the southeast corner of the major intersection in Sebastopol, at the corner of Main Street and Bodega Highway. *101 Main* is the only restaurant in either Marin or Sonoma County Aristide will patronize.

101 Main's owner-chef, Volodya, and his wife Laura manage on a very limited budget to offer food that is, according to Aristide, *"... delicious, imaginative, unpretentious, straight from a French or Swiss country kitchen...."*

Every time we've met each other (except for five or six times at Aristide's home and twice at mine) over the last several years Aristide insisted our meeting place be *101 Main*. At a recent meal (a half-hour after the dessert) Aristide spat out the names of five famous American chefs who " ... do not deserve the dish-washing job at *101 Main*."

Sitting between him and his wife, I pretended to ponder the serious implications of the dilemma Aristide presented me but as often happens when I'm in Aristide's company, I found analysis difficult. I pretended that I not only knew what he was talking about but I also hoped to give him reason to believe that I would, in a moment, come up with a response of comparable intellectual pith. (I warned you there'd be adult content here.)

Priappus rambled and rumbled on while I continued to sip the strong, thick coffee, which Aristide had correctly identified (after his third slow taste), as Gaia from Peet's Coffees in Berkeley. "I detest," Aristide continued, "the uncritical devotion of sycophants."

"Does that *non-sequitur* include me?" Celine asked.

Aristide tenderly pressed a forefinger to his wife's lips, returned it, the forefinger, to his own lips, and pecked it. "Sycophants. One of the reasons I retired from the field. You can't imagine the Freud and Whine fadees who virtually rush to kiss my ring. Pope Aristide the First."

I knew Aristide well enough to be sure a lecture was bouncing on the springboard, preparing for a dive into our conversation. It was sure to be a recitation of a line or a paragraph or a page or several pages from a book or a magazine he had read a year ago or ten years ago or even twenty years ago, and it was sure to be a precise oral duplicate of the printed original.

"Chester, are you familiar with Yeats? His *Why Should Not Old Men ...*"

"No," I said.

"I have the feeling," Celine said, "you are about to be."

Aristide, gazing into the distance, sang it out (his deep basso bringing up the eyes and heads of every diner in the room and, at the end, winning appreciative applause that he acknowledged with sham humility.)

> Why should not old men be mad?
> Some have known a likely lad
> That had a sound fly fisher's wrist
> Turn to a drunken journalist;
> A girl that knew all Dante once
> Live to bear children to a dunce;
> A Helen of social welfare dream
> Climb on a wagonette to scream.
> Some think it matter of course that chance
> Should starve good men and bad advance,
> That if their neighbors figured plain,
> As though upon a lighted screen,
> No single story would they find
> Of an unbroken happy mind,
> A finish worthy of the start.
> Young men know nothing of this sort
> Observant old men know it well;
> And when they know what old books tell
> And that no better can be had
> Know why an old man should be mad.

The poem, you've noted, does not swell with optimism, which prompts me to advise you one last time. Proceed no farther in this chapter if you disagree with what you're about to read.

Aristide Priappus began to study with French chefs when he was fifteen. He served a five-year apprenticeship at Le Trianon in Paris and went on to work for five more years with Jovan Trboyevic at La Perroquet in Chicago. Before he reached his 30th birthday, he was fed up with food. Always a reader, he decided to be an author. Returned to Paris, he served for several years as an aide to Robert J. Courtine, France's most prestigious food writer. Friendship with Courtine led to a friendship with Karen and John L. Hess (former Food Editor for *The New York Times*).

By the time he met the Hesses, back in America, Priappus had forsaken the *preparation and serving* of food and wine. Thanks especially to his respect for John L. Hess' articles, he devoted himself to *writing about* food and wine. A decade later (Hess and his wife now *persona non grata* with the rising *nouvellies* at *The Times* and thus no longer welcome in the offices of that grim *éminence grise* of contemporary journalism,) Aristide, easing away from his interest in food, concentrated on writing about wine exclusively.

Before he was into his forties, Priappus had been crowned and coronated by a consortium of American and European newspapers and magazines. In London, Paris, Rome, Berlin, and New York, Priappus was (he still is, in fact) treated with a respect reserved for chancellors, kings or queens.

Priappus, like myself in his late seventies, is now a man who not only does not think long about what he says, he always says what he thinks. The result of the man's confrontational independence: he has made 43,457 enemies, bettering my record by two.

The Food Section of this morning's *San Francisco Chronicle* contains a boxed "Bulletin" informing the world (well, at least San Francisco) that Chester Aaron's bruschetta recipe has just been installed on the Golden Scroll in the Tri-State (including, according to *The Chronicle*, California, Oregon, Arizona and New Mexico) Culinary Hall of Fame (a former missile silo reshaped to suggest a male California Quail), recently opened to the public in Buffone, California. A note for the record: in a court of Public Opinion, *The San Francisco Chronicle* has been found guilty of self-abuse for referring to itself as *The West Coast New York Times*.

I can only imagine Polly Carpenter's anguish when she sat down to breakfast this morning and, after buttering and jamming her *croissant*, opened today's *Chronicle*. Ever since the bruschetta cook-off a year ago, Polly Carpenter has been pushing long and very sharp pins into the life-size dolls that represent me and my near-twin, Priappus. I say *"near-twin"* because Aristide and I are both short and stocky; and we are both heir to florid faces and bushy eyebrows and big noses. We differ intellectually however. Aristide never forgets anything he hears or reads; I forget everything before I even read it.

Another difference: Aristide dresses like an Armani model, caring not at all that Armani male models, tall and slim and either unbathed or unshaven or both, subscribe to the Milan-born myth that beards and body odors are natural aphrodisiacs to women, all women. Priappus, rebel that he is, shaves every day and sends off a mild scent of old-fashioned British Bay Rum. I shave whenever I find my razor on one of the bathroom shelves and my clothes, if not my body, send off a not quite mild scent of garlic.

Aristide resides quite happily with Celine on a twelve-acre estate on Dry Creek Road near Healdsburg, about forty miles from my home. Seven of those acres are planted in Pinot Noir grapes; and three in Zinfandel. When I tasted his wine three years ago and said that even my palate sang alleluias to his Zinfandel, Aristide's response was one of his brief but intellectual lectures: "Chester, have you ever read Husmann's 1880 book *Grape Culture & Wine Making in California*? Husmann compares the best Zinfandels to the best of any wine anywhere in the world. I have imported primo grapes. I borrowed the best winemaker in California from ..."

And so on.

The two remaining acres of the Priappus estate contain a redwood tower of a house surrounded by an edible landscape designed by our friend Robert Kourik.

The past five autumns Aristide has traded me choice (his choices) wines in exchange for two pounds of each of ten specific varieties of my garlic (again, his choices.) After having tasted just about every garlic I grow, he requests his favorites by name. The first three of his ten personal favorites: the French Germinadour, the Xian from China and, of course, The Red Toch from Tochliavri, Republic of Georgia.

Priappus and I have remained friends through a variety of crises, his and mine. When I finally dared prepare one meal at my house for him and Celine it started (following the usual declarations of my modesty and my incompetence) with a salad of arugula and Cherokee tomatoes (thank you, Darrell Merrell, in Tulsa) pulled from my garden minutes before dining and a dressing of DaVero Extra Virgin Olive Oil with a touch of Balsamic vinegar from Modena, a touch of Dijon mustard, a touch of clover honey. The single entrée I dared present was my version of a soup my father had made when I was a child, a root soup containing mashed beets, turnips, carrots, onions, garlic (Red Toch, of course) and rosemary and cumin (picked minutes before from my garden), and chunks of braised beef brisket. My Russian Jewish *pot-au-feu* simmered for six hours before it was served; but the meat, almost as tender as marshmallows, still tasted of the grill.

Celine accepted a second bowl and two additional slices of my bruschetta. "If I were not married, Chester, I'd claim you for my groom, but no children. I will not dawdle children on these skinny knees."

In late July of 1999, when I decided to celebrate the end of harvest (which would be one month later, in August) and the approach of the planting season (October through November), I decided to celebrate my birthday at the same time. You don't get too many opportunities to celebrate a 76th birthday. The next time around, I'm going to Bali, home of the most beautiful women in the world.

My immediate and tentative plan for the celebration: invite a few people (no more than twenty), display my very simple and very limited cooking talents, sit back and smoke a cigar. But that would mean I'd have to spend time with old friends. No, thanks.

How about new friends? How about people I've never met

and would not be likely to meet again? No, thanks.

How about my former colleagues at Saint Mary's College? "That," as my mother would have said in her Polished English, "makes me to vomit."

I mentioned my ideas to Celine and Aristide. Celine suggested I display my farm, display my garlic; and display my house. "You've just framed and mounted all the jackets of your books, you've painted that big west wall a gorgeous orange, and the fields in late summer are at their most beautiful. Do it. Celebrate your life."

"Only invite us to dinner," Aristide said. "Why waste precious time on crowds?"

"Repeat tonight's proven success," Celine insisted. "Root soup and bruschetta. You make the best bruschetta I've ever tasted."

"I tasted better bruschetta only once," Aristide said, "in the hills of Umbria. Fifty-five years ago. I was a lad of twenty. An old peasant with a long, gray beard who grilled his bread on … I'm teasing you, Chester. I agree with Celine. Your root soup, your bruschetta, are better than sex."

Celine tossed her long black hair and pretended outrage. "I resemble that remark!"

I would certainly invite Celine and Aristide, but invite them to what?

The night following my root soup success I traveled to Berkeley to accept an invitation to dinner at a new restaurant called *Coraggio*. My host was one of my colleagues from Saint Mary's College. He was getting married and wanted me to meet his wife. I went because of all my colleagues Ed was the only one I've thought about twice in the five years since I retired.

Coraggio. It takes courage to name a restaurant Courage. One of the sixty-eight appetizers: bruschetta. As the French say: *"Oy vay! Un disgraziato!"*

Soggy bread. Thin and tasteless olive oil. I'd bet my first pair of socks, which I still own and am wearing at this moment, that the oil was not extra-virgin. It might not even have been olive. It might not have been virgin. The tomato slices were so thick and heavy they slid off the bread and onto the plate and off the plate onto the table with a sound like an arch falling. And dressed with about as much garlic as can be pounded into a humming-bird's toenail. Price: $14.00 for two slices.

I could do better than that. So could *Coraggio's* janitor. Any chef picked at random in the entire Bay Area could come up with ... whoa! Could any chef come up with ...?

How about examining that possibility?

Could other chefs improve upon *Coraggio's* bruschetta? Better yet: how about seeing how much better famous chefs could ... how about having a contest that would honor bruschetta and ... how about giving a few chefs a chance to prove themselves superior to their peers? How about a contest?

A *cook-off.*

How about a bruschetta *cook-off?*

How many chefs? Twenty? No, no. Ten? Make it six because they'd bring helpers, and I only have ten chairs. Make it six chefs.

Question: why would these six chefs deign to enter such an event? Answer: because they'd have something, a lot of something, to gain.

I had to come up with *a something.* Some magnet, some person that would draw, would entice, would lure them up from the Bay Area. "Hey! Julia Child might drop in ... Craig Claiborne's promised to stop by (of course he's dead but who would know?). Didn't Michelle Pfeifer fall in love with Sonoma County when she was married here just before she was divorced? I hear Sharon Stone loves garlic. Sharon Stone's promised to .... Hey, folks! Sharon Stone and Richard Gere might drop by. Tibetans as well as Chinese eat garlic by the wonton.

I decided to call Aristide and run the idea up his seventy-seven year old flagpole.

To hell with Child and Claiborne and "Scotty" Pepin and Stone and Gere. Every chef in the country (as well as Asia, Africa, and both Poles) would give their Culinary Guild diploma to just sit in a room and breathe a gram of the same air inhaled by the great Aristide Priappus.

Celine and Aristide were out when I called so I left a message describing my plan.

Priappus called the next morning to inform me (in a voice

sounding as if he had canceled an evening with Queen Sophia of Bulgaria in order to grace my hut of waddles with his presence) of his and Celine's intentions to appear at my bruschetta cook-off.

Should you ever plan to invite your own collection of food mavens to your own allium festivity, consider as your event's centerpiece my personal, private, individual bruschetta. The recipe follows later in this chapter.

"It is," as my ten year old granddaughter says, "to live for."

Before committing yourself, let me remind you (again) of a few garlic facts of life. Because you and I have different chemistries, you and I will react differently to the same palatal stimuli. Depending on the variety of the garlic, the flavor will range from the hot (for me) Asian Tempest from South Korea to the mild (for me) Inchelium Red from Washington State; from the rich earthy Red Toch from the village of Tochliavri in the Republic of Georgia to the mellow almost-mild Guatemalan Ikeda; from a velvety texture of the Tarne, from France or the Zahroda from Czechoslovakia to my tiny cutie from Chiappas, which yields a pulp as coarse as sandpaper.

An anecdotal but relevant aside. Remember that world-famous food writer at the New York Food Fair? The one who, with her three stooges (instructor/chefs from the American Culinary Institute) at her side, who flipped through the forty different garlics I had spread across the table? The one who offered me a sneer reserved for just-apprehended child-molesters? The doyenne of American Taste who said, "Oh, come on. This is a scam! Garlic is garlic!"? Remember her?

Instead of punching Madame upside the head, I suggested Madame sample the contents in the four bowls of hummus on the table. In front of each bowl was a small card containing details of the garlic used in that bowl, citing name, country of origin, appearance, possible taste-potential; and probable shelf-life. I informed Madame as she moved from bowl to bowl that I had pressed equal amounts of a different garlic into each of the bowls of hummus. Four bowls, four different garlics.

Prepared to slay this ancient dragon standing before her, Madame selected a cracker to use as her dipping tool. After the second bowl (Spanish Roja), Madame's eyes widened. After the third (Creole Red), Madame's mouth opened and stayed open. After the fourth (Red Toch), Madame clenched her hands together (almost in prayer) and said in a whisper of sincere apology, "I didn't know."

I'll say that for her. She did admit her failing, something Aristide and I are constitutionally incapable of doing.

Two weeks after the New York Food Fair I received a letter from Madame, asking for ten or fifteen garlics she might plant in her New England garden. I sent them; she in turn has since sent me three thank-you letters. Note: humbled though she had been and respectful as she remains of the performances of the different varieties, Madame, in her subsequent articles, still uses the generic term *garlic* when she cites the herb-for-use in one of her recipes. I recently sent her a card, chiding her for her negligence. Madame probably has forgotten how to spell *California*.

Shortly after my return from that Food Fair I met Aristide Priappus for dinner at *101 Main*. When asked to defend my silence of the previous month, I mentioned my trip to New York and my experience at the Food Fair with Madame and her three stooges. I was barely into the tale when Aristide not only identified the woman by name, but he also identified each of her three pompous stooges. "The rich pompous *booboisee* — that's Mencken's term, not mine, Chester — the rich *booboisee* who indulge that culture deserve the garbage they are served and for which they pay an emperor's ransom. I quote at length my ally and my friend, John L. Hess, who, in *The Taste of America* (Viking Publishers, 1977, 384 pages) refers to Balzac. 'One does not dine, this is Balzac speaking, Chester, as luxuriously in the provinces as in Paris... but one dines better; the dishes are better thought out. In the far reaches of the provinces, there are *Carêmes* in petticoats, unknown geniuses who know how to make a dish of beans worthy of ... 'End Hess' quote of Balzac's quote. Your New York madame, Chester, is an admirer of, a compatriot of, and a promoter of *la grossa frode*, Julia Child. *La grossa frode*, in Italian and French and Russian, Chester, means one huge fraud."

"Lordy," Celine whispered. "Must you shout?"

At that same meal that evening when Aristide was roused to anger by my left-handed tribute to the *Goddess of Nouvelle Cuisine* (I said something about her being the first to alert Americans to the fact that salads could be more than iceberg lettuce topped with thousand-island dressing), the inimitable Aristide almost stormed out of the restaurant.

Aristide has told me more than once that his beloved John Hess had written (see *Taste of America*, page 173-175) that Julia Child had always put down French women as less than imbeciles in the kitchen. More than once, more, in fact, than twice, Aristide has quoted Hess' quote from *The New York Times* referring to Nancy L. Ross of *The Washington Post* quoting Julia Child as saying,"'French women don't know a damn thing about French cooking, though they pretend they know everything.' See *Taste of America*, Chester. Pages 173-174."

That night at *101 Main* in Sebastopol there was a new reference. "Chester, do you know Marcel Rouff's *La Vie et la Passion de Dodin-Bouffant?*"

"No, Aristide, I can't say I do. Not only do I not speak French, I also never even speak to the French if I can help it."

"I share your sentiments, Chester," Celine said. "The French are so ... so frigging French."

Aristide went on, of course. "I think about Child's comment about French women and I think of Rouff. His book is a tribute to the talents of French women in their kitchens. In his book *La Vie and-so-forth* a Prince invites Dodin to dine. It is a feast of fifty royal dishes composed by a squad of chefs and served by a *maître d'hôtel*. In return, Dodin invites the Prince to a dinner prepared by his, the grateful Dodin's, *cuisinière*."

"What's a *cuisinière*, Aristide?"

"You unfortunate Yiddish hick. His *cuisinière* is his kitchen cook. His household chef. The meal? A single dish, the lowly *pot-au-feu*. But it is such a *pot-au-feu* that the smitten Prince has no choice but to try to steal away Dodin's *cuisinière*. Dodin, to keep his cuisinière, has no choice but to marry her."

"Our story," Celine said, "Ari's and mine. In the movie Charles Laughton plays Ari and Norma Shearer plays beautiful, shapely, talented Celine."

"The entire book," Aristide continued, "is a tribute to *la cui-*

sine de femme, la vrai cuisine de France. And Julia Child says French women don't know anything about French cooking. One would think the so-called Feminists, did they have a conscience, would slam one of Julia's cream pies in her face at every one of her television appearances. But no. Ignorant sick sycophants, they throw flower petals at her feet. Let the feminists check *The New York Times* of June 30, 1975 … twenty-seven years ago, Chester … where the Great One, the Honorable Chef Paul Bocuse informs that male trollop, Craig Claiborne, as here follows. 'Women,' Bocuse said, 'lack the instincts for great cooking. They have one or two dishes they accomplish well, but they are not innovators. The only place for them is in bed. Any man who doesn't change his woman every week or so lacks imagination.' You don't believe me? Go to the library. Check The New York Times of June 30, 1975. Where are the Amazon warriors when we need them? Where are Germaine Greer and Betty Friedan and … and all those other female spear-throwing eunuchs?"

Pause, to gather strength, not to refresh memory.

"I recently talked to three people associated with the Freud and Whine pages at *The New York Times.* I wanted to do an article about John Hess. I wanted to return to and evaluate his judgments and predictions of thirty years ago because almost everything he predicted has come true. Know what the food honcho at *The Times* said? 'Oh, Hess turned into a bitter man as he got older. And mean.' As if mean and bitter men can not distinguish truth from lies, real from fake, decent from villainous."

"What's wrong with bitter?" Celine asked. "Lemon's bitter. And lime. And bitter herbs are served at a *seder* to guarantee the survival of bitter memories. Right, Chester?"

I nodded. "Too true. I make those same bitter herbs into lozenges and suck them daily."

Aristide twirled his glass, dipped his nose into the fumes, dreamed, sipped, closed his eyes, and then opened them. "Chester, if I weren't too old to carry a bomb, I'd … but I don't believe in violence, Chester. Except when it's necessary."

Aristide Priappus is not revered for his lack of passion or his verbal restraint. In fact, in many circles Aristide Priappus is not revered at all. I love the man and admire him. He ain't easy to love, but then (Do I have to remind you?) I'm not made in God's image either.

To protect my reputation, my ass, and my psyche I must make confession here.

I admit that of the eighty-seven garlics I grow I can, by taste, distinguish perhaps five. No great feat. Last year Aristide, by taste, actually identified seventeen correctly. The other sixty received nods or shrugs or grimaces. It could have been this or that, but definitely was not that or this. He will always say, however (and will be correct 95% of the time), "This is a Hardneck garlic," or "This is a Softneck garlic."

My reaction when I'm not sure? I sing or shout or whimper or curse or shake my head or stomp my feet or purr. Anything to distract you from the fact that I might be occupied in a life that does not abide by scientific truth.

Aristide is even more insistent than I am in the conviction that there is no Pythagorean theorem to prove taste correct. The square of the right angle of any clove of garlic is not equal to some of the angles of the other two squares who are eating it.

I do not denigrate science. I grate it every day, every hour.

My much-admired model for scientific objectivity: Professor Everett Koenigsberger, Chief, Bureau of Weights and Measures Dept. of Commerce, Washington, D.C. Professor Koenigsberger, after years of analyses in his laboratories, has documented and proven the fact (fact, mind you!) that the mouth of the actress Julia Roberts is exactly the same width as the Mississippi River at flood stage.

Here come additional facts you must memorize.

Bruschetta can and perhaps even should be served at various levels of taste and intensity. Your success will depend on your treatment of the three ingredients basic to the dish: the bread, the garlic, the olive oil.

First: the bread.

I use a bread called Pugliese (see Italy's province of Puglia) made by Grace Bakery in Berkeley, California. The crust is firm, and the interior dough does not tear when you briskly rub it with the peeled garlic clove. The trademark holes of the Pugliese do provoke a certain amount of aggravation during the preparation, but the resulting total absorption of the garlic-oil mix is worth the effort. It is not too soft, not too oily. A normal slice of the Pugliese, about an inch thick, will accept about a tablespoon of oil. The single acceptable alternate when Pugliese is not available is a flat very crusty loaf of French peasant origin called *Pain Rustique* and available locally (thanks to Sheri Thrower) in Sebastopol, California, at Fiesta Market. *Pain Rustique* (from Nancy Silverton's La Brea Bakery in Los Angeles) is unshaped and free-formed, a special version of the classic Italian *ciabatta*. Like the Pugliese, the *Pain Rustique* has a thin but firm golden crust and a soft, hole-filled interior. If you place the entire loaf on edge and cut down through the middle, forming two broad thin slices, you have two pieces that present a crusted bottom and a spongy doughy surface. The crusty bottom helps hold the oil in the bread. If you don't overdo the oil, you'll have no gloss on the plate at all. The oil is in the dough and soon in your gut. Waist not, want not.

Even after you select your bread, you still have choices.

If using a loaf, how thick do you make your slices? Do you grill the slices of the Pugliese or the halves of the *Pain Rustique* over coals or do you toast them in your counter-top appliance? I prefer the coals because the grilling adds char to the taste, which is one of my personal satisfactions. I char everything, usually including, when I barbecue, my eyebrows. One choice you will resist with all the strength of your convictions: that commercial *focaccia* sold in super-markets and which, warmed in your microwave oven, presents a crust that is the texture of a stale oyster and a dough that has the appearance and the consistency of phlegm.

Second, the garlic.

Which *variety* (some use the word *strain*) of garlic to use?

My own first choice is always, when it's available, my Red Toch from the Republic of Georgia. Second choice: my Persian Star, from Samarkand, Uzbekistan, or my Inchelium Red from the state of Washington, or Creole Red from the Gulf-Creole region.

Third, the olive oil.

Extra Virgin of course. But which from among the many available in the markets? The cheapest possible? The most expensive? Is there a correlation between price and flavor? My friend/informant (see following) convinces me color cannot be used to judge olive oil. "In a perfect world where there is no possibility of fraud, it wouldn't matter. Leaves can be added to the mix during pressing, which will contribute chlorophyll, giving a greener color. Early harvest oils are naturally green because of the greenness of the olives (all olives in ripening go from green to black.) As the olives ripen, the fruit flavors mellow and more oil is available. A fully black olive produces a mellow oil."

Does this woman, Colleen McGlynn, one of two owners of DaVero Olive Oil, impress you? Smart, clear, clean prose that gives very much information in very few words. The kind of writing I love and have to work like hell to accomplish.

I have come to rely on DaVero, which is produced close to home in Sonoma County's Dry Creek Valley. In Italian *DaVero* means *Exactly! The truth! Yeah! Wow! This is it! I'm the best!* The original trees (from Lucca), from which Colleen McGlynn and Ridley Evers' groves received the initial cuttings, produce what one authority has deemed "the holy grail of olive oil."

As a man of resilient faith, that's good enough for me. I've been in search of the Holy Grail since the fourteenth century.

Though anecdotal, I can verify the following story: in December, 1997, the owner of Frantoio, where DaVero mills its olives, took a sample of DaVero oil to Imperia in Italy where, unbeknownst to the tasters, the DaVero was slipped into the judging circle, which was evaluating oils from Italy and France. DaVero won. Why? One theory advanced by Colleen McGlynn is DaVero's crew picks only as much in a day as can be processed the following day, and the mill is thoroughly free of dirt and leaves. Listen closely and you'll now hear me use words and phrases that have brought my eyes into rolling when someone like Aristide Priappus uses them.

For Colleen McGlynn and Ridley Evers and (after much clucking and reluctant concession) for me, the " … combination of four varietals brings a more nuanced oil than the use of a single varietal. Pressed together the four varietals produce the ultimate sensation of fruitiness, warmth, and richness, not in different areas of the palate (which occurs when tasting a single varietal) but all through the mouth."

DaVero's words.

Want more DaVero's words about its oil? " ... taste characteristics are Tuscan style: pepper in back, fruit forward, good nose and a hint of artichoke, fennel, apple."

I have tasted and tasted, and I think I've got it. By George, I think I've got it.

Don't ask me to tell you why I like DaVero. I don't have Evers' or McGlynn's talents or palates; but, like the woman who met Art Carney and said, "I don't know anything about Art, but I know what he likes," I know my favorite olive oil is DaVero. Gracious soul that I am, I offer you DaVero's web site: www.DaVero.com .

I believe it was Jesse Ventura who said that taste, like beauty, is either in the eye or on the palate of the beholden.

Hey, man, serve my original (I stress *original*, remember!) bruschetta, and your guests be holdin' a lot of garlic.

Chapter Twelve

BRUSCHETTA COOK-OFF FINALE

CELINE PRIAPPUS SUGGESTED I FIND SOMEONE TO ORGANIZE THE cook-off. "You have the garlic work, the writing work, the geezer work, Chester. You want to enjoy your seventy-sixth birthday? Get someone to set up the party for you, someone who does this sort of thing for a living. I know who might. There's a woman in Santa Rosa, a cook-book writer, first name's Polly ... Polly, Polly ..."

"If," Aristide said, "you mention the name I suspect you are about to mention, I am getting a divorce."

"Oh, hush, Ari. You'll never leave me. Who else would indulge your silly arrogance? This woman, Chester, this Polly-something, writes cookbooks. Prize winning cookbooks."

Aristide closed his eyes as if prepared to receive not one but several painful vaccinations.

"She writes for magazines and newspapers, too," Celine went on. *"New York Times, Los Angeles Times, Boston Globe.* Restaurant reviews, interviews with people in the culinary world, you name it."

"I'll name it," Aristide said, after sipping his wine. He pursed his lips as if the fluid contained an abundance of alum. *"Nouvelle cuisine.* That's the name of a Black Hole in a neighboring galaxy. Doesn't *nouvelle* have a ring to it, Chester? There is a passage in Beaudelaire..."

Celine, waving aside her husband's advancing lecture, said, "Polly Carpenter."

I did not want to offend Celine but I could appreciate Aristide's trepidation. "I know Polly Carpenter," I said. "We're friends. Well, sort of. I guess. Maybe. Who knows? Polly can be a royal pain in the allium some times. You think she would really take on something as trivial as this?"

"If," Aristide muttered, "there is something in it for her, which, take it from me, my boy, there is. Trivial? Do you realize that in Kazakhstan the word polly *means* trivial?"

"Ari, if you don't shut up, I'm going to shred your wine cellar."

Aristide: *"En garde,* Chester! *Attenzione! Achtung!* Watch your ass! Polly Carpenter is what the French call a *poseur.* Or what the Russians call an *obmanshchik,* used in reference to someone involved in deception for ... for whatever reason, sex, money, food, position, career, whatever. *Poseur* in Russian becomes *posyor,* accent on the last syllable. Before the revolution the language of the upper classes in Russia was French. Incidentally, that is the historical reason for the occasional French words, pronunciation altered, in the Russian language. Pushkin, you will be interested to know, did not speak Russian until he was seven years old."

"You were interested in knowing all that, weren't you, Chester?"

Aristide very carefully poured into his glass the last few drops of the '92 Nuits-Saint Georges Les Vaucrains, which he'd refused to share with either Celine or me. He knew he'd be wasting what he referred to as his liquid gold on me and he also knew Celine would not in the least feel slighted. He'd learned on the eve of their marriage that when she was seventeen Celine had traded her virginity for a glass of Bertani Amarone that had solidified her respect for her Italian heritage, which, by definition, scorns all things French. "Including," she informed me, when she confessed her sin to me last summer, "their so-called *code d'honneur*. To most of the world French *honneur* is even less impressive than their manners."

"'94 or '95 Bertani was *vino* with a capital V," Aristide said. He went on, undeterred. "*Obmanshchik*. Miz Carpenter, like most of your *nouvelle cuisinistas* are *obmanshchiki* in bankers' clothing. In American English: frauds, phonies, fakes, quick-buck artists."

Celine, for her own salvation, had long ago learned when and how to make concessions, but she refused to rely on her lessons this night. "Ari, I am not suggesting Chester marry the woman. I'm suggesting he hire her. He has other things to do, important things. But he deserves to celebrate his seventy-sixth birthday labor-free and stress-free."

Aristide raised the bottle and addressed it as if it were an old friend. "You still hold," he said. "I should have bought five cases, me proud beauty. First mistake I've made in fifty years."

Celine, for my benefit, circled her right ear with an extended right forefinger, rotated it several times and aimed it at her husband. "Ari has programmed himself to ignore the fact that *nouvelle cuisine* is here to stay."

"Young people are also here to stay," Aristide informed her. "That doesn't mean I have to respect them." He gazed at me over the rim of his glass. "*Nouvelle cuisine*, Chester, began in these United States in the '70s as an honest attempt to return to eighteenth and nineteenth century classic French cuisine, which relied on the best fresh foods available and, for texture and body in sauces, on the alliance of butter, egg yolks, or creams, not, as practiced by Beard, Pepin, Claiborne and Child, on quick-fix flour or starch. A crime, incidentally, to which each of the aforementioned miscreants has publicly confessed. Your 19th century classic French chef would have leaped into the Seine before using flours or starches as thickeners."

Celine handed Aristide her bottle of Siro Pacenti Brunello.

"Pop the cork on this, daddy. You have such strong manly fingers."

After pulling the cork, Aristide sniffed it, circled thumb and forefinger and said, "May I?" He poured a bit into a clean empty glass, sipped, and said, "*Che bella!*"

"Chester, do you realize that I have endured forty years of so-called life with this encyclopedia-that-walks-like-a-man?"

"Forty-one," Aristide said, pulling himself out of his chair to cross the room to his wife's side and kiss her cheek. "You deserve a medal, *bambolla mia*. Chester, I award Celine Josephina Sabini Priappus not five but six stars."

I departed the Priappus' house near midnight, trying to convince myself Aristide would not consider me a traitor for what I did nine hours later.

Polly Carpenter wasn't home, or at least she didn't answer her phone, so I left a message. "Polly, this is Chester Aaron. It's nine o'clock Tuesday morning. Please call me when you get in. I'm setting up a special little birthday party (my own) and I want to invite five or six Bay Area chefs. Want to have a friendly competition. Aristide Priappus and his wife will join us. I'd be inviting you as a guest if I didn't have a possible job for you. I'd like you to organize the event. I've never done anything like this so I need advice from an expert. Talk to you soon."

Flattery has always gotten me somewhere.

In my defense I should inform you that over the years Polly Carpenter and I had met at a variety of functions celebrating Sonoma County's farmers, chefs, and writers. Partly because Polly really can occasionally be a charmer and partly because I identify with her near-psychotic drive for attention, I admit to being a member of that diminishing quartet of friends who continue to nourish a mild affection for the woman.

A few years ago at a book-signing in The Palate, an upscale market in Santa Rosa, there were six writers who, over the years, have brought attention to Sonoma County's treasures, especially its farms, wines, restaurants, vacation sites. One writer to a table. Polly's table was next to the main aisle and my table was to the left of hers. The other four tables, attended by their writers, extended to my left.

Polly's was the only table which, under the weight of stacks of her beautiful and expensive cookbooks, was in danger of collapse. In those stacks were five or six different titles, three of them winners of Beard and Claiborne and Child awards. Her line of fans, their checkbooks at the ready, was so long it interfered with customer traffic. The other five writers, including me, busied ourselves with tic-tac-toe.

In spite of her reputation, Polly was quite gracious that day, especially to me, partly I suspect because I was the only man in the group and partly because the other women's books were (in Polly's mind, I'm sure) suspect. I once heard her ask at the home of a mutual friend, "Who could really take seriously a book published by something called *Horse's Tail Press* or *Caliopeepee Press* or *Two Sisters and a Mom Press*?

I must say here that the publisher of my garlic books and my garlic poster, *Ten Speed Press*, is respected by the big traditional houses in the publishing world, as well as, I might add, by Aristide Priappus. In fact, the great man himself has selected Ten Speed to publish his current project (*Drinking and Tasting Wine*) instead of Knopf, Harper Collins, Random House or Doubleday, all of whom would kill to have his name grace their roster.

During a quiet moment at that signing in Santa Rosa, Polly insisted on buying my two garlic books as well as my garlic poster. "I'm going to frame this gem," she said, "and hang it on my kitchen wall."

How can I not respect someone who possesses such elegant taste?

Polly did not respond to the first message I left on her answering machine or over the next three days to my second, third, and fourth messages. I was about to give up and make my way to one of those fabled Head Hunters I've read about, but then on Friday evening she called.

After the usual exchange of mini-nothings, I laid out my plans for the cook-off.

She repeated the words *bruschetta-cook-off* as if memorizing important details for a final exam.

"You're probably swamped," I said. "With all your deadlines I doubt you have the time but I thought it might interest you. I need someone to, well, to take over. This is the time of the year, the time of the month actually, when I have to be out in the field planting. I'll pay. The whole thing's my seventy-sixth birthday gift to myself."

She demurred, for about three seconds.

"It so happens," Polly whispered (she has succeeded after years of rehearsal in matching perfectly the pitch and texture of the voice of Lauren Bacall), "that I am between projects. For the next six weeks I'm not travelling to a single television or radio interview. I've been reading your garlic books and admiring your talents, Chester. I saw you on the Victory Garden show, and I read the article in *Rebecca's Garden* and I saw the cover photos in *Fine Cooking*. You're a Renaissance man, writer, farmer, professor, hunk."

The woman not only has ambition, she also has a discriminating eye.

"Come on, Polly. I'm seventy-five years old. Almost seventy-six. I'm an impoverished writer, a retired professor, an exhausted and failed farmer. Hunk? A hunk of aged salami maybe."

"You're so alive, Chester." (Lauren Bacall again.) "And the party idea sounds grand. I'm sure I can find the time, if you think I could help. Let's talk."

Because Polly lived in Sebastopol, I suggested lunch the following day at Broken Ford Café in Freestone about midpoint between our homes. She accepted the invitation, saying she'd heard such positive comments about the food at Broken Ford that she was obligated to review the place. "And the timing's perfect," she said. "Patsy, Travel and Leisure editor at *The Times*, wants an article suggesting Sonoma County locales that might appeal to travellers. So Broken Ford fits right in."

After we were seated at the cafe (a rusted corpse of a 1951 Ford pickup in the front yard) and before our menu-dispenser arrived, Polly said, "Fill me in, Chester." She dug into her large handbag to remove a notebook and pen.

I informed Polly that next year would be my last year as a farmer. "I'm tired. I want to spend my time writing." Her disappointment seemed genuine. "But," I said, striving for the voice and manner of Aristide Priappus, "after having devoted twenty years to the growing of exotic garlics, I want to go out flying all my flags, all my trumpets blaring."

The extravagant imagery had been meant as a joke, a verbal cartoon, but I observed Polly writing in her notebook, "... *exotic garlics ... flying flags ... trumpets blaring ...* "

"Bruschetta is my favorite food," I said. "I have firm notions about how it should be prepared. I've learned some things..."

She wrote, on her pad, *bruschetta*, and underlined it.

"I thought: Okay, let's have a competition. A bruschetta cook-off. There are about six chefs in the Bay Area who have ordered my garlic over the years so I thought I'd invite them."

"The names of the chefs?"

She nodded approval at each name and, as she wrote them in her notebook she added, after each name and without my help, the name of that chef's restaurant.

"Is there a format you want them to follow?"

In suggesting various conditions that might be imposed for the preparation and presentation of the bruschettas, I admitted that I was not comfortable with my own ideas. I not only never did this sort of thing, but I also did not have the time to sit down and organize my thoughts about what I wanted or how I wanted it done. "First of all, Polly, I'm not satisfied with the term *cook-off*. It sounds too much like *shoot-out*." I took on a young-ganger voice: "Hey, man, my bruschetta is bigger than *your* bruschetta!"

"Chester, chefs thrive on competition."

"So we keep the term *cook-off*?"

"Absolutely. That's one of your two motifs. The other being *garlic*. First question an editor asks about an article or a book I propose is *what's the motif*? Every time I pitch a book or an article that's the first thing I fix in my mind before I meet with the editor. What's the *motif*? I love *cook-off. A Bruschetta Cook-Off*. We change it for dramatic effect to *The Great Bruschetta Cook-Off*. That says it all. I have one question."

"Only one?"

"Well, a major one. Will Aristide Priappus be involved? I

know you are the only person in Sonoma County who has access to him."

I came this close (tips of thumb and forefinger touching) to canceling everything then and there. "I don't think of it as *access*, Polly. We're close friends. Aristide, his wife Celine, me."

"I envy you. If I brought my editor Aristide Priappus they would..."

"Hold it. Hold it, Polly. Aristide Priappus is not John the Baptist and neither you nor I am, are, Salome. No exploitation of Aristide's name in this, in any of this."

"I wouldn't think of it. But you know that even if Aristide is just going to pass through the room the chefs will beg, absolutely beg, to help you celebrate."

"Repeat. No mention of Aristide."

"Trust me. I'm proud to help celebrate your birthday. Chester, every chef in the country, every writer of cookbooks, including me, reveres your work with garlic. Now what are the details I can tell the chefs?"

Out of somewhere Aristide's advice to be cautious with Polly Carpenter came slinking up behind me. And then came Celine's advice to relax and celebrate. "You can inform each chef that the bruschetta I judge to be the best gets its creator three bottles of '95 Williams & Sellyem Pinot Noir."

Polly's mouth dropped open and stayed open so long I count-ed the number of gold fillings in her rear molars, three on top and two on the bottom.

"That, Chester, is a ransom for a king. Are they stored in a vault? Are they insured?"

"They are stored in Aristide Priappus' wine cellar. Aristide gave me a case for my birthday. I'm donating three bottles. Aristide knows."

"Chester, I will do this for you for no fee. Normally, I charge. But for this grand occasion, I am your servant."

"Polly, I don't expect you to do this as a favor. I'm very will-ing to pay."

"Hey, this is an adventure. This will be a learning experience for me. I will never be too proud or too old to learn. Think of it this way. I love garlic but I've never dared write about it with you, the master, living in the neighborhood. This partnership could get us together on a special book. Wouldn't that be a hoot?"

"I'm willing."

"Aristide Priappus. For those of us in the food world it's like being in the presence of Brillat-Savarin."

"He played goalie for the Canadians, right?" If I could not distract her by direct and firm warning, perhaps witty satire would work.

She laughed. "You can't fool me, Chester. I'll tell you the truth. I would be offended if you decided to leave me out of this event. I usually ignore messages left on my machine, but thank God I called back on yours. Look at what I'm into."

"O.K. What do you need from me?"

"Before I leave, I'll get the dates and your parameters for the bruschettas, things like that. I'll deal with the chefs. I'll get the wording set up. Sit back, chill out, Chester. You have important work to do. I'm already thinking about the book you and I will do. Not just a grower-and-chef thing, a writer-and-writer thing, a man-woman thing … you see? Two motifs. Fun fun."

Polly's high school cheerleader persona failed to impress a somnolent young woman who approached the table, who studied Polly, studied me, thought for a moment. Remembering her role, she shook herself and muttered, "I'm not, like, your wait-person but, like, you'll need these." She dropped two menus and a wine list on our table.

Polly surveyed the wine list as if it were a road map to heaven. "I hardly ever drink at noon," she murmured, "but our contract deserves to be celebrated. There's a Red Horse Zin here that … "

"I always have a glass of their house-white."

Polly almost managed not to gasp. "Please. Let me order a wine for you. They have a Red Horse '94. Best Russian River offering in the last ten years. I'm paying homage to this very wine in *The Times* next week."

The '94 Red Horse zinfandel came accompanied by the usual commentary devoted to *the nose* and *the oak* and *the cork* and the virtues of the '94-compared-to-the-'95 compared to the-'97, etc., etc.

Why do I have trouble with this, as Aristide calls it, *épater des booboisee*? I'm sure I irritate people when I talk so self-right-eously, so pompously, about farming, about writing, and about being in debt: topics near and dear to me. Why can't I indulge similar failings in others? Is it because I'm just no damn good?

Aristide always laughs when I confide to him my suspicions about the language that accompanies the celebration of wines. "Blather, dear boy, pure blather, most of the time; and I emphasize *most*. But when I'm with an extraordinary wine-maker whose dedication and imagination I admire, I listen to him with the same attention I'd offer Shakespeare were the Bard to appear and lead me by the hand through the intangibilities of *Hamlet* or *Lear*. In a vineyard, I never go near owners, investors, those … those … those investors." He spoke the word as if it fouled his tongue. "This sounds like rhetoric out of the '30s, but I want to be with the little people, the so-called salt of the earth. Those workers who put the vines in the soil and observe the grape and listen to the wind and test the sun on their wrists and measure the sugar and perform their art-in-action pressings. Those are moon-struck geniuses to whom I'd entrust my soul."

Polly brought me out of my reverie. "I wonder what I should order. A small hole-in-the-wall cafe can almost always be judged by one item; its salad dressing."

I felt a chill as, again, out of the recent past came Aristide's cautionary whisper.

Polly, shaking her head, suddenly looked somber. "Very sad," she said.

I glanced up, thinking she'd spied an old friend in the room, someone balanced on the edge of death. She was indeed appraising the room, the other diners, the almost arrogantly laid-back wait-per-sons and the hip-hopping staff in the open-to-view kitchen. "Don't like it," Polly whispered, jotting notes. "Funk's OK in clothes and music, not in food. If that monsterette with those greasy dreadlocks and snotty nose-ring is our server, I'm not touching the food."

I said, "They're young, Polly. They think they're rebels, but they work hard for low pay. And the food's not only tasty here, and filling and varied, it's inexpensive."

Fortunately, the waitress so offensive to Polly was not responsible for our table. Rochelle, whom I've known from several visits

I've made to the cafe, was clean, neat, considerate, and professional. I ordered my usual polenta (topped with local turkey sausage and pine nuts and a tomato-basil sauce), but Polly ordered a small green salad and a bowl of soup.

"You're a cheap date," I said.

"I'll possibly have something later."

After one taste of her salad, Polly, writing as she talked, judged the dressing to be "slightly better than adequate." The cream-of-artichoke soup with jalapeño peppers? "The chef has a heavy-hand with potent herbs. Subtlety is an art."

I did not seek additional comments, but that did not mean I did not receive them. Near the end of the meal, to find at least minimal satisfaction, I drew Polly's attention to the price of the lunch (including the wine.)

Polly said, yes, the prices were fair. "But can I recommend this funk to readers of *The New York Times* just because the prices are fair? Trust me. I'll find something positive to say."

Aristide's whisper in both of my ears: *Tempted to cancel yet, Chester?*

While I waited at the counter to take care of the check, Polly toured the shop at the rear of the café. When she joined me, she was visibly upset. I walked her to the car, wondering if I'd said something that offended her; but when she opened the car door, she was all smiles and hugs. "This will be fun," she said. "Relax now and we'll talk tomorrow."

Time out.

I want to explain that reference (some pages back) to my *not having had time to sit down* and my prompt and willing surrender of responsibility to Polly Carpenter.

When Polly and I met at the Broken Ford Café, it was the end of summer. All the garlic had been harvested. Facing me, virtually the following day, were the first steps in the preparation of the boxes for next year's crop. And then, after the preparations (two weeks of seven eight-hour days each week), come the planting of the first cloves.

Preparation of the boxes meant that those eight boxes that had been invaded by gophers had to be emptied, the boxes turned over, the wire repaired or replaced, the boxes turned upright again, and filled again with new soil and new compost. All of it had to be wheel-barrowed from a hundred yards away. New soil and compost had to be added as well to the other fifty-four boxes and mixed with the remnant soil that had not been washed away by the winter rains. The maze of drip lines feeding every single box (and all their fittings) had to be checked and tested, and, where necessary, be repaired or replaced.

Planting of the first cloves meant that the best cloves of the best bulbs of all eighty-seven varieties had yet to be selected out of the approximately two thousand bulbs I'd stored in special mesh bags hung in the shadiest and coolest breezeways. It also meant that, once the 32,000 prime cloves were selected they would, over the next two months, starting October 1, be planted one-by-one with this thumb and this forefinger.

Oh, and between now and October 1, the last parcels of still viable garlic had to be mailed (at reduced prices) to those subscribers who had contacted me late in the season.

Can you appreciate my swallowing my pride and accepting the help of Polly Carpenter, whose credentials threw a long dark shadow over my own?

Consider.

Polly Carpenter has been a force in the Food World, local and national, for twenty years. Her reputation as a chef could win her a position in any one of the ten best restaurants in the country. Her recent book *Root Vegetables I Have Known* (still on *The New York Times* best-seller list,) has earned the James Beard Award, The Craig Claiborne Silver Chalice, the Julia Childhood Medallion d'Honeur, and the Jacques "Scotty" Pepin diploma, each honor guaranteeing at least 10,000 new readers. The original proposal for *Roots* (as Polly refers to the book on her talk-show circuit) had earned her a $50,000 advance, but a firm savings account and wise investments have not swelled her head. She remains an impassioned supporter of Sonoma County's small farmers and small wineries. Remember what she said to me at that lunch that day at Broken Ford? You probably didn't hear her. "I have little interest in the big guys, the Gallos, the Mondavis, the Kendall Jacksons. I like the small wineries, Chester. Like you and me, they live on the edge."

Aristide Priappus, when I informed him of Polly's comment, nodded like the wise old sage he is and murmured, "Anyone who lives on the edge, Chester, is leaving too much space behind his back. Polly Carpenter lives in the center. From there she can see where she came from and where she's going."

Two days before the scheduled cook-off, I asked Polly if I might see the memo she'd composed for the chefs because I had not heard anything and needed to know. Polly informed me that the material had been e-mailed to the six invited chefs several weeks ago, and all six had promptly, and with great delight, accepted.

"But I never saw the material you sent out. You said you'd show it to me."

"No problem. Here. Chill out, as the wee ones say. Let the record show…" and she handed me a copy of the e-mail, a single page: text on the front and a map of Sebastopol on the back.

Yo, friend and fellow participant in the Great Bruschetta Cook-off

Aristide Priappus and Chester Aaron have selected the six of you from among thousands of the nation's most prominent chefs to present for judgment one representative bruschetta. One entry each, so make it your very, very, very favorite. To the winner (are you prepared for this?): three bottles of '95 Williams & Sellyem Pinot Noir from the cellars of Aristide Priappus.

Map is enclosed. Be at Chester's home by noon. His kitchen will be available. Entry on the table under the arbor by one o'clock at the latest. All present to be guests of Chester Aaron and Aristide Priappus at 6:00 p.m. at the Sebastopol restaurant, 101 Main. Volodya, owner and chef, is reserving three tables for the evening for the exclusive pleasure of the participants in this grand signature event of the season.

Signed: Aristide Priappus, Chester Aaron, and your humble servant, Polly Carpenter.

On the map, a circled X at the intersection of Main Street and Bodega Highway identifying the location of *101 main.*

You will note, as I did, that after all of my admonitions Polly Carpenter had used Aristide Priappus as the lure. What could, should, would I do? It was, as one of my students at Saint Mary's College had written in a term paper about Napoleon's defeat at Waterloo, a *fête accompli.*

The evening before the event Aristide and Celine invited me to dine and relax at their home. I permitted myself to grieve.

I could not go so far as to admit to Aristide that I had not disputed Polly's design of the *cook-off plan.* I had not even seen it until a week after it had been received by the chefs, and the chefs had accepted the invitation. "Aristide, I don't give a damn if this cook-off is or isn't successful. I just want it over with. I have work to do. I'm sorry I involved you in the whole damn mess. I will never do this to you again."

Aristide never gloats, except in jest. "You're correct, Chester. It is a mess." He was not in the least melancholy. In fact, he was chuckling and wringing his hands like a child on Christmas morning. "This," he said, "is going to be fun."

Fun?

Fun for me is reading old copies of *Garfield* or *Peanuts* or especially *Pogo.* Fun for me is listening to tapes of Jack Benny or 1940 programs from Nashville's *Grand Ole Opry.* Fun for me is watching Mel Brooks' *Blazing Saddles* or *Young Frankenstein.*

When I was preparing to leave their home, Celine was solicitous, almost humbled. "OK, I was wrong. As usual, the Great One was correct. So what do we do now?" She put an arm around my shoulders and kissed my cheek. "Everything will work out. I know it will. See you tomorrow, Chester."

Aristide embraced me, too. "*A domani, friend.* I give you one last bit of advice. Nothing in life is as serious as death. Just remember the inscription on W. C. Fields' tombstone. *All things considered, I'd rather be in Philadelphia.*"

The early morning breezes were balmy.

About eleven o'clock the sun turned hot. Then, shortly before noon, winds coming over the hills from the ocean were so cool I thought I might have to offer sweaters and jackets to the more vulnerable. As I (glum, silent, morose) and Polly (bright, cheery, giggly) prepared the tile counter in my kitchen and arranged the various pots and pans and dishes and platters for easy access, the breezes turned warm again.

Aristide and Celine arrived before the others. I introduced them to Polly who (I'm presuming here from her face and what is currently called *body language*) was having multiple orgasms.

Celine pitched in to help the setting-up, but Aristide retreated to the deck at the western side of the house. In one of the reclining redwood chairs he read or reread in French, Stendhal's *The Red and the Black*. He could have read it without effort had it been in Spanish, Italian, Russian, German or Swahili.

The chefs arrived in a single cavalcade. Two came alone, two came with their significant-others, two with assorted children, aides, culinary students, cousins, aunts and uncles. They all raved about my kindness, they all raved about my contributions to the attack on world-hunger, they all raved about my farm, raved about my solar home, they certainly, all of them, raved about my garlic. In between they all raved about each other, then they raved about Polly Carpenter.

The chaos was slightly less impressive than the D-Day landings on Normandy Beach and a bit more benevolent. Everyone appeared to have been consuming Happy Pills.

Inside the house the music Polly had selected to set the tone: Sarah Brightman and Andrea Bocelli singing *Time to Say Goodbye*. Set on repeat, it repeated six times. On the beginning of the seventh, repeat Aristide beckoned me to his chair "Chester, can you do something about that pablum that has seeped into your sound system?"

I went in, removed the Brightman, and replaced it with a CD picked at random.

"Ah," Aristide said." Handel. *The Marian Cantatas and Arias*. Anne Sofie Von Otter." He waited. "Musica Antiqua Koln. Reinhard Goebel directing." He leaned back, closed his eyes, and ignored the revelry at the front of the house as the chefs and their battalions moved their completed bruschettas from my kitchen to the grape arbor.

When Von Otter moved into *Haec est Regina virginium*, Aristide sang in harmony and in Latin, of course. At the first long break between bands, he said, *"Ah! Che troppo ineguali."* His eyes closed, and his right hand directed the orchestra. "Pity," he murmured, "we won't be hearing the heart of the recital, the aria *Sventurati mieisospiri*. Four solo violins, a viola and a continuo. A representation of the Seven Sorrows of Mary." He was starting to join Von Otter in the *recitative* when Polly, running back to the deck where Aristide, Celine, and I were preparing ourselves, screamed, "We're ready! We're ready!"

On the first piercing note of the scream, Aristide had grabbed at my arm as if someone had stabbed him with a dull needle. Polly's repeated scream — "We're ready! We're ready!" — ripped the voice of Von Otter into fragments.

"A perfect illustration," Aristide muttered through tightly clenched teeth, "of wines mixed but unmatched. To the barricades, Chester."

Time to Say Goodbye was floating through the open windows once again and up through the grape arbor where the barricades were being manned and womaned.

Aristide led the way. Celine followed her husband. I, the birthday boy, followed Celine, thinking, hoping, praying that in six more hours the cook-off would be over, the dinner at 101 Main would be over, and I would be home in my 'jammies.

Climbing the steps to the floor of the arbor where the crowd waited, Aristide Priappus' appearance was only slightly less impressive than Pope Paul's arrival at Saint Patrick's in New York at sunrise Easter Sunday.

Aristide wears no jewelry so no one could kiss his ring, but I have to admit that even I, the C.E.O. of Cynics Anonymous, was overwhelmed. I knew Aristide Priappus was a *mensch* (that's not French for *important personage*), but I was not prepared for such trills and bows and eye-rollings and burblings and bowings and curtseys of respect and devotion and sheer surrender. Perhaps the presence of Julia Child would have stirred such religious fervor but I doubt it. Beard? Not at all. "Scotty" Pepin and Craig Claiborne? Yawnsville, as *The Hollywood Reporter* might inform us.

I have never granted Aristide credit for a talent for clowning, but there he was, strutting toward the arbor (Celine groaning and then bursting into laughter) with outstretched hand moving in pontifical benediction as he intoned: "Hear Ye! Hear Ye! I pronounce a world absent of gar-ar-lic a heaven absent of Gaw-aw-ed." He chanted the sentence four times: in French, in Italian, in Spanish, in English. Then, after intoning a benediction upon me, insisting that Chester Aaron deserved sanctification for his years of devotion to the merging of the worlds of art and labor, he turned to touch the top of my head with the tip of his forefinger. With Celine stifling her laughter in the background, Aristide (face purple with constrained laughter) bowed to me; I bowed to Polly; Polly bowed to me; we both bowed to Aristide, who, in turn bowed to the chefs and their retinues, all of whom bowed to Aristide and to each other.

For lack of anything further to say or do, I said, "Let us begin."

On the long table were six platters of bruschetta. Around the border of the arbor the aides unslung their cameras and popped their flash bulbs.

Aristide stumbled. Or had he only pretended? Balance regained, he laid his head on my shoulder. "My God," he mumbled into my ear. *"Disgustoso!"*

Was he laughing or was he weeping? I could not be sure and did not especially care to know.

The audience — the chefs lined up like a white-jacketed, white-touffed honor guard, wide open eyes gleaming, wide open mouths filled with teeth — waited for the inevitable declarations of praise. Poor lads, and lass.

Step by step, the great Man moved the length of the table, pointing to one platter and then to the next. "Beluga Caviar!" he said, failing or refusing to mask his shock. "What … what pomposity." He had difficulty breathing. "Zebra Oysters! One hundred dollars a pound." He glared at the horde of felons shivering before him. "The reason these precious little beasts are protected is that they are almost extinct!"

Celine, at his side, said, "Ari, relax, dear. Remember Dr. Corning's advice."

A sputtering Aristide advanced two steps. "Truffles! Canned truffles! Surely you know, whoever composed this … this monstrosity … you probably don't know … truffles are at their best in midwinter and this is September! "

Was it Celine or Chester who said, "It's not important, Aristide."

"*Foie gras!* On bruschetta, the ultimate peasant dish. The mark of peasant food is simplicity, you bunch of stupid … stupid … "

Could Aristide Priappus be at a loss for words?

No.

"And look at this … this … pyramid of self-indulgence. *Korushka!* Russian smelt. Hundreds of ice-fishermen out of St. Petersburg die every year searching for *korushka*, thousands are cast adrift on ice floes and you … you … comfortable little, protected little … you *dared* place this egregious display of self-indulgent arrogance on bruschetta … This is Vanderbilt bruschetta! These are bruschettas out of John Jacob Astor's kitchens! *Quel fucking chutzpah!* "

He stared at them all, he stared (face purple) at them one by one; and he would have raised his fist at Polly Carpenter had he not stopped it halfway in its upward arc to chew on his knuckles. "Chester, don't you dare let even one of these criminals so much as sniff the cork of even one bottle of your precious Pinot Noir."

It was at that moment that one of the chefs covered his face and burst into tears and raced to his car. Another chef scurried about, weeping, trying to gather up her platter and accouterments. A third chef staggered into the table that held the twenty-four bottles of wines that had been carried from the Bay Area. The table collapsed. At least fifteen of the bottles and just about all of the glasses crashed on the wooden floor. The remaining participants, young and old, men and women, scurried, retreated, weeping, a gang of Jobs and Jobsesses bemoaning and begroaning their varied pestilences.

* * * * *

Twelve minutes later the last of the cars had disappeared.

Ten minutes after the last car departed Aristide, Celine, and I stood alone in the grape arbor.

"I'll help you clean this mess up," Celine said. "I'm responsible, I'm afraid."

I mumbled something that should have sounded like, "It was my stupidity, Celine."

The Great Man, exhausted, lowered himself, with a long sigh, into a chair. "There's enough stupidity to go 'round, but that had to be my finest performance. Sir Ralph Richardson or Sir John Gielgud? I played the raging *Lear* once. In London. This performance was superior."

Celine, at her husband's side, put an arm around his head and hugged it to her breast. "Tell Chester, Ari."

Tell Chester? Tell Chester what? That he has the brain of a fragment of concrete?

"Are you ready for this, Chester?"

Chester was ready for nothing short of self-immolation.

"Polly Carpenter appeared at our door three days ago."

Celine, lovely Mother Superior Celine, put her arms around me.

"The lady—no, no, the female — pleaded with me to write an introduction to her new book, the book she signed a contract for the day you called her to ask her to organize the cook-off. I excused myself, went into my study, and called her editor, whom, of course, I know quite well. Polly Carpenter had demanded and received an advance of $100,000 for her proposal for a new book, $50,000 more than she'd received for her current *magnum opus*. I called Shaughnessy, at *The New York Times*, editor of the Freud and Whine section. She informed me my colleague Polly Carpenter had promised a long article for the Wednesday food page about a unique event in Sonoma County, California, which honored the dean of contemporary culture urban-and-rural, one Aristide Priappus. I alerted Shaughnessy to what would be happening at that event in Sonoma County. Shaughnessy suggested that rather than Polly Carpenter writing the article she would be delighted to have Aristide Priappus offer his perceptions in his own inimitable prose. Aristide Priappus told

Shaughnessy what she could do with next Wednesday's Freud and Whine section and subsequent issues of *The Times*, especially the ten-pound Sunday editions. Shaughnessy grunted in pain at the prospect, and said she hoped to live long enough to see me regret my holier-than-thou attitude. 'Holier-than-thee,' I informed the woman."

Celine, tightening her arms about me, said, "Sometimes Ari tries the patience of his friends, Chester, even those friends who love him and whom he adores in turn. Please forgive him if you feel punished for…"

"Why did they come, Aristide?"

"Why? Not for you, Chester. Not for me. For themselves, dear boy. Do you realize what these three bottles of Williams & Sellyem Pinot Noir are worth, Chester? Not just in dollars but in sentiment? In history? This wine was made by the renowned Bert Williams when he and Ed Sellyem still owned the joint and when Williams was the wine maker. These bottles are the last of the very best before the new pagans raise new barricades. Good wine, wine with a legend, wine with a history, wine never to be equaled, is worth more, Chester — to me, to sincere and knowledgeable admirers of the grape — than an original folio by Shakespeare. To possess this '95 Pinot Noir is comparable to riding with Christopher Columbus on the Santa Maria. The admiral was not, as historians maintain, on the Nina or the Pinta, Chester. My research proves he graced the prow of the Santa Maria."

Aristide pointed a finger at the table, covered now with an array of platters covered with a collection of flower-draped, rose-bedecked, ribbon-bewrapped bruschettas I might have met in a garbage dump.

"*Drech!*" Aristide said. "*Schisen! Merde!* Shit! Manure! Haul it away! All of it. I won't go near that collection of *schmata*." Celine and I cleaned up while Aristide, ensconced on his chair on the western deck, read his Stendhal.

After a compulsory shower in the hottest water I could endure, I drove the three of us into Sebastopol, to *101 Main*. I'd been prepared to beg forgiveness for loss of customers and of income, but the restaurant was full. One table was empty, having been reserved for a party of three. Us.

Volodya came to our table from the kitchen and waved off my apology and my offer to pay for the reservations that had not been honored.

"They were honored," Volodya said. "After Aristide called yesterday and canceled today's plan, we adjusted."

Aristide pretended to buff his nails. "I'm a prophet in my own time," he said.

To help celebrate my seventy-sixth birthday, Volodya and Laura placed on our table their crisp walnut pralines. Who would dare try to describe the spray of *glace* that shielded them from view but not from scent? I'll try: *Apricot clouds*.

Celine sang *Happy Birthday* to me in Italian, and Aristide sang the same tune, slightly off key, in five different languages.

On the way home Aristide delivered tidbits of additional information gleaned from his calls to New York.

When Polly Carpenter had called her editor and made her pitch, describing her *motif*, and demanding twice the amount of her previous advance, her editor promised to call her back in twenty minutes. He discussed Polly's ultimatum ("If you can't give me a firm yes, I'll go to Hollie Constable at Harper/Collins tomorrow.") with the Executive Editor. Polly's editor called her back in fifteen, confirming the grant of Polly's required advance. Within twelve hours there was a variety of supplemental offerings including a series of five-minute spots twice a week on the PBS scam called *The Lehrer Report*. Polly Carpenter, groomed and cosmeticized to resemble a vampy Celine Dion, would guarantee the addition of a new and substantial audience to PBS's current classy-unconscious audience already being bored from within by well-paid dullards.

Another plan was set in motion that day Polly received the commitment of the required advance: photographs of Polly Carpenter, in discrete make-up and Victoria's Not-Very-Secret lingerie, to appear on the covers of *Gourmet* magazine, *Saveur, People, Elle, O, Vogue, Ladies in Waiting, Ladies Standing, Ladies Lying*.

"Are you prepared, Chester? Can you guess Polly Carpenter's title for the new book?"

Chester waited.

"*Taming the Wild Bruschetta*. Sub-title: *Blessing Sonoma County's Terroires.*"

"Terroires?"

Aristide shook his head, unwilling to believe his own commentary. "*Terroires*," he said, his perfect French making me too aware of my own stilted English. "Another term beloved by the Freud and Whine faddies. When a chef cites an ingredient from a *terroire* that means he will be doubling or tripling his prices tomorrow night. Forgive me. Let us go on."

"Please," Celine said, her hands folded in prayer before her Sicilian-queen face. "Please, Ari, bring this to an end."

"This, Chester, is the end. At the peak of the advertising splash dedicated to *Taming the Wild Bruschetta*, Polly Carpenter will, in collaboration with the winery of her choice, be opening an exclusive and very expensive restaurant in Healdsburg, the heart of the heart of Sonoma Wine Country."

I waited.

"Name of the future restaurant?"

I waited.

"*Bruschetta.*"

In your dreams, Polly.

Last year Aristide Priappus, interviewed by editors of four European newspapers, invited me to attend the luncheon he would be serving but only if I would offer his guests my bruschetta. I accepted the invitation and the terms. My bruschetta was prepared exactly as I have already described it in the early pages of the preceding chapter, detailing the requisite and precious items: the bread, the olive oil, the garlic.

The bread I used that day was the *Pain Rustique* from Sheri Thrower at Fiesta Market in Sebastopol. I grilled the slices over my own carefully prepared oak coals. The garlic? Red Toch, from the Republic of Georgia. The olive oil? DaVero, extra-virgin, of course.

Spread on the oiled and garlicked grilled bread: slices of just-picked Cherokee tomatoes from Darrell Merrell and just-picked leaves of green basil from my own garden. Sea salt. Pepper.

That is, was, it.

The editors raved so loudly their songs were heard in Rome, Paris, Berlin and London. Not to mention San Francisco. One of the editors could have been the beautiful Anne Sofie Von Otter singing (singing is not a word exultant enough to describe the experience) Monteverdi's *Orfeo*. A third could have been Paul Robeson, whose voice God created to teach the human spirit to soar.

No wonder my bruschetta has made it into California's Culinary Hall of Fame.

That was the classic bruschetta Aristide had met in Umbria, the classic bruschetta I had met in Tuscany. Both specimens, in both of our closed minds, the original, the true bruschetta. Unblemished by ambitious modern wannabes.

But.

But but but. Butt butt butt.

After my return from Tuscany ten years ago, I'd found in every pseudo-Italian restaurant in New York, Boston, San Francisco and, especially in Los Angeles, versions of bruschetta that could have been designed (and probably were) by Calvin Klein. Cold soggy bread slices topped with garish wet chunks of various colors, all of them red.

For the next ten years Chester, the purist, treated himself and his various guests to the original, the unadulterated, *peasant* bruschetta.

A week after receiving the notice that my bruschetta recipe was to be enshrined in the California Culinary Hall of Fame in Buffone, California, a book happened into my possession. A friend, Janice Dent, who owned a very small café in Occidental (Aristide shed real tears when Janice's cafe gave up its ghost), gave me the book as a gift.

Title of the book: *Bruschetta*. Authors of *Bruschetta*: Ann and Franco Taruschio.

Bruschetta had been published in 1995 in London by Pavilion Books Ltd., and in the same year in New York by Abbeville Press.

Make a mark on your wall. Make two marks.

In the seventy-sixth year of my life I was humbled. Maybe

even humiliated.

And Aristide Priappus was humbled. Not, however, humiliated.

The Taruschios own a restaurant (once a little country pub called The Walnut Tree) in, of all places, Abergravenny, South Wales. The Taruschios and the food they offer are now honored by *cognoscenti* from all six corners of the globe.

Bruschetta, Taruschio, South Wales. Go figure.

I learned from the Taruschios that bruschetta originated in the central part of Italy, in the general vicinity of Emilia Romagna. The Italian dialect word *bruscate* means *abbrustolite*, or *toasted*.

This is a brief excerpt from the front flap of the Taruschios' book, but it explains everything, including how one, someone, anyone, can humble two great men such as Aristide Priappus and Chester Aaron, one greater, one humbler, than the other.

> *The essence of bruschetta (of which crostoni and crostini are variations in size) is ... a slice of bread ... toasted, rubbed with garlic and seasoned while still hot, with sea salt and olive oil and topped with a selection of intense flavors. The possibilities for experimentation are almost infinite. ... although originally bruschetta was toasted by peasants over a wood fire, excellent results can be obtained with a griddle or even just a basic broiler ..."*

I found a copy of the Taruschio's book for Aristide.

Celine read it first and practically strapped Aristide in bed while she read it to him. She interrupted herself constantly to show him the dramatic photographs.

A week ago, a month after having received the book, Aristide invited me to dinner. One course. Bruschetta.

To each of the three of us: six slices of toasted Pugliese bread, rubbed with garlic and oiled. On each of the seven slices a different topping. Aristide introduced each of the seven bruschettas in two languages. His recipes came directly from the pages of the beautiful little book *Bruschetta* by Ann and Franco Taruschio.

Bruschetta con Pomodori e Rucola (with tomatoes and rocket, or arugula.)
Bruschetta con Porcini Trifolati (with porcini mushrooms in garlic and parsley.)
Bruschetta al Caprino e Noci (with Goat's Cheese and walnuts.)
Bruschetta con Frutti di Mare (with seafood.)
Bruschetta con Aringhe alla Calabrese (with herrings Calabrese.)
Bruschetta con Peposo (with peppered beef.)
Bruschetta di Polenta con Uova Strapazzate e Funghi Porcini
(polenta bruschetta with scrambled eggs and Porcini Mushrooms.)

Now, two years after that historic event called *The Great Bruschetta Cook-off*, I sit on my deck, smoking my Hoyo de Monterey and loving my life because I remind myself this glorious summer evening that my gift to myself for my past seventy-sixth or maybe my approaching seventy-seventh birthday is learning, finally, to eat humble pie. Not a tempting delicacy.

Aristide has joined me at the table. "That event, my behavior," Aristide confesses, "was the second mistake I made in my life."

Celine, with a toss of her long still jet-black hair: "Number 54 a, sub-1."

The Hoyo de Monterey is the best I've ever smoked.

I use Bombay gin this night in my gin-and-tonic, not the cheapo supermarket stuff. The Bombay moves through my veins like the elixir Ponce de León was searching for.

I look down across the field at the spread of boxes, at the garlic growing tall and green, at the hardnecks just beginning to send up their scapes, and I line up all the joys that have shared my life here in this home, in this field.

I am at peace, I am in love with my life. I do not inform Celine or Aristide, when I excuse myself and go inside, that I intend to call Polly Carpenter.

I will invite Polly Carpenter to dinner tomorrow evening.

Forgive and forget.

You have a Ph.D. in *Forgetting*, Chester. Start earning one now in *Forgiving*.

Do Polly Carpenter a favor. Take her eight or ten bulbs of Persian Star.

Persian Star from Samarkand, Uzbekistan.

A perfect garlic for bruschetta. Even better, perhaps, than Red Toch.

Sorry, Poppa.

THE RECIPES

Recipes

999 OUT OF EVERY THOUSAND COOKBOOKS ARE DESIGNED TO attract the eye and the wallet. 998 out of every thousand cookbooks have photographs and jacket designs that hurtle the cost of the books too far beyond their value to the kitchen cook. 997 out of every thousand cookbooks rely on the names of famous chefs and famous and/or expensive restaurants to convince you that owning the books gives you the right to announce yourself a premier guest of that restaurant and/or a personal friend of that chef and/or his/her significant other.

To prove I am not contemptuous of all chefs or all cookbook writers, I cite two people I've met recently and whose books I'm delighted to have read and admired even before I met them. Paula Wolfert and Carol Field bring the objective dedication of a scientist and the passions and imaginations of the best poets to their areas of interest (Wolfert, mainly but not exclusively to Eastern Europe and Morocco; Field to Italy and all things, not just food, Italian). But to call the books by these two authors "cookbooks" is like calling "La Boheme" or Beethoven's Ninth Symphony music. I read Wolfert's and Fields' books the way I read the best novels: with gratitude for their ability to not just involve me in their adventures but also to provoke me into adventures of my own.

Both authors are highly sensitive to cultures past and present. Perceptions and responses and interests of each author are, of course, different. Though those differences produce unique prose styles, they share a rare gift: their judgments are continually driven by that joyous curiosity that defines young writers but which often fades or even dies as cynical middle age approaches. Both authors retain their youthful joy as they continue to experience and write about new adventures. I dream, fantasize, about joining them on their next exploration just as when I was a child I used to fantasize accompanying Amundsen to the North Pole or Martin and Asa Johnson to Africa or Rogers and Clark into Indian country.

For my two previous garlic books I followed the pattern set by successful predecessors: soliciting famous chefs for recipes, but not anymore. In my travels over the last ten years, I have met men and women dedicated to feeding friends and family, not just with the tastiest but with the safest and, if possible, the least expensive foods. The sources for the recipes in this book are people like you and me: decent, unassuming, loving, hard working. They are people who cannot afford to subscribe to the monthly magazine How to Make Lots of Money Easily and Fast and a List of Restaurants to be Seen Spending it on Yourself.

The recipes in the last pages of *Garlic Kisses* vary from quick-and-simple to prolonged-and-exotic. Several have flowed down from parents and even grandparents while a few have been regenerated after a newborn interest in lost cultures. Two or three are on-the-spot creations. Only one is not related to food. I offer them as they were offered to me. A few spelling changes, a few words changed, but the voices are the voices of my friends.

First things first. A few prefatory comments now about - what else? - garlic.

Every contributor (except one) used the routine super-market garlic (California Late from Gilroy, California.) Given each recipe's ingredients, I will now and then recommend, as a substitute, one of my own eighty-seven varieties. Very few of these garlic varieties are available in the local supermarkets. If you do track down a grower, the garlics are usually much more expensive than the supermarket product.

Do yourself a favor, not so much for this year as for next year and the following years. Spend a small amount now for a few pounds of five or ten of these "exotic" varieties and grow them yourself for next year and then every year after. Garlic will grow no matter where you live: cold or hot weather, on a city lot, on a farm, in a penthouse. There are many books out there (including two by this author) that can guide you should you be moved to grow *Allium sativum*.

The span of taste in supermarket garlic is limited almost to zero. The resident taste will be destroyed by the extreme heat. You might as well use a Habanera pepper. When working with these recipes (or any others), you will decide to accept or alter the amount of garlic suggested. In my suggestions I choose a specific garlic that will enhance but not overwhelm the inherent taste or texture of the dish.

Example: in a dressing for salads or in a sauce to accompany seafood, I do not want to destroy the appealing and necessary (for me) scent and taste of fresh greens or seafood. I will use mild garlic such as Creole Red or Inchelium Red or Guatemalan Ikeda. They offer more garlic flavor than heat, and the flavor is not heavy or overwhelming. A second example: I would not use the very hot (after hundreds of taste-tests I can say that most people judge Asian Tempest the "hottest" I grow.) Should I put Asian Tempest on arugula or radicchio? My mouth and palate would burn for so long that I'd lose the sharp sweet specific flavors of the green and red leaves I love so much. I would not use Russian Salvation, the taste of which is strong and earthy and long lasting, on salmon or scallops, because I want to savor that taste/smell of ocean. Inchelium Red will not only offer a background taste of garlic but it will also remain in the background. I will hold that mussel in my mouth and realize that Oh, this tastes more like ocean than the last time when I didn't use that garlic.

Tied to all this is a biological truth to remember: Because we all have different body chemistries, we respond in different ways to the same and different stimuli. A garlic that is hot to you can be mild to me, and what is spicy to me can be sweet or almost tasteless to you. Some of my friends can't stand the smell or taste of anchovies; other friends are raised to heights of ecstasy by the sight and scent of a single fillet of anchovy on their Caesar salad.

I've never met a cat or a dog or a garlic or a red-haired Irish woman I didn't like. I just like some garlics (and some Irish redheads) more than others. My favorite Irish redheads? Maureen O'Hara, Edna O'Brien, Milly O'Keefe, and sweet Molly Malone. My favorite garlics? In the order of the strength of their support of my taste-chemistry: Red Toch from the village of Tochliavri, Republic of Georgia; Armenian, from the village of the family of Silva Baghdassarian, Hadrut Karabagh; French Germinindort; Xian, from China; Guatemalan Ikeda; Russian Red Streak from Leningrad; Japanese, from, so far as I can track it down, Hokkaido. I have another called Hokkaido Zai Tai which is not as beautiful, not as hot, but with a very distinct taste of its own.

Three important notes. 1. In the glitz commercial cookbooks and in the glitz food magazines and in those newspapers that offer food pages, there is a fixed format for the printing of recipes. No fixed format here. What you see is what I got. 2. As to order-of-appearance (soups to salads to main courses, etc.:) there is no order because I myself am disorderly in my conduct and my appearance. Like super-market garlic, it leaves much to be desired. 3. Many of my friends work twelve hour days and six day weeks for less-per-week than Spago or The French Laundry charge for a bowl of soup. (Do you know how to say rip-off in French? ... *c'est de la tricherie!* or *une escroqerie!* You put in the accent marks.) In Russian? ... *moshenichestvo or obmanschik* !) For lack of time and lack of money and lack of pretensions, my friends occasionally rely on canned or packaged ingredients. So do I, for the same reasons. You will find a few of the enclosed recipes very brief and without reliance on rare or elegant ingredients or techniques. Example: look at the recipe for Baba Ghanoush by the Jordanian Palestinian, Khader Hussary. He refers to supplements called tahini and hummus. For your information: tahini is sesame seed paste; hummus is cooked and mashed chickpeas with tahini added.

For an informative and impassioned discourse on Baba Ghanoush, see Paula Wolfert's *The Cooking of the Eastern Mediterranean* (Harper Collins, 1994.) ("... To infuse a smoky flavor into eggplants during the winter months, I use a trick that I learned from a Greek cookbook author, Vefa Alexiadou. I wrap a large eggplant in a double thickness of foil and set it over high flames on top of the stove." And Wolfert on tahini: "Dips and sauces based on tahini ... are rich and creamy, and excellent on broiled meat, chicken, fish, and shellfish. They are also good over vegetables -- such as cooked cauliflower, crisp fried eggplant and zucchini, kibbeh, potatoes and Swiss Chard; hard-boiled eggs; and boiled snails; and they can simply be used as a dip for pita bread. Tahini is very healthy with plenty of B vitamins; and it is also an excellent source of calcium, phosphorous, and iron."

That was tahini. Now Wolfert on hummus: " ... A good plate of hummus is never presented undressed. It should be spread on a plate, then smoothed down from the middle outward with the back of a spoon to create a wide well in the center. A sprinkle of ground cumin and a little drizzle of olive oil and lemon are then added. An exceptionally pretty presentation is achieved by heating some hot paprika in olive oil until the oil turns red; strain the oil, then drizzle over half the hummus while sprinkling the other half with a few dots here and there, finally finishing with a thin line around the dish."

Remember what I told you about Wolfert's scholarship, passion, and prose?

My favorite way to eat some garlics is raw, but I eat almost all garlics (even that stuff from the super-market) on bruschetta. My own recipe for bruschetta, and a discussion of that holy eminence, can be found in the preceding text. Find it, read it, obey it. Alter it if you dare, but eat it. Carol Field elucidates the origin of the food and the word itself in her Celebrating Italy (1990, William Morrow.) "Wherever olive oil is produced," Field tells us, "it is traditional to celebrate the harvest with bruschetta, thick slices of country bread grilled over a fire, rubbed with garlic, and drizzled with pungent fresh green olive oil." … *"Bruciato,"* she goes on, ("burned" in Roman dialect); *fett'unta* ('oiled slice" in Tuscany); *soma d'ai* ('brushed with garlic" in Piedmont, although in Piedmont it is not bread but fat wands of crisp grissini called rubita that are dipped in a shallow bowl of olive oil and then rubbed with garlic…). Peasant wisdom has it that the father who plants a vineyard for his sons, plants an olive grove for his grandsons because olive trees begin to bear years after the vines; but once well rooted, may survive for centuries."

Remember what I told you about Fields' scholarship, passion, and prose?

Hello, hello, it's time to go. My farewell wishes are two: may you enjoy the food mentioned in these pages as well as the food that is not; and may the god of *Allium sativum* bestow her or his or its blessings upon you and in you.

Chester Aaron
Occidental, California
September, 2000

ADAMS' GARLIC ELIXIR

My garlics are usually gone by March or, at the latest, April. "Gone," meaning they have begun to rot. I then have to rely, like you, on supermarket garlic.

At the beginning of March this year I had about a thousand bulbs from perhaps ten different varieties still in my shed. I could not plant them, I could not sell them, and I could not give them away. I could search among them and find perhaps enough cloves to keep me free of the supermarket. At this time of the year, the subtleties of taste differences among whatever garlics I still have are just about lost. The span of taste-variation is at its widest in the first three or four months after harvest, say October or November. The longer those varieties survive, the more they taste alike.

I have had numerous meals at the home of Suzanne and Roger Adams. Suzanne, a chef of serious distinction, has created dishes that would reduce the Romeos and the Romeas of the food world to suicide were they to try to match her.

I mentioned my garlic dilemma to Suzanne and Roger. They grow different varieties of garlic too, though not in such quantity as I do. They also had some bulbs remaining that would be usable for only a week or two. Then they too would have to buy the ordinary Gilroy garlic that is in all probability sprayed with toxins and without the subtleties of taste our garlics offer. Suzanne came up with the idea which, after several tests, resulted in what she refers to as "my *elixir*."

Roger, a retired engineer, now a grower of fine foods and flowers, came up with a method that made the preparation of the garlic cloves faster and easier.

We simply collected all our bulbs and broke them apart into cloves. Those cloves already rotten or seriously on their way were discarded. They would go onto the compost pile. The remaining cloves were dumped (about a hundred or two hundred at a time) into a metal vat with a mesh bottom. Roger then power-washed those cloves. The water ran out onto the field. The skins of most of the cloves were cleared away from the body or loosened sufficiently so that they could be easily removed.

Of the remaining now-white cloves we removed those whose

color and texture suggested degeneration. Of those remaining, we cut away the brown spots.

Now they were ready. This was when Suzanne relied on her food processor.

GARLIC ELIXIR
Suzanne Adams

1 cup peeled garlic cloves
1/4 cup parsley

Process above ingredients until chopped fine or to your liking.
Place in a mixing bowl.
Add the following to the bowl.

1 tsp. salt
1 tsp. pepper
1 Tbsp. Red Wine vinegar
1 Tbsp. lemon juice

Stir in olive oil until it permeates the mixture: about 1/2 - 1 cup.

Place in glass jar and cover with 1/4 - 1/2 inch of olive oil to seal.

Store in glass jars in refrigerator.

OPTIONAL ADDITIONS BEFORE PROCESSING

Chopped black olives
Red pepper flakes
Anchovies
Capers
Your choice, Etc.

I met Suzanne and Roger Adams at a gathering at Robert Kourik's house. (See Robert's books: *Your Edible Landscape, Drip Irrigation, The Lavender Garden, The Tree and Shrub Finder*.) The Adamses live in the hills west of my home in Occidental, not quite midway between the Pacific coast and me. Over the years I have bestowed on Roger various garlic varieties which he is very successfully growing in his magnificent garden, along with greens and herbs that would make a French Chef's (not THE French Chef's) mouth water. Suzanne, who has studied with various chefs, has served me so many magnificent meals I stopped counting. Our published reviews of a few of her meals have made journalistic history.

The garlic used for this Elixir was not one variety but many. At that late date all garlics taste alike so the twenty or thirty varieties could be treated as one.

Money, Sex, Garlic; What Else is There?

Notes

FUSILLI LUNGHI ALL'AMALFITANA
Margot Fanger

Margot Fanger, born and raised in California, lives abroad in Boston. Among her varied careers she is a mental health clinician at the Harvard Community Health Plan; a lecturer on psychiatry at Cambridge Hospital, Harvard Medical School; a master programmer in neurolinguistic programming; a certified hypnotist; a co-author with Steven Friedman, of the book *Expanding Therapeutic Possibilities: Getting Results in Brief Therapy* (Lexington Books/Macmillan, 1991.) Margot has cooked so many hypnotic meals for me over the last fifty-five years I stopped counting at 237. Her husband (I forget his name) sent me the following recipe with a hand-written note: "Hey, izza great!"

FUSILLI LUNGHI ALL'AMALFITANA

1/2 cup extra-virgin olive oil
4 anchovies
1 1/2 lbs. ripe tomatoes, peeled, seeded, cut into strips
(Canned peeled and seeded tomato chunks are fine)
(Also a few cherry tomatoes added at the end)
3 Tbsp. black olive paste
1- 6 1/2-ounce can tuna, drained
10-12 oz. imported long fusili
Salt
1/2 lb. fresh mozzarella, cut into small dice
Freshly ground black pepper
1 bunch fresh basil leaves, coarsely chopped

Place 1/4-cup olive oil and the anchovies in a large sauté pan. Cook over low heat until the anchovies melt. Add the tomatoes, raise the heat to medium, and cook until the sauce thickens, about 10-15 minutes. Combine the olive paste, tuna and 2 tablespoons of olive oil in a small bowl. Blend well with a fork. Cook the pasta in abundant water. When *al dente,* drain well and place in a heated serving dish. Dress with the remaining olive oil. Add the olive and tuna mixture and toss to coat the pasta. Add the tomato-anchovy sauce and toss. Sprinkle with the mozzarella and basil, toss again, and serve immediately.

Garlic I'd recommend for this recipe: Creole Red.
Other garlics and anchovies would fight for superiority.
Creole Red is not strong but it will be there.

Garlic lovers do it: ARO-MANTICALLY!

Notes

CALABACITAS ("Diminutive Squash" Stew)
Avesa I. Rockwell, New Mexico

"My Minnesota Swede, Pennsylvania Quaker and Irish Catholic ancestors were farmers in cold wet places. The concept of hot spicy food was alien to my nature. I received a third degree burn trauma after nibbling on one deep-fried tortilla chip dipped in a watery homemade salsa. To soothe the burn my stepfather used a honey-soaked sopapilla (deep-fried bread pillows). It did not work. For years, as I grew up in New Mexico, I avoided chilies until I tried the sweeter green. Now I crave its simple taste here in the land of pickled jalapenos and tomato/cilantro salsa.

I arrived in New Mexico in 1977 with my rebellious young mother and her new husband, who was to manage a solvent recycling business. They bought one acre on a corrugated dirt road that led up the west mesa above the village of Corrales, an agrarian community then 15 miles north of a sprawling Albuquerque. My mother created a garden by replanting the native sage and chamisa and wild flower beds bolstered by rocks stolen from mountain rivers. I played in the cottonwood forest that lined the Rio Grande, swam in the spring-fed "Clear Ditch," caught crawdads in chocolate *acequia* ditches. My first grade class represented the village's mix of traditional Hispanic families, Pueblo Indian "ex-pats", two Mormons, and a handful of "*rubia*" rag-tag white children with creative hippy-dippy names like mine whose parents raised goats and sold jewelry at the local art galleries.

After I grew up and went away to college, my mother became a very efficient activist protesting a semi-conductor factory's contamination of local air, soil, and water. She organized a meeting that received record-breaking attendance from people who, like her and me, were always sick thanks to the effects of the industry's ongoing pollution. She won a partial victory with the company installing minimal abatement equipment to protect the residents.

Calabacitas is a traditional recipe common in native kitchens in New Mexico but rare in restaurants. For that reason it remains a "best kept secret". It is remarkably healthy and vegetarian. Prepare this stew in the late summer/early fall using the freshest ingredients. The dish is derived from the triumvirant crop of corn, beans and squash, cultivated in a clever symbiosis: the corn grows straight, providing a trellis for the beans, which in turn give needed shade to the delicate zucchinis.

The green chilies are ubiquitous in New Mexico. On I-25 you can order a Big Mac with "red" or "green". The standard roadside question, when you order, is, "Red or green?" To say "Christmas" means you want both at the same time. Green chilies are the unripened version of the red, which is dried for "ristra" decorations or ground into an earthy rich spice. Farmers sell raw chilies in bushels. They roast the green "Big Jims" in a 50-gallon barrel grill over a blistering manure fire. Green chilies are more densely packed with Vitamin C than any other.

CALABACITAS

1 large yellow onion, minced

2 Tbsp. olive oil

10 cloves of New Mexican garlic (red pungent little buggers that grow as volunteers in mother's garden)

4 cups peeled and chopped summer squash (zuc or crookneck)

2 cups cooked pinto or lima beans

4 ears freshly shucked white corn, with raw kernels cut from cob

3 fresh tomatoes, chopped

6 N.M. Green Chilies, roasted, peeled and seeded (*see guide below)

A few pinches of dried oregano

Salt (salt increases the heat of the chile, use caution) to taste

Pepper, to taste

Sour cream for garnish

Serve with steamed tortillas or fresh corn bread

(*Guide how to roast green chilies): place raw green chilies on a cookie sheet. Broil until blackened on each side. Remove from heat and cover with a damp towel. The resultant steam will separate the skin from the meat. When they cool down remove stem, peels and seeds unless you want your stew HOT. Save the whitest seeds to add to the stew and toss the brown ones.

In a large Dutch oven or stew pot, on medium heat, sauté onions and oil until translucent. Add squash, garlic, corn, tomatoes, chopped green chili meats and spices. Add water. Cover and simmer on low for 15-20 minutes. Serve warm with sour cream and corn bread.

The garlic I'd recommend for this recipe is the garlic Avesa refers to, the Hardneck that grows wild in the Mountains of New Mexico. I have used Spanish Roja and Mazatlan varieties and like them both, though the Mazatlan is much hotter with a lingering taste.

Live to eat garlic —— Eat garlic to live

Notes

STIR FRY WITH GARLIC CHUNKS
ROAST LAMB
SPAGHETTI & MEATBALLS
Joan Padro

Joan Padro was born in New York City and grew up in the shadow of the Empire State Building. Never, during those years, did she even once see King Kong. Joan spent part of her childhood in Havana. Back in New York, she attended Columbia University, majoring, mastering and Phding in Slavic Languages. She traveled extensively in the old USSR and in Russia. She attended the Moscow Olympics but not as an athlete. She has lived twenty-eight years in London where she monitors Moscow's Channel One news for selected clients. She reports on Russian politics and life for the BBC and writes a column for a British newspaper. Joan's hobbies: cooking and gardening. Her enslavement by two Epicurean cats —Dvushka and Gorby — has been recorded in the London Annals of Cat Crime.

Joan is writing a book about her work and her experiences. Her prose is serious but her poetry is both serious and funny, full of pith and vinegar.

STIR FRY WITH GARLIC CHUNKS
Pour olive oil, one onion (chopped fine) and 1 1/2 heads of garlic (cloves cut in half) into a wok. Fry until garlic and onion are brown. Add soy sauce and then add diced or stripped pork or chicken. Cook until meat is well done. Add Chinese leaves or pak choy, mushrooms, corn. While this is cooking boil water for rice or noodles. When rice or noodles are ready, drain and add to the wok. Stir, mix and serve piping hot. Variants can be snow peas, water chestnuts.

I'd suggest, of course, Asian Tempest or Xian garlic, both of which are not just very very hot but very very tasty.

ROAST LAMB

Lamb shanks or half leg-of-lamb. Use one head of garlic. Place two sheets of aluminum foil criss-crossed on bottom of roasting pan. Slice one onion and place slices on aluminum sheets and cover with the leg of lamb. Crush half of the cloves and rub on the lamb. Place the remaining cloves, whole, around the lamb and add fresh rosemary and bay leaves plus oregano.

Fold the aluminum foil over the lamb and over the lamb and seal to make a parcel. Do not open until lamb is done. Roast at medium heat for 2-1/2 hours. Serve piping hot. Small potatoes can be roasted with the lamb or rice can be cooked separately.

With lamb, I'd suggest a mild garlic, such as Inchelium Red

SPAGHETTI WITH MEAT BALLS

Start with any spaghetti sauce to taste. Add sliced garlic, onions chopped fine, oregano (optional), spices to your taste. Simmer gently on low heat. Form your chosen meatballs but place crushed garlic in the center of each meatball as it is shaped. Place meatballs in the sauce and turn periodically. Simmer very slowly for 90 minutes. Serve over spaghetti or other pasta of choice.

I'd suggest the hot but tasty Tuscan White or Montesi - yeah, try and find it!

Notes

PASTA ALA VONGOLE
ARTICHOKE DIPPING SAUCE
Brett Roberts

Brett Roberts was born in Southern California. He started cooking after the family beach parties ended. He long ago traded in his marshmallows, charcoal and coat hanger for sirloin, Calphalon and Henckels. A self-taught cook, Brett entertains his friends at his San Francisco home where he enjoys small dinner parties.

When Brett moved north to San Francisco in the late '70s to study marine biology at the University of California at Santa Cruz, he traded in his microscope and scuba gear for pencils and a straight edge. He completed his architectural studies at the University of Illinois at Chicago. He currently works for an architectural firm in San Francisco designing large commercial projects.

How did I meet Brett? His lady friend is an editor at *Sunset Magazine*. She, Amy McConnell, was at a meeting of editors where I performed my garlic dance. We liked each other. She visited me one day at the end of summer when she and Brett were bicycling through the hills. They called and though I rarely submit to unplanned visits I made an exception. We sat on the deck and before they left I loaded them up with apples (Arkansas Black) and Asian pears (Hosue) from my trees. They invited me to a dinner in Tiburon, at the home of Amy's mother, Betinna. Brett served the above, the Pasta ala vongole and the artichoke dipping sauce. Everyone else, I gathered, was as impressed as I was.

PASTA ALA VONGOLE

Sauté, over low heat, about 8-10 sliced cloves of garlic in about 1/2 cup of olive oil

After garlic softens, add about 10 sliced scallions (the white and the green)

Add 1 Red Bell Pepper, chopped

After the vegetables have softened, add the juice from a 6-oz. can of whole baby clams (I use the Geisha brand)

Hit the mixture with salt, pepper, 1/4 tsp. crushed thyme,
1 Tbsp. crushed red pepper

You can also, if you wish, add sliced black olives here

Add 1/2 cup white wine

Let sauce come to simmer

(During this time you will have added to boiling salted water
1 lb. of pasta - fusilli or linguini)

After sauce simmers a few minutes add lots (about 1-1/2 cups
chopped Italian parsley)

As parsley wilts, stir down the sauce

Turn off heat and add 2 Tbsp. butter (let it melt into sauce)

Drain pasta and place in a warm bowl

Dress pasta with juice from 1-2 freshly squeezed lemons

Pour sauce on top of pasta

(Yo! Don't stir or all the good stuff falls to bottom. And if
guests ask for cheese, throw them outa ya house!)

Garlic I'd recommend: again a mild but tasty
Inchelium Red or Chet's Italian Red so as not to
overwhelm the delicate flavor of this dish.

ARTICHOKE DIPPING SAUCE

1/2 cup fresh mayonnaise

Crush a couple garlic cloves, add to mayonnaise

Add fresh ground pepper and crushed sage to taste

Add 1-2 tsp. Red Wine vinegar or lemon juice

You will want to prepare and chill more artichokes than
you think appropriate.

I'd recommend a French Messadrone garlic, which is
sweet and nutty when cooked, complementing the
nutti-ness of the 'choke and the chef.)

OLD-FASHION GARLIC SAUCE
Roxanne Castro

Roxanne Castro is Assistant Vice President at National Bank of the Redwoods in northern California. She lives in Windsor. She is married. A devoted member of the Church of Christ she belongs to a choral group-worship team.

At the age of five Roxanne won a children's bake oven, a little stove with an oven, heat generated by an electric light bulb. She was changed forever. She did not leave the kitchen until she was 21. She has recently disclosed a secret. One of the so-called preservatives in the following recipe is the citric acid. Should you be reluctant to use citric acid you can (as Roxanne did once) use a package of commercial Italian dressing. Don't be a snob. Try it.

I met Roxanne after I transferred my estate from Wells Fargo and Bank of America to National Bank of the Redwoods because I'd heard the people there, from askers down to tellers, were human. They were indeed. Going into NBR is like going into the home of a favorite uncle or aunt. Suzie Braga, at the Sebastopol branch of NBR, knowing about my obsession with garlic, introduced me to Roxanne, who, later, during a business trip to Sebastopol, visited my farm and gave me several jars of her sauce. It was gone in two weeks. I later gave Roxanne some of my garlics and she used them in that year's production of the sauce. She is now growing several varieties of my garlic and will soon be self-sufficient.

You will realize, once you make and use it, why this sauce, offered at the Santa Rosa Harvest Fair a few years ago, won "Best-of-Show". If you meet Roxanne you will vote her the Very Best to Show.

OLD-FASHION GARLIC SAUCE

3 lb.	Garlic - finely chopped
6 cups	Canola oil
1 1/4 cups	Red Wine vinegar
1 bunch	Parsley - finely chopped
1/4-cup	Green pepper, minced

1/4-cup	Red pepper, minced
1/2-cup	Garlic granules (not salt)
1 Tbsp.	Sugar
1 Tbsp.	Citric Acid

Salt & pepper to taste

Heat oil slowly, add all other ingredients. Let simmer over low heat for 10 minutes. (Just enough time to slightly cut the bite of the garlic and blend the flavors.)

I hot-pack the ingredients into the jars via standard canning process, keeping jars in boiling water for 10 minutes. The shelf life is then indefinite. Once opened, jar must be kept in the refrigerator. The flavors mellow over time. Shelf this for at least a month before use.

Makes a wonderful gift for friends that like garlic. Is great for garlic bread, added to pasta, or any other idea you come up with no matter how crazy it sounds.

Two choices of garlic for this sauce: Creole Red, which is mild; Armenian, which is strong and earth.

Gold Glitters, Sex Thrills, Garlic Stinks—All are Good

Notes

CARROTS IN YOGURT GARLIC SAUCE
Meral Bozkurt

This recipe came from my aunt. I ate it in my childhood.

My family, Crimean Tartar since anyone can remember, lived a hard life. Stalin and Communism brought famine to the bread belt and fertile land my family came from. Then the Nazis invaded and placed my father, a young Soviet soldier, in a prisoner of war camp. My mother, a young woman, and her family were taken to Germany to work as forced labor on farms.

After the war my mother's family and my father were all located outside the Soviet Union, and became official refugees to the Allied Forces because they could not return to their homeland. Stalin had forcibly exiled all Crimean Tartars.

My parents, as refugees, lived in different countries in Europe, longing for their homeland and clinging to their culture. While living in Luxembourg, my grandfather decided it was time his teenage daughters were married. A devoted Muslim, he would never permit them to marry Christians. So he decided to migrate to Turkey, raise his family in Muslim culture and marry his daughters to Muslim men.

To starving people with a strong culture, food is always important. In Istanbul my aunt learned new and different recipes. This carrot dish for example. The Turks fried their carrots. My aunt decided to merely braise them until they are soft and golden.

My aunt and my mother learned different recipes for different foods in different countries. I remember going to the dinner table and having different dishes with names such as "the German casserole" or "the Italian sauce" or "the traditional Tartar dish" or "the Luxembourg roast" or "the French dish" or "the Russian salad."

As a teenager, wanting to be assimilated into the American culture, I did not eat foreign food. I wanted hamburgers and Chef boy'r Dee. Only now do I appreciate the connection of my family's dishes to their culture and to their trials and tribulations. Food with a Tartar twist connects me to my ancestors.

My love to you. Meral, child of a refugee.

I met Meral Bozkurt three years ago on a cold rainy afternoon in Occidental. She was with another woman named Carmella Bolgetta, and a teen-age boy. They chose me out of several people standing on the sidewalk and spoke to me in Italian, asking me to recommend one of the local restaurants. I advised them. They asked me to join them. I did, humiliated at my having forgotten most of my Italian. Finally Nina, from Naples, said, in perfect English with a Bronx accent, "You've forgotten your Italian." I could have killed them. Instead, I invited them to my home where we watched a video of the movie taken from Carlo Levi's "Christ Stopped in Eboli."

I fell in love with both Nina and Meral. But Meral stayed in communication with me and she also loves cats so I'll only marry her when I grow up.

CARROTS IN YOGURT GARLIC SAUCE

1 lb. large carrots - preferably organic
1/4 cup olive oil
1/4 Tbsp. salt
Water
1 cup fresh yogurt
4 cloves garlic-grated

The Carrots:

Cut carrots into 3 to 4 inch pieces,then slice lengthwise into 1/4inch slices.

Place sliced carrots in pot. Carrots should cover bottom of pot. A 9" pot will probably do.

Add water to pot but do not cover the carrots.

Add olive oil.

Add salt.

Braise under medium-low heat until water is absorbed into carrots and carrots are soft. The oil remains and the carrots are slightly golden.

The Sauce:

Grate garlic into yogurt
Add pinch of salt
Mix and let sit while carrots are cooked and cooling
Add to carrots when they have cooled.

This dish is best when served cold. It is great in the summer.

Having no garlic from Crimea I went next best:
Ukrainian White, a garlic that is the first to harvest
and the last to fade on the shelf. A big garlic, strong
and hearty.

Got Garlic?

Notes

SU MEI DUMPLINGS
Michael Smith

Michael Smith started his career as a chef by washing dishes. He moved up through the ranks in a variety of restaurants including The Mandala Café, Blue Heron, and the Courthouse Café. He moved to San Francisco and graduated from the California Culinary Academy in 1985. Catering for four years enabled him to travel extensively in Africa and Asia. Back in Sonoma County he worked as an organic farmer for three years. He and his wife Thia owned Café Dahlia for several years until 1997, when he took over the management of the employee-café concession at Industrial Light for Lucas Digital, Inc. Michael and Thia have two children and live in Sebastopol, California.

Su Mei is part of a traditional Dim Sum meal, which is usually eaten at brunch time. They can be enjoyed as appetizer or a full meal. It is hard to stop eating them. Makes about twenty dumplings.

1/2 lb. ground pork
1/2 lb. prawns
6 small dried black Chinese mushrooms
2 Tbsp. cilantro, chopped
2 Tbsp. ginger, minced
3 green onions, chopped
2 Tbsp. sherry
1/2 tsp. salt
1 Tbsp. corn starch
1/2 tsp. sesame oil
1 packet fresh won ton skins

Put dried mushrooms in hot water for ten minutes to rehydrate them. Peel and chop prawns until about the same consistency as the pork. Combine pork, prawns, cilantro, ginger, green onions.

Chop the mushroom fairly fine. (You might have to remove the tough stems first.)

Add mushrooms to pork-prawn mix. Also add sherry, salt, cornstarch, sesame oil.

Mix well and set aside.

Put about 1 Tbsp. of filling into the middle of a won-ton skin. Wet rest of skin around the filling with water. With wet fingers, pick up filled skin with both hands and push skin together and mold until skin sticks together. (BUT YOUR DUMPLING MUST BE OPEN AT THE TOP.) There are different styles you can rely on: a pleated look or the smooth wrap look. As long as it sticks together and is open at the top.

When you put the finished product on the plate, push them down a bit so they will stand up on their own and not roll around.

Repeat filling of skins until filling is gone.

Cover with a damp towel or paper towel on so they don't dry out and put them in the refrigerator until you are ready to seam and serve them. They can also be frozen.

DIPPING SAUCE

1/4 cup Red Wine vinegar
1/4 cup soy sauce
4-6 cloves garlic

Mince the garlic and add to vinegar and soy sauce.

Steam the dumplings for six-to-ten minutes, depending on their size, until firm. It's best to oil your bamboo or aluminum steamer first so the dumplings don't stick.

If served as an entree, accompany with steamed rice and asparagus.

I met Michael and Thia when they owned Café Dahlia in Graton, six miles from my home. We became friends immediately. Over the years I have unloaded various garlics on Michael's porch. He is growing them very well. Michael and Thia offered simple but imaginative and varied meals to the patrons of Café Dahlia and friends and I miss them and Dahlia desperately.

The town just ain't the same. Of course it never was.

Michael's choice of garlic: Yugoslavian Red.

BAKED WHOLE WHEAT FUSILI PASTA WITH ROASTED GARLIC - BECHAMEL SAUCE
Linda Preciado

Linda's career in food started in 1979 at a private Gestalt Psychotherapy Training Institute at Big Sur, California. She moved to the Bay Area and began working as a cook and baker. That experience led her to restaurants, where she worked as a pastry chef. She has offered cooking classes to both children and adults.

Linda enjoys cooking the cuisines of Mediterranean countries, especially Italian and Southern France.

Since 1997 she has worked as a private chef.

BAKED WHOLE WHEAT FUSILI PASTA WITH ROASTED GARLIC - BECHAMEL SAUCE
(Yield: 4-6 Servings)

8 oz. fresh mozzarella balls
2-3 Tbsp. olive oil
1-cup Parmesan, freshly grated
1-cup fresh bread crumbs
12 oz. dried whole-wheat fusilli
Salt, pepper, pinch of nutmeg

(optional: broccoli and cauliflower florets may be added.)

ROASTED GARLIC BECHAMEL SAUCE

3 Tbsp. butter
3 Tbsp. flour
Sprig of thyme
3 cups milk, heated
1 head of garlic
1 Tbsp. olive oil
Salt, pepper, pinch of nutmeg
First, prepare the sauce and set aside to cool.

Preheat oven to 350 degrees. Slice top off of garlic bulb and drizzle exposed garlic with olive oil. Lightly salt bulb and wrap, tightly, in foil. Bake 45 minutes. Garlic is done when it is soft all over. Be careful not to overbrown.

While garlic is roasting, melt butter in a saucepan and add flour. Cook over low heat for 2-3 minutes, stirring constantly. Add hot milk and sprig of thyme. Using a whisk or wooden spoon, stir until thickened. Remove from heat and stir in soft garlic squeezed from roasted bulb. Season with salt, pepper, nutmeg. Let cool.

While sauce is cooling, cook pasta in plenty of boiling salted water. When al dente, drain and rinse in cold water.

Toss breadcrumbs with olive oil. Add Parmesan. Mix thoroughly.

Preheat oven to 375 degrees F.

Cube mozzarella. Generously butter a 9x13 inch dish. Pour in sauce. Stir cooked pasta with mozzarella. You may now add optional vegetables (the broccoli or cauliflower florets.)

Smooth top and spread breadcrumb mixture evenly over the surface.

Bake 45 minutes to 1 hour.

Casserole is done when breadcrumbs are evenly browned.

I met Linda Preciado when she was working at an upscale market in Oakland, California and, at the same time, working as a chef-caterer. Over the years she and her friend Birgitte Krogh (whose recipe follows) have visited me here in Occidental. I have visited them in Berkeley. They have helped me with fieldwork and verbal massage. It's better than the best compost.

The garlic(s): Celaya Purple, from Mexico, with
a fiery taste when raw; and Acropolis, from Greece
which hits hot at the back of the mouth but fades
fast and leaves a fine garlicky taste.

A QUICKIE
GARLIC GINGER SAUCE
Birgitte Krogh

Birgitte was born in Denmark and lived in Copenhagen until, at the age of twenty-three, she moved to California. She grew up in a food and animal-loving family that often started the day by discussing what they would cook for dinner that night.

Birgitte has cooked and baked professionally for nearly twenty years. She has worked in many aspects of the food business, even owning her own much acclaimed restaurant in Berkeley. For the last three years she has had her dream job: working for a Bay Area couple as their private cook.

Birgitte has lived in Berkeley for the last twenty years, sharing a home with her husband Tony and various other animals. She is about to harvest her second crop of Chester's garlics. In the evening Birgitte loves to chew raw garlic. En garde, Tony!

BIRGITTE'S QUICKIE
Birgitte Krogh

Delicious served with salad and ripe tomatoes.

2-3 slices of bread
4 ounces fresh mozzarella or other mild cheese, shredded
1 egg
1 Tbsp. flour
1 Tbsp. milk
1/2 tsp. salt
1/4 tsp. paprika
1 large clove garlic, peeled and mashed or pressed
1 Tbsp. Aquasvit, vermouth or white wine (optional)
Olive oil: enough to cover bottom of frying pan
Mix all ingredients (except bread) together with a fork.
Spread on one side of each bread slice.
Heat olive oil in pan until hot but not smokey.

Fry bread cheese-side down until golden.

The garlic: Medidzhvari, from the Republic of
Georgia (hot at first, then heat fades fast) or Mon-shanskij
(from Czechoslovakia), which is moderately hot and very
tasty.

GARLIC-GINGER SAUCE

This sauce is wonderful poured over hot al dente pasta mixed
with steamed or sautéed vegetables or served with grilled meats.
Sauce can be made in advance and stored in refrigerator for
about 3 days.
Recipe makes about 2 cups of sauce.

1 egg
2 Tbsp. rice vinegar
1 tsp. Dijon mustard
2 Tbsp. lemon juice
1 tsp. Sesame oil
1 Tbsp. soy sauce
2 cloves garlic, peeled
1 piece peeled raw ginger (approx. 1 cubic inch)
1 1/2 tsp. Lan Chi black bean sauce (with garlic or chili,
available in Asian section of most markets)

Using a food processor, blend egg, vinegar, mustard, lemon
juice, ginger, garlic, soy sauce for about 30 seconds.
Slowly pour in sesame oil, olive oil and black bean sauce.
Run for another 30 seconds.
Mix sauce into hot pasta of choice a little at a time, approximately 3/4-cup per pound of pasta.
Birgitte and Linda Presciado (see previous recipe) are old
friends. I met Birgitte before I met Linda because I occasionally
dined at Birgitte's restaurant in Berkeley. Later, when Linda drove
north to get out of Berkeley, Birgitte accompanied her.
I will not forget one rainy day when Birgitte and I worked in

the field and Linda, fighting a cold (I think) stayed inside by the fire and read. Out in the field I looked up and Birgitte was kneeling in the grass, a slicker covering her body, rain pouring down her face. She is a working fool.

The garlic, with all those spices: Red Rezan, from south of Moscow. Strong flavor that lasts and lasts

Eating garlic is a breathmaking experience.

Notes

MUSHROOM OR CHICKEN PROSCIUTTO TORTELLINI
Sheri Thrower

Sheri Thrower graduated from the California Culinary Academy in 1987. She has worked as a chef at Sonoma wineries (Veranza, Iron Horse) but for the past few years she has worked at Fiesta Market in Sebastopol, California. There, at Fiesta, she is free to create new and exciting dishes, of which, I can personally testify, there are many, they are varied, and I have been delighted with 99% of everything available. Patrons can receive taste-samples of any creation in which they are interested. Much of the success Fiesta Market has achieved is due, in no small part, to Sheri.

In 1990, while working in a fresh progressive deli in Marin County, Sheri was asked to create something "out of this world" using garlic. These were the days of the "aioli" rage. Sheri put the following salad together, introducing a garlic-basil aioli dressing. She first used the dressing on chicken-prosciutto tortellini. Next on a Portabella mushroom tortellini with fresh red and yellow cherry tomatoes. Sheri suggests serving the salad chilled on a warm summer evening. With a garnish of fresh basil.

Sheri has served the salad as a side dish with an extra-sourdough baguette and she has also used it as a side dish for grilled fish, meat, vegetables or poultry. A wine enthusiast, Sheri favors a Pinot Noir or Merlot to accompany her creation.

This salad won the gold medal at the Harvest Fair in Sonoma County in 1998 the salad won the gold medal.

MUSHROOM OR CHICKEN PROSCIUTTO TORTELLINI
20 Servings

12 - 8 oz. packages fresh pasta (see note*).

Cook 4 minutes in boiling water, strain, rinse with cold water, set aside.

DRESSING
(In Cuisinart)

2 bunches parsley, no stems
1 bunch basil, no stems
1 cup garlic cloves
Black pepper, salt
4 cups mayonnaise.
1 cup white wine vinegar
16 Roma tomatoes, halved, seeds removed. Halves cut into bite-sized pieces.

Start Cuisinart. Add all ingredients except tomatoes and wine vinegar.
Add wine vinegar to blend.
Add sauce to tortellini and top with tomatoes.
*<u>NOTE</u>: Sheri recommends your using your favorite recipe for preparing your own tortellini if you do not buy the ready-packaged (such as Di Giorno or Mallard's) mushroom or chicken tortellini. For your information: the difference between tortellini and tortelloni is size. By linguistic rule tortellini is smaller than tortelloni.

I've made this dish with Tuscan White garlic
and Tarne, from France. Which was my favorite?
Both.

Garlic isn't perfect, it's much better than that

Notes

BABA GHANOUSH
Khader Husary

Khader Husary is a Palestinian from Jordan. He owns and manages, with his son and four daughters, a Texaco station-deli-market at the intersection of Occidental Road and Highway 116 in Sebastopol, California.

I stopped at the station one day and asked Khader Husary if he liked garlic. Gentle, calm, dapper, elegant, he replied with the gentlest voice, "I eat much garlic. Especially in Baba Ghanoush."

He'd said the magic words.

His recipe follows.

The dapper elegance of the man has been relayed to his daughters and his son, all of whom, in their quiet but courteous efficiency, operate the very busy complex, catering to every type of human God spent a busy weekend creating: business people of all genders, cowboys, construction workers, students, teachers, migrant workers, me.

No matter the chaos at that intersection, the handsome son and beautiful daughters remain pleasant, calm, and efficient. Like their father.

BABA GHANOUSH

2 eggplants.

Bake until they're soft.

Take them out of the oven and peel them.

Put remaining eggplant in a bowl. Add ½-tsp. salt. Squeeze in juice of 1 lemon.

Add 2 Tbsp. of tahini.

Mix together.

Press in 1 clove of garlic.

Eat.

HUMMUS

Put 1 can of garbanzo beans, drained, in blender.
Squeeze in juice of 1 lemon and add 1/2-tsp. salt, 2 Tbsp.
Tahini. Blend.
Add garlic in the amount you desire.
Serve with or without olive oil

Garlic eaten is an investment in the future.

Notes

GARLIC CRISPS, CHIPS, FRIES
Kandis Kozolanka

Kandis was born in Ottawa. A descendant of Romanian Gypsies, Kandis can trace her heritage back to Transylvania. At birth, Kandis was given a garland of garlic to wear. She says she would still be wearing it around her neck if her *buntza* (grandmother) were still alive.

She has lived in various countries but is settled in northern California. After accumulating vast experience as a baker and caterer she now is in charge of the kitchen for Tea & Tarot (an English Tea Room in Sebastopol).

The following is her favorite recipe, which says a lot because her collection would fill a large library.

Kandis occasionally works with Suzanne and Roger Adams when they have catering jobs but she also works alone. Less frequently now, however, because Tea & Tarot is more than full time.

"This is deep fried garlic. I use it mostly to garnish a meat or fish entrée. But if Chester is over for dinner it rarely makes it past appetizer. We can't stop nibbling on it. The task is easier if you have a small garlic-slicer; otherwise, use a thin very sharp knife."

I met Kandis through my friendship with Suzanne and Roger Adams and Robert Kourik.

GARLIC CRISPS, CHIPS, FRIES
Heaps of peeled garlic, sliced very thin
Olive oil
Sea salt

Cover the bottom of a small fry pan with 1/4 inch of olive oil. Heat until olive oil speaks to you (it crackles and smokes)

Add garlic and fry over medium heat until golden and crispy. Not too dark or it will taste burnt.

Do a small batch first to see it works. It will get dark fast after the golden stage so be prepared to remove all of it quickly onto a paper towel.

While it is still hot sprinkle with sea salt.

Eat as an appetizer or garnish garlic mashed potatoes, salmon, anything roasted or barbecued.

Go ahead. Try to eat just one.

I have used all varieties of garlic, including
California Late from Gilroy.

Garlic is in the nose of the beholder

Notes

GARLIC AND ROSEMARY LAMB MARINADE
Jeff Creasey

Jeff lives in Custer, Washington.

After high school, Jeff tried college but gave it up. About sixteen years ago he settled into doing concrete work. For the last ten years he has been a self-employed concrete finisher.

Jeff and Kris have been married for fifteen years. Kris is a supervisor at a local medical insurance company. For the last four years Jeff had been gardening. About two years ago, after reading my garlic books, Jeff called me and we have been friends ever since, though we have never met. He has been planting my garlics as well as garlics from other growers Last year he planted 4700 cloves.

Every two or three months one of us calls the other to compare notes about problems, about weather, soil, compost, tricks for winning against the odds. On occasion Jeff has caught fish up north, smoked them and sent them to me overnight express. I will eat it in various ways but my favorite: in pasta, with a light garlic-oil sauce, pine nuts, tomatoes, torn leaves of a green such as arugula or kale or even basil.

Like me, Jeff is organic. Unlike me, he is going to continue growing garlic for the next thirty years. The International Association of Concrete Workers reports that Jeff Creasey is the only member who invited friends, neighbors, relatives in to sample the tastes of his various garlics. "Jeff is a rare breed in our membership. He will never talk about his tools or his trucks or his construction jobs but he can talk for hours about the most artistic way to tie a beautiful and successful trout fly, or the benefits of organic gardening, or the origins of each of his various garlics. If you'd let him he would talk for days about he various qualities of tastes that distinguish the Yugoslavian Red garlic from the Creole Red or the Spanish Roja or the Bejing Pink or the Mucdi. The man is awesome."

That's a direct quote from the Newsletter of the International Association of Concrete Workers.

Jeff (friendly, open, hard working, generous, loving of humans and animals) is one of those people someone — Whitman? Emmerson? Aaron? — has called the "salt of the earth."

GARLIC AND ROSEMARY LAMB MARINADE
Serves 4 (8-10 lamb chops)

2/3 cup balsamic vinegar
1/4 cup honey
1/3 cup chopped fresh rosemary
1/4 cup water
3 Tbsp. crushed or chopped garlic
1 Tbsp. olive oil
1 tsp. lemon juice
1/4 tsp. coarse ground pepper
1/8 tsp. Sea salt or Kosher salt

Whisk all contents together very well and set aside. But stir occasionally.

Remove sinew and fat from each lamb chop, leaving only meat attached to bone. (By doing this you expose more meat surface to the marinade and no further trimming is necessary).

Give the marinade a good whisk and pour into a flat-bottom glass dish big enough to hold all the chops laying flat.

Lay chops flat in dish and moved around to coat both surfaces.

Cover and refrigerate 4-6 hours but turn and recoat chops at least once. Marinate at least two hours but not more than eight.

I use the barbecue, on medium high heat, with the chops 7-8 inches from the flame. Cooking time varies with the thickness of the chops and how rare or well you want them. Chops we get are about two inches thick and take 8-10 minutes a side. They come out just a touch past medium well.

A couple of minutes before removing the chops from the heat sprinkle with a very small amount of salt.

A garlic I have used on lamb or veal is a relatively
strong garlic without too much heat, such as the
Xian or the Armenian or the Yugoslavian Red.

BLOODCLOT BUSTER
Annie Lanzillotto

What can I say about Annie Lanzillotto that has not already been said by Dante, Silone, Pavese, Levi, Magnani, Morante, Loren, Sylvana Mangano?

Annie was born in the Bronx in 1963 but she has since migrated to Brooklyn, where she is a writer, director, and performer. She curates literature at The Kitchen. Annie's grandmother, Rose Pettruzelli, was born September 6, 1900, in Acquaviva delle Fonte, province of Bari, Italy. Rose Pettruzelli, who will be 100 years old this September, is currently performing on stage in video works by her granddaughter, Annie.

The recipe that follows — the only offering unrelated to food — is a tribute to Annie and Rose, young and younger representatives of the Italian gender.

How did I meet granddaughter, Annie? I think — correct me, Annie — we met on e-mail. Or through e-mail. One thing led to another and I realized I had an Italian tiger by the tail.

It turned out that Annie is not only garlic oriented, she is garlic obsessed. Much of her writing and theater work involves, in one way or another, garlic. Her props and costumes are made of garlic. She wrote and performed a show called "Pocketing Garlic". The heroine of the story: her grandmother Rose, who always refused to pay money for garlic. Instead of buying garlic at the market she would "pocket" it. The Pettruzelli-Lansillotto family quote: "Some things in life you shouldn't pay for. Garlic is essential. Garlic is the essence of life. You don't pay for garlic."

Annie's show was commissioned by an organization called "Franklin Furnace" for their "In Exile" series. It was performed at The Knitting Factory in NYC in 1994.

As Annie and I talked — via e-mail — I learned that she was about to depart for Italy. For one whole month. Filled with envy I acted in pique: "Send me a recipe tonight!" She submitted the following recipe with the following preface: "When the doctor says amputation is the next step for your 99-1/2 year old grandmother, and her blue marble leg is getting colder by the day, due to bloodclots, you …

1.CRUSH three bulbs of fresh garlic in a blender with good olive oil.
2. APPLY a thin coat of Vaseline over the leg.
3.APPLY the poultice over the entire leg, foot, between the toes.
4.WRAP the leg in a white cotton pillowcase.
5.ELEVATE slightly.
6.WARM the leg using your hands.
7.LEAVE on overnight.
  In the morning, gently pat the crumbling mixture off the leg.
  Repeat this procedure eight nights, until circulation is completely restored."

  Rose Petruzzelli, Annie Lanzillotto: *voi saluto*!   Or is it *saluti? Tu*? No matter, I salute you both!

  The garlic of choice? Montesi from northern Italy

Garlic--A Heavenly Taste, but not Heavenly Scent

Notes

FOCACCIA
Dianne Naber

Dianne and Gene Naber live up the hill behind the Union Hotel in Occidental. They are old friends who, when I need advice about anything (from food to computers to traffic laws) are there to help. Dianne is a lifetime member of the Gonnella clan, one of the three major Italian influences in local history.

Last year the Nabers traveled to northern Italy and returned with a jar of local olive for me as well as two bulbs of garlic. From a town called Montesi. I planted twenty-two cloves. But first I tasted two cloves. I distinctly heard Enrico Caruso singing. Or was it Mirella Freni? Tebaldi? Today, Sunday, June 18, 2000, at breakfast in the Cafe: payback time. I gave the Nabers three bulbs of Montesi I just pulled from the ground. They will eat one head, plant the cloves from the other two. Garlic and life goes on.

Dianne worked for the County Legal Services until she retired two years ago so she now works twice as hard at the same job. Gene, formerly one of the head honchos in Sebastopol's Radio Shack, thinks up schemes for expanding his mind and his home and his universe. On Sunday mornings Dianne and Gene saunter into the Café at the Union Hotel about a half-hour after I do. They have their breakfast, read the paper and go on to church. They are dedicated Catholics.

Were I in need of anything — advice, labor, money, love — I know I can call Dianne or Gene at any hour, night or day. Especially if it's around mid-afternoon.

Dianne offers this recipe.

FOCACCIA
2 cups lukewarm water (85 to 95 degrees F.)
2 tsps. active dry yeast
4 cups unbleached bread flour
2 to 3 tsps. salt
2-3 tsps. olive oil
2 Tbsp. chopped fresh rosemary
1 tsp. Kosher or Sea salt

Pour water into large warm bowl. Sprinkle yeast over water and stir until dissolved. Stir in 2 cups of flour and the salt. Stir briskly until smooth (about 2 minutes.) Dough will be somewhat wet and tacky. When dough pulls away from the sides of the bowl and forms a loose ball, it has been stirred enough. If the dough is still too tacky, add additional flour. (I use regular flour and I know I will need to add more than the listed 4 cups. I statt with 4 and add until the dough is the consistency I want.)

Cover bowl with plastic wrap and let rise in a warm place until doubled in volume. 30-40 minutes.

Pour dough onto baking stone or cookie sheet. Divide into two parts. Brush dough with 2-tsp. olive oil. Dip fingers into cold water or olive oil and insert into dough. Make holes in the dough by pulling it to the sides about 1 inch at a time. Pull holes at random to form craters. Stretch dough into two 1-inch thick ovals.

Brush ovals with olive oil. Sprinkle one oval with herbs and sea salt. (See choice of toppings below.) Sprinkle the other with seeds (see below) and sea salt.

Note: flat bread does not need to rise. It will bake beautifully no matter what you do to it.

TO BAKE

Preheat oven to 500 degrees. Reduce heat to 450 and place bread on oiled or non-stick baking sheets in oven. Bake for 15-20 minutes, until bread has a gold-brown color. Cut into wedges and serve warm with olive oil for dipping.

TOPPINGS

Seed: use a mix of any of the following seeds to produce an aromatic and flavorful crust: anise, caraway, dill, cumin, fennel, sesame, Nigella. (Nigella is sometimes called black-onion-seed. It is found in Middle Eastern shops.)

Herb: rosemary, basil, Greek oregano, Italian seasonings mix or Zatar (a mix of thyme and sesame seed). These herbs can also be blended into the dough for excellent flavor. Caution: breads containing herbs must be watched carefully so they do not burn.

Hiding garlic aroma is like hiding a fire in the dark

Notes

YES! Send me *GarlicKisses* for only $19.95, which includes handling and postage. Call for prices of five or more (419-499-4604) or e-mail mgarlicm@accnorwalk.com . Also, credit card orders at www.mostlygarlic.com or www.booksamerica.com or call 1-800-929-7889.

Makes an excellent gift whether a garlic lover or not

Garlic Kisses

Love, Chester

NAME _____
PLEASE PRINT

ADDRESS _____

CITY _____ STATE ___ ZIP ___

MAIL TO: MOSTLY GARLIC, 19 E. CHURCH ST., MILAN, OH 44846 USA